Info-Rich – Info-Poor

Info-Rich – Info-Poor

Access and exchange
in the global information society

Trevor Haywood

BOWKER
SAUR ●

London • Melbourne • Munich • New Jersey

HM
221

H 395
1995

British Library Cataloguing in Publication Data
Haywood, Trevor
   Info-rich/Info-poor: Access and Exchange
   in the Global Information Society
   I. Title
   302.23

ISBN 0-86291-631-3

Library of Congress Cataloging in Publication Data
A catalog record for this book is available from the Library of Congress

Published by Bowker-Saur
Maypole House, Maypole Road
East Grinstead, West Sussex RH19 1HH, UK
Tel: +44 (0) 1342 330100 Fax: +44 (0) 1342 330191
E-mail: lis@bowker-saur.co.uk

Bowker-Saur is part of REED REFERENCE PUBLISHING

ISBN 0 86291 631 3

Cover design by Juan Hayward
Typeset by Florencetype, Stoodleigh, Devon
Printed on acid-free paper
Printed and bound in Great Britain by Bookcraft (Bath) Ltd

About the author

Professor Trevor Haywood began his career as a metallurgist spending his early years testing big and small chains to destruction. During one of the many sea changes in his life he moved out of metallurgy to work in public libraries. After a time as Acquisitions Librarian at Aston University he moved to the newly formed Birmingham Polytechnic taking up a post as a Lecturer in Management in the School of Librarianship in 1971. He became Dean of the newly created Faculty of Computing and Information Studies in 1986 and was confirmed as a Professor and Dean of Faculty when the Polytechnic became the University of Central England in 1992. His research interests are broad and embrace: Information and Wealth Creation, Information Access, the Economics of Information and Public Policy with regard to Information issues, all of which he has covered in lectures and papers delivered in many parts of the world. His most recent publications include *The withering of public access* for the Library Association in 1989 and *Changing faculty environments* for the British Library in 1991. He has been a serious photographer for over thirty years and his work has been published in a wide range of publications including his own 1986 award-winning book *Walking with a camera in Herries Lakeland: a journey through the lakeland novels of Hugh Walpole*. He lives with his wife Susan at Workhouse Cottage, Kidderminster, Worcestershire.

For Lena

Some burn books for telling lies,
Some say that they are the only truth.
I do not make lies,
I do not make the truth,
I make a book!

Daniel Hechsetter
1872

Contents

Preface

We are all avid consumers of information. If physically we are what we eat, mentally we must be the information we have absorbed. The quality of our mental diet is no less important to our general wellbeing than our physical diet. This book explores some of the processes and influences that affect the way we access information, the value we give to it and the vehicles we use to share or exchange it. Whether it be in the social, the political, the economic or even the spiritual arena, the world can be seen as an information system, and events the product of a long series of 'information moments' that have cumulated in the knowledge domains that distinguish between or unite individuals, activities and communities.

Commentators on information, and on the increasingly exciting technologies that we use to disseminate it, often divide into 'optimistic' and 'pessimistic' when it comes to considering current and future trends in its access and exchange. I confess to belonging to both camps, sometimes at the same time and over the same issue. I am pessimistic when considering the future information resources that will be available to peoples currently outside the wealth-creating countries of the northern hemisphere and the Pacific Rim: I cannot see how they can ever catch up. I cannot see a will among wealthy nations to share their bounty unreservedly with poorer ones in order to give them the liberating effects of information at little or no cost, despite the domino-type prosperity that this would inevitably bring over time. I am optimistic that technology will continue to bring increased benefits and convenience to the citizens of wealthy countries, both in support of entertainment and escape and in mobilizing information as a major source of future wealth creation. The title *Info-Rich – Info-Poor* was chosen to emphasize the fact that the opportunities access to information can bring have never been, and are unlikely to be, distributed evenly among the members of any community, rich or poor, large or small. What is probably more important is that, despite the convergence of a whole range of new information technologies, access to information that can really empower and liberate people still looks set to be the preserve of an affluent minority. Unless the uneconomic sharing of *all* kinds of information becomes commonplace this discrepancy could occur to such an extent in the future that it will become impossible for the inhabitants of Info Rich and Info Poor countries to communicate or transact with each other using the same assumptions. The latter will suffer the same frustrations, with regard to accessing information, that they currently do with regard to consumer products and lifestyles.

World advertising expenditure has tripled since the 1950s [1], and its relentless messages remind millions of people every day of what they have not got and will never get. The face of a Sudanese or Somali delegate at an international conference called specifically to share information and knowledge between the attendees will often display the same kind of frustration: the frustration of not having started from the same point, of not having had access to the same kinds of libraries, of not being able to afford the same kind of hardware and software, of not having had teachers who could prepare the ground so well, or of not having had access to as many colleagues to discuss the issues with in any depth. The paradox is that such information poverty coexists alongside the extreme richness of information infrastructures developing elsewhere in the world. Despite a growing expectation in the west that increasing political democratization and powerful technological capacity will make more information available to more people for their better enrichment, welfare and wellbeing, the squeeze on the Info Poor shows no signs of abating. New Media, particularly satellite television and wireless communications, are beginning to penetrate where few pages were ever turned as their costs come down and the infrastructure to support them is put into place. The debate about their role and value in supplying information, in among the new opiums that they also peddle, is one that is set to continue for many years. What follows is a highly personal selection of themes and perspectives from a world where information is now deeply embedded in every activity that makes up the fabric of human endeavour. Sometimes the lack of clear boundaries makes the containment of such a selection more difficult than would be the case in a more precisely delineated discipline. I realize this and accept the incompleteness that is the inevitable result.

Benjamin Disraeli is reputed to have suggested that a person should only set out to write a new book whenever they wanted to read one. In the light of this chastening thought I would justify my selection of the issues that follow by wishing that I had been able to read about them, in the order that they are presented here, in another place. Information gathering, processing and transmission between generations has always been the fundamental basis for human action, and despite the boundaryless nature of the challenge, the 'wide-angle lens' of the information perspective does offer some interesting insights into the human search for value and meaning that are often not available to more domain-specific approaches.

I hope that you enjoy reading this as much as I have enjoyed putting it together.

1. Nicholson Lord, D. (1993) Is today so much better? *The Independent On Sunday*, 3 January

Trevor Haywood, October 1994

Acknowledgements

Being boundaryless, the range of sources that might help inform a trip around the world of information exhibits an exceptional diversity, some of which can be discerned in the references at the end of each chapter. I would like to record my particular thanks to the following authors, whose ideas and approaches I found both stimulating and helpful: Steven Rose, *The Making of Memory*; Tom Stonier, *The Wealth of Information*; *Information and the Internal Structure of the Universe* and *Beyond Information: The Natural History of Intelligence*; Barry Jones, *Sleepers Awake, Technology and the Future of Work*; Mike Connor, *The Race to the Intelligent State*; and Mark Hepworth,*Geography of the Information Economy*.

Other publications that I used regularly and which were often a source of very useful information include: *The Guardian*, particularly Will Hutton, Victor Keegan and Suzanne Moore. *The Economist*, its supplements and specialist surveys; also the *Financial Times* and its special features, *The Times Higher Education Supplement*, *The Independent*, *Business Age*, *The Harvard Business Review*, and BBC2's 'The Money Programme'.

In addition to the above I would like to acknowledge the particular support of the following:

Paul Embley at UCE for our discussions, over many years, on some of the issues covered here; Professor Judith Hitchen at UCE for her critical and fastidious reading of the evolving manuscript; John Leighfield, Executive Chairman of AT&T Istel and Bill Brown of Lucas Aerospace for valuable discussions on issues around the 'knowledge surplus' idea; Stuart Atkin for his generous guidance and help in Tokyo during December 1992; also during that hectic time my thanks to Richard Hinder, then at the British Embassy in Tokyo, Adrian Jenkyn, Mr Sato, Managing Director of Fujitsu

Research and Development, and his many patient colleagues who coped so well with my naive questioning at Kawasaki in December 1992; also Professor Heinze Wolf of Brunel University and Professor John Goddard and his colleagues at the PICT Research Centre at Newcastle University. Thanks to Val Ellis of Information Services at UCE for her many kindnesses in seeking out material for me, often armed with only the vaguest of clues as to what it was I was looking for; Fleur Meredith, postgraduate student in the School of Information Studies at UCE, who helped me collect some material for Chapter 2 and Linda Latimer for her valued help and advice with regard to the organization and presentation of the text. My thanks also to Geraldine Turpie of Bowker Saur, who started me out on this particular journey and to Val Skelton who, on taking up her editorial role, chivvied me just enough to get the final manuscript delivered before the end of the decade. Thanks also to Professor Diana Green, Pro-Vice Chancellor at UCE for supporting some time away from the university during June/July 1993 and my visit to Japan during December 1992.

And last, but by no means least, heartfelt thanks to my wife Susan, whose love and support during the more frustrating parts of this journey made all the difference to the destination. I hope that all those who have helped me in any way, accept my gratitude, enjoy the end product, happily take a share in any credit and quite naturally remain blameless for any faults.

Chapter 1

The information–knowledge chain

Any discussion of information, its social and economic value, its role as an agent of change, its transmission, retrieval and accessibility, is bound to fall foul of the challenge of precision as regards definition. The subtle differences between data, information, knowledge, insight and wisdom have given fundamentalist commentators in this area many hours of pedantic fun and my attempts to begin this work with some ideas on the connections between these concepts are unlikely to satisfy the fiercest of these. What follows is a simple example to illustrate how humans seem to construct the highest levels of their understanding, together with some reflections on the efficacy of such a step-by-step approach. I would like to suggest a mental journey that begins with the presentation and acquisition of data, moving on towards wisdom and insight via the key stations of information and knowledge. Human beings are great parallel processors. During everyday transactions and exchanges many of the states noted below will coexist in a seamless jumble of activity, gradually making more sense as they are shuffled from one mental filing cabinet to another on the journey to construct a satisfactory meaning. This step-by-step example should therefore be seen as an aid to signposting and reflection, rather than a precise order of activity.

Data

Data is the first stage in the evolving information–knowledge chain, usually represented by shapes in the form of letters, words, numbers or symbols that require cognitive skill to decipher, and the recall of previously assimilated information to help give them meaning. A set of Japanese characters set out on a page requires a prior knowledge of

Japanese before they can be processed as the written representations of a language. Someone unfamiliar with the style and layout of written languages might see them as having no meaning at all. Depending on their similarity to previously observed patterns, they could be invested with a novel meaning totally unconnected with writing or language. Investing symbols with meaning is easier if we know the context, but this has only so much power to illuminate. Despite knowing the context, and despite being armed with a rail-map of the city, any non-Japanese reader using a Tokyo railway station knows the bewilderment that can arise from written language. We also know that different people using the same language and the same rules can still come up with different meanings. The rules are important but they are only a part of the process. Rules help us organize information, but in the hands of the unimaginative they can also inhibit the development of its full potential. Humans always bring more to interpretation than a precise knowledge of the rules. Constable's painting of 'The Hay Wain', a sophisticated representation of humans in an English landscape, would offer few clues as to its meaning to an Arctic Eskimo. Shape, texture, colour, size, thickness would all convey something, but the intended meaning would require a completely different history of clue acquisition.

The same can be true even within a compatible, clue-laden culture. For example, the random collection of numbers 1891 1831 1861 1851 1801 1811 1821 1871 1841 1881, set out like this, do not mean much. A person's ability to give them meaning will depend on their cognitive skills, including knowledge of any rules which they might recognize as operating on these kinds of symbols, the context in which they are presented and, not least, their mode of presentation, e.g.

1831
1891
1861
1851
1801
or 189118311861185118011811 etc.

We may not have access at any one time to all the clues that we need for complete understanding, and under such circumstances it is not unusual for us to try and guess at meaning. Given our natural curiosity and desire for meaning, such guesses are likely to be fuelled by recall information that generally expects numbers to be arranged in some kind of order, i.e. they should comply with one or more of the rules of association we have been taught to remember.

Guessing is an interesting aspect of human data processing, and very important to us in our daily struggle to give meaning and to help reduce uncertainty. We use the term 'guessing' to indicate that we do not immediately recognize the patterns of data that we have been presented with and cannot retrieve enough information from our memory to help us handle them with confidence. Instead, we put together the fragments of the presented data that we think we can recognize and make a guess. Given more time to reflect on the material, we may discover that we can recall having processed patterns or symbols like these before. When this happens we are able to return with a more confident opinion.

Returning to our collection of numbers, we know that without the use of commas or, as in the first series presented above, spaces, we would not even be sure whether we were dealing with one large number or ten separate numerical values. The way that data are presented and the way we perceive them to be organized are important conditions for acceptance or rejection. We expect certain codes and disciplines to govern the modes of data presentation, and these embody important clues about intended meaning.

Information

If the next document we receive specifies that each of the numbers separated by a space is a discrete value, and that the order they should follow is: 1801, 1811, 1821, 1831, 1841, 1851, 1861, 1871, 1881, 1891, then the application of some simple mathematical knowledge tells us that this is a mathematical progression with a difference of ten between each of the values. An educated person, used to seeing the dates of years set out in this way, might deduce that they did indeed represent dates at ten-yearly intervals. If a third document noted that these numbers represent the first ten dates of the official British Census, then we are well on the way to turning this collection of symbols into meaningful information.

The transformation of data into information is thus a process of reception, recognition and conversion, made possible by our cognitive history and our ability to decipher symbols within a particular culture. Interestingly, accurate conversion of data to information can only take place when we are able to add value to it from stores of information that we have access to. These may be held in our own memory or in books or electronic devices. This raises an interesting question: when did the first recorded set of data become information and where did the information come from that helped make the conversion? Perhaps the answer is somewhere among the first 'information moments' explored in Chapter 2. If, just for fun, I set out the following symbols as raw data for you to process:

you will be hard put to make sense of them. No expert, no book, no electronic device, no one close to me holds the information necessary to illuminate my intended meaning. It is a unique set of symbols that you can only construct the meaning of, a meaning that will be drawn from similar patterns that you have come across elsewhere.

Just having seen similar patterns at other times will encourage you to assume that they are meant to mean something, that they represent information that someone wants to convey to someone else, that they are not just meaningless marks on the paper. We therefore need access to other information stores before we can begin to unravel the signs and symbols that we are presented with. This minimum-information state forms the 'base camp' from which we set out to discover the meaning of new data. Furthermore, this meaning is given shape and substance by a variety of other processes that derive from all the events in our lives so far. This includes our personal history, the values we have come to hold, how the information is eventually presented to us and, most importantly, what we have come to expect from information presented in this way. An interesting complication has arisen with regard to modern information presentation: recipients now often expect there to be a subtext or hidden meaning within many modes of presentation which, if not explored or interpreted correctly, could lead to serious misunderstandings. The public face of information presentation is often heavily influenced by status and roles in relation to others, irrespective of how the information was acquired and processed. This may lead to typical or untypical postures and declarations, depending on the public circumstances. There is also the important private formation of views and beliefs, which is often denied a public face. This latter, embedded and unseen, lies at the core of our information processing and, more to the point, how we decide to present it. Sometimes even the most experienced of communicators will be unaware of the range of interpretations that can be placed on the information they present. Every one of us constructs a private version of public information and a public version of private information. Our use of language, the values we hold, the responses we desire and our previous experience all influence us as presenters and recipients of information. Those of us who work in organizations where information is regularly presented to us as part of an argument for change are very familiar with the private–public/public–private information tightrope. Whether information is doubted or believed is largely determined by the way it is presented. Perhaps to the detriment of human engagement, the possible motives that lie behind even the most innocuous public presentations of information are never far from the recipients' thoughts as they begin to process it.

Knowledge

Some of these insecurities may affect the way we see our original array of numbers: we may be looking for something that is not there, but which would not surprise us if it was. If we were subsequently informed by a trusted friend or colleague that there had been a general election in Britain in 1841, and that it was the first time that a party in opposition had succeeded in forming a government after a general election, the discrete date of 1841 in our array would begin to take on much more meaning. This meaning would be further embellished if the same colleague also explained that all voting in a British general election before 1870 was held in public, and that the votes cast by an individual were actually recorded in public view. If we were also told that records of voting were often published by local printers in 'poll books' that sometimes gave the occupation and address of the voter, we can see that the number 1841, when read as a year, could be further supported by at least two important sources of sociopolitical information, i.e. the published census returns and any surviving 'poll books'.

Using these sources we could build up some interesting and informative pictures, for example about the voting behaviour of people following particular occupations during the first half of the 19th century, thereby creating some quite specific new knowledge. Note how this latter part of the journey has been more and more informed by a mythical 'colleague'. This is an intentional device to reinforce the point that we live in a world already populated with people who have acquired information and converted it to knowledge. As well as recognizing the 'personal' aspect of information and knowledge acquisition it is important also to understand that our knowledge is as much mediated by other people as it is by our own experience. That 'one person's knowledge is made up of other persons' knowledges and other people's determinations . . .' [1].

Wisdom/insight

Researching these issues among a number of primary sources, we might discover some concerning the general election of 1841 that had not been examined before. If we added to this information the study of other eminent commentators on 19th century electoral behaviour in secondary sources, including any electoral trends that might be highlighted by published reference works, we would be well on the way to becoming experts, having acquired a high level of information about the social and political dynamics of the year 1841 and, more particularly, the issues affecting the general election of that year. This would enable us to begin to speak with authority and confidence on some very specific aspects of the year 1841.

Depending on our skill at handling it this knowledge could enable us to share with others previously unrecognized insights, connections and perspectives on the year 1841, and its relationship to preceding and subsequent years. This confidence and connection-making ability would eventually be perceived as 'wisdom' by others. Our continuing ability to demonstrate deep knowledge on this subject, and to illuminate other, seemingly unrelated, dates and issues via our use of it, would also be recognized as acts of great insight. Our communication of this wisdom, via books, articles or television interviews, might eventually change the way that the year 1841 was understood and perceived by a whole range of observers. At various stages in this process, access to additional information sources, including our own cognitive history, enabled us to organize the information into new or familiar patterns, giving us the opportunity to validate and confirm the credibility of previously accepted views and ideas and to explore novel and untried associations and meanings for the first time. Stonier [2], in seeking to differentiate between 'physical information' and 'human information', also considers the human data–information–knowledge chain as a spectrum, with simple symbols at one end and complex human processing at the other:

> . . . with a single bit in the binary system as the smallest unit of information, while knowledge, insight and wisdom would comprise the other end, exhibiting increasing levels of complexity. Patterns of information, at whatever level of complexity, need sensors to be perceived, and 'intelligence' to be analysed and processed. It is processing information into new patterns that the human brain is so good at. Knowledge, insight and wisdom represent the increasing complexity of organized information in people's heads.

The information journey, then, can be seen as one of increasing complexity, often covering a long chain of human intellectual activity ceaselessly seeking to give meaning to what it finds. Drawing lines or distinctions between components in the chain, as in the journey to '1841' described above, is just a device to help us appreciate the levels of complexity that we might be dealing with at any particular point.

Narrowing for fit

The human ability to process information into new patterns and, over time, to grow new knowledge in the steady, building-block way noted above, often forms the basis of our differentiation between one person and another. It is what we look for when we select someone to carry out a particular job or task. Their success in having navigated a recognizable path is what helps separate them from other contenders:

> He's been a chemist for ten years, he can't possibly understand the level of thermodynamics that we need!
> She's been managing a group similar to ours for six years, it's a natural move.
> We really need someone who has several years in finance!
> He does have a wide range of experience but is it focused enough for us?
> She has travelled a lot, but selling gas turbines is quite a different matter from selling advertising.

We sum up the qualities that we need using the shorthand term 'experience', and we look for a curriculum vitae to confirm that someone has the kind of experience we think we need, gained over a timespan that seems appropriate. In this kind of selection process we often use 'timespan' as an analogue for depth of knowledge. All other things being equal, we naturally expect some serious information and knowledge acquisition to occur over time. This is known as the 'track record' and is proof that someone has absorbed information and developed new knowledge in the specific domains required by a potential employer, and that they have applied it successfully in a similar arena. Indeed, the modern curriculum vitae has become a major test of information 'squeezing': squeezing whatever varied experience people have acquired into the sometimes very narrow requirements of a particular job specification. This is 'narrowing for fit', and suggests an obsession with narrowness that is likely to exclude large chunks of acquired knowledge because it does not obviously fit the specification. Specific human knowledge is held as a subset of a big general knowledge database with which it constantly connects to produce rich and diverse solutions to problems. Narrowing for fit could miss the desired potential by fixing the template too tight.

The straightforward linear information–knowledge chain and the wisdom that emerges from it may now be facing a crisis of appropriateness. Too much of yesterday is embedded in the journey, producing 'standardized' knowledge outcomes that offer little or no preparation for tomorrow. The build-up of often very highly rated experience in order to secure the rewards that accrue from narrow expectations may also be encouraging us to retain a lot of dead information. We feel insecure about dumping it because it reinforces the comfortable narrowness that the world seems to want. Thus encouraged, we fall back on reviving our old information stores in the mistaken belief that this will be enough to help us cope with entirely new situations.

In 1944, as a global war that had changed so many old patterns and behaviours that had once seemed immutable, was coming to an end, T. S. Eliot elegantly set out the transience of what is currently celebrated as 'known':

> There is it seems to us
> At best, only a limited value
> In the knowledge derived from experience
> The knowledge imposes a pattern, and falsifies,
> For the pattern is new in every moment
> And every moment is a new and shocking
> Valuation of all we have been.

It may be that the relentless ambiguity, uncertainty and 'new and shocking valuations' of modern challenges now require substantial unlearning before we can successfully address the proliferation of non-familiar patterns.

The gentle progression through the information–knowledge chain mediated by our traditional approach to education could now be too narrow, cramped and overly heavy with rules and protocol to support the successful navigation of many modern challenges. To paraphrase Rousseau: 'Information was born free and everywhere it is in chains'.

The challenge of 'freeing it up' will still require support from well developed information stores, but it will also require states of mind that can dump some of the constructions of our old knowledge. The creative openness needed to address repeated uniqueness will require us to be hospitable to new kinds of wisdoms, wisdoms of holism rather than reductionism, of expansion rather than confinement, wisdoms that can break out of the old information–knowledge sequence and embrace unexpected futures with greater enthusiasm. Achieving this will require us to acknowledge and give a place to types of creativity that we may have difficulty in explaining by traditional information–knowledge routes. This will sometimes seem unreasonable:

> The reasonable man adapts himself to the world; the unreasonable one persists in trying to adapt the world to himself. Therefore all progress depends on the unreasonable man.
>
> Bernard Shaw, *Man and Superman*

The key role of memory

The human brain operates within strong contextual and cultural dependencies and the information–knowledge journey is an important part of this context. The principal source of information for all of us lies in the regular and repeated presentation of patterns which we are taught from birth to recognize as being linked with certain kinds of sensation or outcomes. These repeated patterns provide the brain with most of its compass bearings, and as we grow from childhood into adulthood we expect our capacity to recognize patterns and to understand things to improve. Memory plays a major part in our ability to achieve this, and after a number of years of growth, it is probably not too strong an assertion to say that we are what our memory allows us to be.

All new information is stored in short-term memory, from which we carry out much of our immediate day-to-day recall, often drawing on new information within a few seconds or minutes of storing it. Some of this information will later be dropped into long-term memory, but most of it will be discarded.

Information dumping is an important activity. It is a characteristic of biological information processing systems that they operate with a limited store that can soon become full. Without the capacity to dump, our speed of retrieval would be severely impaired. As we constantly receive a great deal of information, some dumping or instantaneous selection has to take place otherwise we would soon be overwhelmed. By a process of constant reorganization and restructuring, a healthy human memory manages to retain only a partial history of what was presented to it. By modifying its existing structures in the face of new experience it seeks to introduce a hierarchy of significance and relevance to guide information retention. Factors other than 'fullness' also affect our ability to retain and retrieve information (see below). Some of the information that we do retain may be lodged so far back in long-term memory that only quite extraordinary feats of pattern recognition will fetch it out again, and then often inexplicably or accidentally. These deep subconscious memories have stored everything we have ever consciously dropped into them, and there the information rests until triggered by a request for validation.

Long-term memory seems to be better at retaining information concerning tasks that we refresh by repetition, e.g. swimming or riding a bicycle. It is also good at retaining information about situations that inspire intense emotions, e.g. danger, joy, anger, pain of love. These two neural 'triggers', refreshment and strong emotional association, seem to play a key part in strengthening the initial information 'footprints' within human memory. It seems likely that a particular stimulus will both activate the chemistry of transient short-term memory and begin the build-up of more stable long-term memory. However, if the build-up of long-term memory is interrupted, perhaps by a period of disturbance or deflected concentration, all memory of the stimulus will be lost once the information stored in short-term memory has declined.

Long-term memory needs time to develop from the small and continually emptying reservoir of short-term memory. Lacking time and the two 'Rs' of recurrence and rehearsing to strengthen neural connections, neural pathways lack nourishment and the memories associated with them decay more quickly. Steven Rose, a bio-chemist at the Open University, has spent two decades researching the chemical changes which take place in different kinds of memory in an attempt to understand how they are formed, how recall is facili-tated and why it sometimes fails. In his award-winning book *The Making of Memory* [4] he notes the difficulty of identifying a unit of information within the brain. He postulates that the components of even a small piece of information might be drawn from a number of different locations across the physical area of the brain via an almost infinite number of synaptic connections. This 'plasticity' is at odds with the common belief that the brain is a kind of computerized information store, which adds a bit here or deletes a bit there with something akin to microelectronic precision. Instead, the brain seems to be constantly reforming the connections that make different memories possible:

> If you assume – as we do – that memories are stored in the brain in some way as patterns and connections between individual cells, if you have got a constant flux of connections and pathways and activities running around in the brain you'll scan and pick up semi-random information of that sort. [5]

This is why we surprise ourselves when we recall something apparently unrelated to our current memory search, or when a memory of a past event seems a little less precise than we think it ought to be. Rose is also well worth reading for his outline of a taxonomy to help explain different memory roles: the semantic memory – informing the ordering of things; the episodic memory for the placing of things in a time sequence; the declarative memory for the naming and recognition of things; and the procedural memory for the how-to-do functions.

We have all plodded through the kind of sequence set out below, convinced at first that we had no memory of the thing inquired for, only to finally make the magical connection:

You remember that kid who lived five doors up from us?

No.

He had red hair.

No.

His mother had one leg slightly shorter than the other?

No.

You must remember him. Roger Bell his name was.

Roger Bell, yes, he did have red hair and he had a rabbit that was always getting out. Yes I remember him.

Not unusually among humans, the name was the connection that had been strengthened just enough to prompt accurate recall; the other information, although stored, had not been refreshed enough to respond. Rosenfield [6], via a summary of Edelman's theory of neural Darwinism, also emphasized the importance of strengthening neural connections:

1. During embryo development there is laid down an extremely complex neural network. This constitutes the primary anatomy of the brain.
2. Learning involves the superimposition of patterns of connections onto this primary network. Such patterns are not created by creating new, or more, connections, but by strengthening existing pathways.
3. Pathways compete with each other. Patterns of connections are nourished by stimuli and grow stronger at the expense of weaker ones, which decay and are overridden. Note it is the weaker connections which disappear, not the neurons themselves.

The message, then, is clear: that all learned patterns decay with time unless reinforced by intense or repeated messages. This may be a blessing. Meadows [7] notes that the brain, however 'good' it is, can retain only a small portion of the information that it receives from the senses. That these:

> . . . may be the equivalent in computing terms, of 10 million bits per second. Over a lifetime of a billion seconds, we receive 10 million billion bits. The brain has a storage capacity of perhaps 100 billion bits – 100 000 times smaller than the total information output.

Now you know why you forgot the milk!

Some researchers [8] are attempting, via sophisticated scanners, to construct visual representations of a human brain while it is actually engaged in routeing signals around the physical network of the cortex to call up information from memory. During these experiments live subjects are injected with a tiny amount of radioactive oxygen and given a list a words to recognize. As the subject attempts to recall items from the list specific parts of the brain become active and use more oxygen. The scanner, by detecting these traces of radioactivity, can identify which part of the brain is working hardest. It then stores the data describing the increased activity, which is later converted to a visual image which can be retrieved for examination on a screen. These observations of short-term recall confirm Rose's belief that the brain is host to a number of different memories, short-term, long-term, audio and visual. They also suggest that these different memory functions are located at different points in the physical mass of the brain, and that any one or more locations might be called into use when recalling particular information. Equipped with repeated experiments designed to test the effectiveness of human recall, rather than brain scanners designed to show circuit activity, cognitive psychologists strive to observe how human recall behaviour is influenced under different sets of conditions. Using techniques such as the 'Brown–Peterson task', developed in the UK and the US during 1958/59, they examine issues such as short-term forgetting, delayed recall, filled and unfilled retention intervals, rehearsal and memory decay. These are the very real phenomena that affect us all in our day-to-day information recall, from elusive telephone numbers to the name of the vaguely familiar person walking towards us with a look of recognition on their face. The concept of filled and unfilled retention periods utilized by cognitive psychologists to help identify influences on recall is one that most of us can relate to. The 'Brown–Peterson' task is often conducted by asking a subject to memorize a set of unrelated letters, followed by a short list of numbers. During recall it is common for people to forget some of the letters. If the experiment is carried out without adding the numbers to the information presented, and recall is required after a short 'unfilled' delay, responses are typically perfect.

If the delay between memorizing and recall is filled with additional information or other mental activity, then recall again deteriorates. An unfilled retention interval allows us to rehearse the information that we have memorized: we can repeat the information over and over in our head and keep it to the front of our mind. Fill up the interval between memorizing and recall with other information, and we seem to have too much to handle. Greene [9] has noted a weakness in some of these experimental techniques that paradoxically seems to replicate more the kind of day-to-day conditions of recall that we are subject to. He notes that it is quite usual during 'Brown–Peterson' experiments to carry out a number of recall trials one after the other, with only quite small time periods between each. Under these conditions one of the key factors at work may be confusion rather than memory decay, i.e. the subject, in trying to recall the information from the most recently completed trial, suffers 'interference' from the information stored from earlier trials. During the first trial in a group of experiments, subjects invariably demonstrate excellent information recall whether or not the time period between memorizing and recall is filled or unfilled. Similarly, if some completely new information unrelated to that being currently used in a trial is suddenly introduced, recall of this new information is not affected by a filled delay. This poses the question, do we ever forget? It suggests that we do not, that once we have absorbed information it is always in our memory. Our problem is that in trying to locate a particular piece of information we suffer interference from similar and competing information, almost like the crackling that we get from a badly tuned radio.

The kinds of experiment noted above are also about learning. Listening to the lists of numbers and letters, recognizing them and storing them are all acts of cognition. However, we should always be careful how we treat laboratory-based measurements of learning and remembering. The state of our emotions plays an important part in conditioning our receptivity at any particular point in time and the different ways in which we have grown to see shapes and symbols will also condition many of our responses to the information that we are presented with. Our personal development will differ from that of others, as a result of different social and cultural experiences. We thus all carry our own non-standard 'interference' at the point of reception, and it follows that the results of any learning situation should take account of this.

Some cognitive psychologists work on the creation of circumstances and conditions that will help improve information acquisition and reduce certain types of recall interference. This could be by the design of the receiver's environment, by developing new approaches to learning or by carefully controlling the nature and timing of information presentation. Such approaches are particularly helpful to people engaged in tasks where the rapid assimilation and recall of complex information, e.g. air-traffic controllers, is fundamental to safety. The careful person-centred design of environments to help mediate the increasingly complex information and data transactions between humans and electronic devices is destined to become a growth industry in the 1990s.

Non-human memories

A lot of human ingenuity has gone into compensating for the limitations of human memory and recall by storing information in more durable, high-capacity 'containers'. Together these constitute the collective intelligence of humankind, and originally consisted of 'hard' records such as marks or inscriptions on clay tablets, stones, monuments, stone circles or cave drawings; later they took the form of writing stored in devices such as books, newspapers, magazines, computer disks, audio and video tapes and, most recently, compact discs. Since the mid-19th century the exponential growth in the production of these 'containers' has often required them in turn to be contained within formal institutions for their preservation and economic availability, e.g. public record offices, patent offices, art galleries and museums, archives and libraries. The end of the 19th and the early part of the 20th century saw the rise of the library as a key instrument of collective memory. In the US and northern Europe public, private, academic and national libraries began to grow dramatically and new library services began to appear in large numbers. Liberal benefactors, such as Andrew Carnegie in North America and the UK, often provided funds for new library buildings. Indeed, so fundamental was/is the idea of a secure place as the storehouse for these particular collective memories that librarians still belong to one of the few professions to be named after a building. This deep association with a place makes it difficult to de-institutionalize access to information. Librarians have to fight to convince the world that the library is just one place from where an information journey can start and that, aided by new technology, the destination can now be anywhere. The supply of books to large urban populations, such as that accomplished by the New York Public Library in the early part of this century, prompted revolutionaries who had never even seen the Manhattan skyline to take an interest in their achievements. In the early hours of 9 November 1917, amid the bustle to set up the first Soviet government, Lenin stopped Lunarcharsky, the People's Commissar for Education, in a corridor of the Smolny Institute in Moscow:

> I attach great importance to libraries; you must take personal charge of this work. Convene a meeting of librarians. In America a lot of good work is being done in this field. Books represent a tremendous force. There will be a much greater thirst for them as a result of the Revolution. We must provide readers with large reading-rooms and also with mobile libraries so that books can go to the reader . . . [10]

If this were updated to read 'So that all information will be accessible to every citizen', it could still sound like a revolutionary call to arms! Libraries are, of course, still full of books. The book as a serious part of our collective memory looks set to be a survivor well into the next century, and as we shall see later, any doubts as to its continuing role as a key cultural artefact, in the face of alternative information packages, will be dealt with by a growing cult of fierce protectionism. Schemes to transform the books currently stored in libraries into pocket-sized electronic packages pop up now and then, but the friends of the book will not lie down.

There are, however, now many more devices for storing information, most of which require electric power to secure their apparently limitless memories and to carry out the formidable manipulatory tasks we ask of them. Such devices can compensate for the limitations of human memory, and the technological advances seem to be unending. These are the fruits of the electronic revolution, and therefore where there is no electricity the capacity to store and gain access to information and intelligence is limited. In developed economies electronic memories have become a critical part of our collective intelligence and it is almost inconceivable to think of a modern community without access to them. The need to store the information in a backup device to prevent loss due to power cuts can also cause problems. The explosions at the Baltic Exchange in London in 1992, the New York World Trade Centre in March 1993 and the City of London in April 1993 highlighted the vulnerability of electronic memories to terrorist attack, the massive expense involved in reinstalling them if they are not backed up, and the near impossibility of securing their complete safety.

Electronic memories also pose a challenge to a new breed of vandal, the 'hacker'. These are usually bright, technically minded and ingenious people who tap into computer systems via the telephone network, wreaking havoc in databases, spoiling programs, withdrawing money, planting misinformation, passing on computer viruses and, last but not least, often running up massive telephone bills for their victims. In May 1993 a judge in England jailed two young men for six months (the first custodial sentences under the UK 1990 Computer Misuse Act) for hacking into databases in Russia, Canada, Taiwan, Singapore, Sweden, Norway, Germany, Iceland, India and Australia, for running up £25 000 worth of telephone bills for other computer users and for causing more than £120 000 damage to computer systems. In branding them as 'intellectual joy-riders' he further commented:

> There may be people out there who consider hacking to be harmless, but hacking is not harmless. Computers now form a central role in our lives, containing personal details, financial details, confidential matters of companies and government departments and many business organizations. [11]

Both of these info-delinquents were university graduates. It is a chastening thought that computer departments in universities all over the world may be inadvertently training people to carry out electronic theft.

However, despite the ubiquity of the electronic memory we still like to believe that certain kinds of information can only be transmitted in person. This is what we call oral history, e.g. grandmother's special way of making shortbread, grandfather's technique for growing tomatoes. In southern Portugal the proper way to cut cork from a mature tree so as to ensure a continuing harvest from the same growth, has been passed down from father to son with some precision in this way. Such examples have something of a romantic appeal, particularly in an increasingly inanimate electronic world. The idea of passing on techniques or skills from one person to another is something that we cherish, partly because we believe that such information cannot be transferred to machines and partly because its insightful and intuitive components celebrate human distinctiveness and protect us from mechanization. Over generations this kind of information transfer represents a little slice of immortality for the human memory.

In some circumstances, orally transmitted memories might be all that is available. This is a chastening thought. Most of us will not be followed by biographers, and our personal diaries, if we keep one, will probably be brief and incomplete. Our activities, ideas and beliefs will largely disappear with us and our 'intelligence' will completely disappear. Victoria Wood, a British comedienne, describes life even more starkly and briefly:

> Born in the north.
> Told a few jokes.
> Spoiled two bras in the tumble dryer.
> Died! [12]

Serious memory decay may set in over quite short periods of time. Almost everything that we do in a day will be forgotten within a few weeks, and as the ability to retrieve a memory decays exponentially more than 85 per cent of our experiences will have slipped out of our minds within a month [13]. Recognizing the problems that this causes for busy people, researchers at Rank Xerox's EuroParc laboratory in Cambridge have set themselves the challenge of developing pocket-sized devices to help people to augment their memories. So far they have confined themselves to monitoring the movements of their own staff, who wear 'smart' cards as they move around the premises within a 'wired' environment. Using a combination of video snapshots and computer-recorded data they have been able to provide no more than memory-joggers. Nonetheless, using this quite simple information they were able to make some progress, improving people's recall of activities during the previous day from 15 events (unaided) to around 35 (aided). The proportion was even greater after the passing of a month, with 12 events being recalled aided compared to only two unaided. Not only did the researchers remember more when prompted by the aids, they also learned that what memories they had retained were often unreliable [13]. Misfiling of data is as common in humans as it is in offices:

A favourite example of memory's reconstructive capacity among psychologists comes from the Watergate hearings, in which President Nixon's legal aide, John Dean, was asked to recall dozens of meetings he had with Nixon as the bugging conspiracy unravelled. Dean's recollection of these meetings seemed so detailed that it earned him the nickname of the human tape recorder. But when Nixon's own secret tapes from the Oval Office meetings were discovered, it turned out that Dean had got the gist of the conversations right, but the actual words and dates were very different. [13]

Given the above, expecting people to recall accurately events that took place 20 or 30 years ago may seem rather optimistic; however, some time ago I had no choice but to try. I was confident that as I was seeking information about the disappearance of a major building, i.e. something that should, on the posing of the question, prompt some powerful memory triggering, I should not have too much of a problem. During the early 1980s I was carrying out some research for a book about the Cumbrian landscapes of Walpole's *Herries Chronicle*. He had used a great house as the location for some of the action in one of these novels, and only a few stones of what I believed to have been a once grand Victorian edifice now remained. I was interested to discover what had happened to it and, more importantly, to put a date on its almost total disappearances from the landscape. I struck out for the nearest village to make enquiries. The answers I received went something like this:

'Burnt down!'
 'When?'
 '1960 or thereabouts.'
 '1952, they was burning out dry rot in the roof when it all went up.'
 '1956 I think it was'.
 'I'm certain it was the Coronation year.'
 'Yes, I was one of those up there burning out the rot, it was definitely 1954, I think!'

Pick any year between 1952 and 1960, and imagine the replies to the same question that someone will get from the adult descendants of these villagers at some future date. Unfortunately, although I explored all the local record sources, none of them was able to provide the date I wanted. The collective memories of the villagers were the best I had to go on. I chose 1956!

This is a story typical of the joys that face researchers into the disappearing past, but there is an important moral: however romantic the notion of handing down information from one person to another may seem, such information must be recorded and the record stored where it will be safe from interference if we are to retrieve it accurately in future years. How safe are the local newspapers in your public library?

The construction of urgency

The issue of interference in memory recall is basically one of biological limitation, a human property clearly related to the finite mass of the brain and the capacity of its neural networks. Urgency, on the other hand, particularly within organizations, is clearly a property constructed by humans, and anyone who is anyone (or wants to be someone) seems to have to show good reason why they are not constructing it at every possible opportunity. It is generally assumed that people are happy to regard this as normal. I mentioned earlier how we often resort to guesswork in order to reduce uncertainty, and suggested that this was largely because the time we were given to take important decisions was often too short to enable confident recall. Add to this pressure of constructed urgency, the interference from competing information during recall, and it is a wonder that we are able to carry out any successful pattern recognition at all. This is a modern phenomenon. Urgency used to be reserved for life-threatening situations where a slow response could prove fatal. Nowadays our minds too often have to respond to trivial definitions of urgency, which results in inadequate recall, guesswork, poor outcomes and stress-related illness, generating more urgency, more pressure and more stress. It is often said that computers 'burn memory' to gain speed and simplicity; this is increasingly applicable to human memory, and it would be useful to ask ourselves who is constructing the urgency that is forcing us into these situations and why? Scientists and researchers often suffer from urgency constructed by a need to be first, or by a desire to check everything that has been produced so far which is relevant to what they are doing. They are often hampered in this by having to access so much information that their ability to be original or creative is stifled. Because of the exponential rate of growth in scientific information, the pressure for speed may, paradoxically, be slowing them down and they are becoming hostages to information overload. The desire to 'check out everything' is a particularly academic failing that often leads to a mad, infinite hunt that can destroy all the joy of subsequent discovery and put off publication dates forever. Those who suffer from this particular desire are constantly reminded that they might have missed something. The feelings generated by this kind of library or information sickness were summed up by Lynch in 1989, describing how a prominent sociologist felt the need of 'protection' from the library:

> My search procedures are disorderly and accidental . . . The main thing that I require of libraries is that they build ever stronger brick walls to keep that mountain of literature from engulfing me. I require libraries to

hide most of the literature so that I will not become delirious from the want of time and wit to pursue it all . . . The problem is not access, it is the reverse, containment. And when I need to poke a small hole here or there to tap a tiny possible matter, I will send someone else on that risky mission, someone indifferent to all that is left behind in the alleyways when they leave . . . Were I now to browse the stacks, as I could do in the luxurious days of student status or that of a very new assistant professor, I would drown, or panic, and certainly lose my way. [14]

It cannot be denied that the selection of information to ensure comprehensivity within any domain is becoming more and more difficult and expensively time-consuming.

Information overload

Sometimes, as with the near-meltdown of a nuclear reactor at Three Mile Island in 1979, the urgency is very real, memory recall is put under serious pressure, 'interference' may fuel panic and the ability to process and interpret the information becomes a life-critical issue on a grand scale. Ford [15] and Burns [16] have comprehensively reported the sequence of events that triggered this information management disaster. My inclusion of the incident here has less to do with the actual technical breakdown than with the kind of information that the operators were expected to process, the way it was presented and the meanings it held for the different people involved. The sequence of events that follows is taken from Burns [16]. Like so many disasters before and after 1979, several written warnings about the possible failure of a number of key components in the plant had been given to the operating authorities, warnings about cooling system valves, the status of the emergency pumps, a potential for failure in the feedwater system, and not least about the design of the main control room:

> In the same year [1977], Aerospace Corporation reported to the Nuclear Regulatory Commission that the control room at Three Mile Island was very poorly engineered from a human-factors standpoint and that it would be a severe handicap if ever a crisis were to occur. This report was stamped 'for future resolution' and forgotten.

At 4 a.m. on 28 March 1979 all of these warnings were to come home to roost, when a valve that regulated the feedwater system inside the reactor stuck open and water began to drain out of the reactor at the rate of 220 gallons a minute. Five hundred lights and gauges were activated and clearly signalled trouble to the operatives in the control room. A few minutes later 800 more indicators were set off, but as there were more than 6000 gauges, meters, lights and alarms on a panel that ran for 900 square feet around the room, the operators had difficulty in extracting information to help them assess the potential cause. During all this, a key red light, designed to show when a valve had stuck open (the plant had a history of sticky valves), did not show. Computer printouts were available to give more precise information about the meaning of each alarm, but as it took 4 seconds to print out each message, the system soon fell behind and after one hour and two minutes the printer jammed. The two operators on duty in the control room were 'bouncing around from panel to panel'; they reacted to each of the alarms but they were still not really sure what was causing the emergency. They did, however, start an orderly shutdown of the reactor which, because they did not know that a valve was stuck open, would, if they had been successful, have caused a major discharge of radioactive water into the Sesquehanna river. The temperature in the reactor was rising, the automatic pumps kept kicking on to pour water in to cool the reactor, while the bemused operators, convinced that this was a system error, kept turning them off. Their information told them that the water level was rising when in fact it was falling. In order to help remove this phantom water they also opened up some emergency drains to let more out. The plant was now on the way to a major systems failure. The core was exposed, the temperature soared from a norm of 600°C to 2000°C and eventually on to 4000°C. Information from a working thermocouple near the reactor only reported data in the normal range; after 700°C it just printed out question marks.

As the crisis deepened the messages conveyed to outside authorities carried all the signs and signals of a small routine crisis that would soon be sorted out by normal internal procedures. These messages were designed to indicate a problem while at the same time insulating the recipients from the real nature of the crisis. Amid these misunderstandings, internal confusions, the lack of precise engineering drawings, a general shortage of confident leadership and some astonishing breakdowns in telephone communication to key groups outside the plant, the men in the control room were still trying to read the information they were being given in order to discover precisely what had gone wrong. Working on the night shift, when their biological alertness could be operating at well below optimum, the controllers were in various emotional states. They were worried, anxious and suffering from information overload. Too much of it was coming at them too fast and much of what they were receiving was not reconcilable with what they had been led to expect. Their view of the validity of the information they were getting and their confidence in the devices that were presenting it was being seriously damaged by this, and the severe emotional strain exaggerated the impact. Burns suggests that there are three main limits to information acquisition:

> First, most people can understand only seven choices – as on the radio dial or, in the extreme, on cable – he or she will settle on the favourite six or seven and forget that the others exist.
>
> Second, the brain is capable of processing only a limited number of symbols per second. When the rate is increased the brain begins discarding them according to their sources, in the same way that we shut out other conversations in a noisy room, or, in a complex business the way managers learn to listen carefully to a few people and ignore others.
>
> Third (and this is the good news) the amount of information the symbol carries does not seem to affect the processing speed. Very complex subjects can be discussed using sophisticated symbols, acronyms and technical language that make the topic incomprehensible to non experts . . . [16]

Despite the ubiquity of these ideas in the literature of behavioural science and ergonomics by the late 1970s, the planners of the control room at Three Mile Island seem to have ignored most of them. Perhaps they regarded them as only marginally relevant. At Three Mile Island there were clearly too many gauges requiring too much integration of small detail by the operators, which left them floundering under pressure. A smaller number of devices, capable of processing some of the information before it was presented, leaving the operators time for reflection rather than having to make complex connections between them on the spot, would have reduced the stress level considerably. Most probably the design of the control room emerged from a somewhat over-confident nuclear engineering culture that saw the information systems as only a 'back-up' for a process that was not expected to go wrong. Why spend a lot of time and money designing failsafe add-ons for something that is never expected to fail? The planners and the operators at Three Mile Island were, as we all are, prisoners of yesterday's certainties. New causations, new relationships and new information unrelated to and unreconcilable with their previous expectations became unhandleable.

The operators pulled forward the tried and tested patterns of the past to cope with the current challenge. When these patterns did not fit or could not be used to explain what was happening they moved into denial mode. Accepting that things can go wrong and that a serious crisis could result when it does, is one way humans overcome the worst effects of this mismatching. Education and training to help prepare people to face highly ambiguous or uncertain situations is another. The limits of human information receptivity under 'normal' conditions are known, and these should form the basis for the design of life-critical information systems. That human receptivity under abnormal conditions will be different again is also known, and allowances, via generous safety margins, can be made and incorporated into all information systems that affect health and safety. In retrospect we can see how the planners of the information vehicles and the potential recipients of the information at Three Mile Island were trapped from the start – trapped in expectations formed by their previous experience and previous evidence of reconcilability.

None of this 'previousness' was to offer satisfactory solutions to the crisis that began at 4 a.m. on 28 March 1979. Fifteen years on we know so much more; the computers are more powerful, the databases more flexible. Intelligent knowledge-based systems can now be installed to assist in the processing of a mass of complex information, sort it into options and package it so as to offer simple and straightforward choices. Operators working in the control room of a modern nuclear power station will thus never lack the evidence that they would need to cope with a similar crisis effectively. The explosion at Chernobyl on 26 April 1986 was, of course, a different kettle of fish: experimental tests being carried out on the reactor early in the morning by a team of tired electronic engineers who had been on duty for over 13 hours; prior knowledge of a design flaw affecting the way that the control rods worked in the event of a shutdown; incredible design parameters etc. – there was really no comparison!

Every day, managers in complex organizations have to juggle with recall interference, requests for immediate responses, the output from human or electronic memories and internally generated paper-based information in a desperate attempt to reduce the uncertainty of potential actions. In these environments 'reducing uncertainty' usually means getting it right first time, but the odds are against them. They simply cannot handle the expectation that they should consider all the available information before they act, the pressure is too great and the expectation too unreal if they are ever to go home! In 1890 it might just about have been possible; today it is not, so most managers live on marginal information. They make serious decisions with incomplete information, they answer questions with guesses and respond to urgent requests by quickly constructing their 'best shot', scoring just enough hits to get by. Cronin [17] noted the importance of distinguishing between 'real' and 'ideal' information worlds:

> Consciously (or unconsciously), most managers resort to a strategy of disjointed incrementalism, meaning that in practice a restricted number of options are examined and only a few immediate consequences considered – 'best-guess' estimating, in other words. In an ideal world we would aspire to perfect synoptic rationality, based on a thorough-going evalua-

tion of all information pertinent to a given decision-making situation. In the real world it makes more sense to aim for an approach mid-way between disjointed incrementalism and synoptic rationality – mixed scanning to use a term coined by Collingridge and Douglas – [18] which attempts to achieve a balance between the concern for operational data and information inputs from the macro environment in which the organization functions.

Mintzberg [19] has argued that organizations tend to grow and that this can cause serious imbalances which in turn lead to superficiality; that 'thick' knowledge has given way to 'thin' knowledge about organizations and their relationship with society. Aware of this thinness managers are more and more tempted to fall back on their intuition rather than the analysis of what they see as poorly validated sources of information:

> ... that superficiality, epitomised by the computer-printed report, is the unavoidable lot of managers, especially those in large organizations. It is the manager's separation from the true 'thickness' of what is being managed that is unbalancing. Superficiality, he says, is the problem.

Too much information is thus paradoxically leading to too little. Because of cost and time constraints what is available cannot be collected together, and even if it could the interference and recall limitations noted above would severely limit the ability of most humans to remember and process it. Although hardly mentioning the handling and processing of information in his intriguing book *The Twenty Four Hour Society* [20], Moore-Ede does draw attention to human failure in contexts where information handling is the most prominent activity. The world now operates non-stop around the clock, and requires human attention to highly technical and often life-critical matters at all hours of the day or night, irrespective of our biological capacity to handle it:

> At the heart of the problem is a fundamental conflict between the demands of our man-made civilization and the very design of the human brain and body. Fashioned over millions of years, we pride ourselves as the pinnacle of biological evolution. But the elegant organization of cells and chemistry, structure and systems, sinews and skeleton, that is the human being, was moulded in response to long-outdated design specs that we seem to have forgotten. Our bodies were designed to hunt by day, sleep at night, and never travel more than a few dozen miles from sunrise to sunset. Now we work and play at all hours, whisk off by jet to the far side of the globe, make life-or-death decisions or place orders on the foreign stock exchanges in the wee hours of the morning.

Many of the failures in Moore-Ede's examples relate to human alertness or fatigue at a crucial information-processing moment. He notes how some of the most notorious accidents of recent times – Three Mile Island, the Union Carbide disaster at Bhopal in India, Chernobyl and the Exxon Valdez oil spill – all occurred in the middle of the night when the judgement of the operators involved stood a more than even chance of suffering from fatigue. His plea for a move towards a more human-centred approach to working environments adds fuel to the arguments of those who seek to develop 'electronic minds'. These pioneers see the burden being lifted from tired and fatigued humans by devices that never need to sleep. They will never be impaired by too much light or too much dark, they never have emotional problems, take drugs or get drowsy. They stand alert and intelligent at all times, able to process huge volumes of information without ever making a mistake.

The search for electronic minds

The proliferation of information, the limitations of human memory and brain processing power and the requirement that information handling and processing often be carried out in antisocial environments around the clock, have prompted the search for electronic memories that can also think like humans. These would not just store information but would manipulate it, learn from it, reason with it and solve problems with it. In the late 1930s the English mathematician Alan Turing strove to give a very precise mathematical characterization to the intuitive concept of computability. The successful breaker of the German High Command's 'Enigma' code during the 1940s, Turing had, in a seminal paper in 1937, described an idealized computer, the 'Turing machine', which only a few years later would be realized in the shape of a working computer. Regarded by many as the father of artificial intelligence, he had no doubt that humans would eventually construct machines as intelligent as themselves:

> My contention is that machines can be constructed which will simulate the behaviour of the human mind very closely. There will be plenty to do in trying, say, to keep one's intelligence up to the standard set by the machines. For it seems probable that once the machine thinking method had started it would not take long to outstrip our feeble powers. There would be no question of the machines dying and they would be able to converse with each other to sharpen their wits. At some stage therefore we should expect the machines to take control. [21]

That last sentence sounds so certain and so ominous.

During the mid-1970s the creation of interdisciplinary groups in universities and corporations to link psychologists, computer and behavioural scientists and workers from other disciplines such as logic and mathematics, heralded the maturing of Turing's embryonic ideas on 'artificial intelligence' (AI) as an accepted discipline. The challenge was to simulate human reasoning and the kind of human memory that supported it.

The aim was to model the human mind via explicit sets of instructions which, in theory, could be varied until the team got it right. Such memories would be able to store infinite collections of information unaffected by problems of recall, interference or information overload, and they would theoretically be capable of making all the required connections without fatigue, without error and without breakdown. Despite the failure of AI to keep most of these early promises, experience gained from the wilder reaches of AI has provided the framework for the much more pragmatic exploration of expert systems (ES). These 'aids' to decision making can capture and store large bodies of expert knowledge in data structures for the purposes of symbolic computation. Some have been used very successfully in helping doctors treat blood infections, in the automatic configuring of new computers, in selecting the correct procedures embedded within complex legislation or regulation, in handling credit evaluations, airline ticketing systems and in solving problems in newtonian mechanics. The protagonists of ES have always emphasized their value as an aid and adjunct to the practitioner, pointing out the main choices or highlighting a range of solutions to select from, given a particular set of circumstances. These systems work best in conjunction with rule-friendly knowledge, where logical selections from the knowledge base can be made, according to fixed rules, and offered as a likely solution. Such a system might have helped the operators at Three Mile Island by preprocessing much of the information that they received and offering them a much more handleable range of choices. The development of computer programs has so far followed the quite understandable route of attacking problems that humans find very difficult, e.g. complex mathematical calculations or the reformatting of massive stores of information around a range of potential enquiry points. Where they have difficulty is in addressing what that most humans find comparatively easy, e.g. recognizing one voice among many, picking out a particular colour or recognizing one particular picture from a host of pictures. We are discovering that the way that humans use information, construct knowledge and enact what they know cannot always be represented by the logical, rule-friendly modeller. Indeed, a number of commentators have noted how much of the human capacity for problem solving, recognizing and understanding the things around them is only partly derived from the logic of rule-based reasoning. They note that human problem solving often emerges from inexplicable reasoning that is only capable of explanation after the event, and that often, only working back from the outcome can illuminate why a decision was taken. Twenty-six years ago Polanyi [22] called this 'tacit knowing', and described it as the kind of knowledge that we use to recognize a human face in a crowd. If it is true that logical thinking funds only one part of our understanding, that we engage in many more unique instances of reasoning than is often thought to be the case, then the computer programmers of the future are in for a tough time. At the moment they write programs that emulate the analytical, logical side of repeatable human behaviour. If it is true that whole chunks of behaviour cannot be reduced to a logical explanation, that much of it is inexplicable, they may never be able to replicate it via a computer program. Like many management theorists computer scientists have been the prisoners of a way of thinking that generally views all intelligent practice as an application of information or knowledge prior to the decision or the action. This premise lies at the heart of nearly all machine–human interaction.

Schon [23] in an antidote to this prior knowledge imperative describes what he calls 'knowing-in-action', 'reflecting-in action' or a 'conversation with a situation':

> Common sense admits the category of know-how, and it does not stretch common sense very much to say that the know-how is in the action – that a tightrope walker's know-how, for example, lies in, and is revealed by, the way he takes his trips across the wire, or that a big-league pitcher's know-how is in his way of pitching to a batter's weakness, changing his pace, or distributing his energies over the course of a game. There is nothing in common sense to make us say that know-how consists in rules and plans which we entertain in the mind prior to action. Although we sometimes think before acting, it is also true that in much of the spontaneous behaviour of skillful practice we reveal a kind of knowing which does not stem from prior intellectual operation.

The idea that we are all researchers as we practise what we do independently of established theory or technique, seems like a death knell to the concept of professionalism. Professionals draw their influence from their privileged access to technical expertise which is underpinned by a body of accepted theory. If it is credible that we construct new, important and immediate theories from our current situation, we may need to re-evaluate the tenacity with which we cling to the precepts so often set down as being vital prerequisites to membership of professional clubs. Lewins [24], while recognizing the large number of hours that teachers spend planning their teaching programmes, also notes how demanding and time-consuming 'reflecting-in-action' can be in classrooms:

However, decision-making is also considerably time-consuming, with teachers encountering decision situations at two-minute intervals while teaching, the greatest proportion concerned with students (39–50 per cent), then instructional behaviour and procedures, content, materials, and learning objectives. Able teachers develop cognitive skills which enable them to move back and forth between implementing pre-planned routines and adjusting their actions to new information and situations which occur during the course of a lesson. Experienced teachers are distinguished by their ability to obtain and retain new information in interaction with students while continuing to maintain control. It is experimentation over a period of time which builds up a store of personal practical knowledge about how to teach effectively.

Schon's ideas owe a debt to the important but difficult quest for an understanding of 'being' articulated by the German philosopher Heidegger in his famous work *Being and Time*, first published in 1927 and first translated into English in 1962. In this complex book Heidegger argued that the old philosophical search for a proof as to whether anything exists outside our individual consciousness was futile. For him there could be no separation between a human mind and what it perceived: they were one and the same. Distinguishing between the subject (mind) and the object (physical thing or action) was just stepping back from the primacy of experience and understanding that operates without reflection. Heidegger was also suspicious of the emphasis given by scientists and philosophers to detached theorizing. He believed that a kind of deep scientific snobbery had set in, only valuing information arising out of the study of logic, language or thought, which was derived from detached contemplation. He, by contrast, and very much as Schon does, stressed the primary role of unreflective experience and action in gaining access to information about the world, a phenomenon he called the 'ready-to-hand'. Heidegger also argued that our implicit beliefs and assumptions cannot all be made explicit, that we do not relate to things primarily through having mental representations of them and that meaning is fundamentally social and cannot be reduced to the meaning-giving activity of individual subjects:

> Heidegger rejects both the simple objective stance (the objective world is the primary reality) and the simple subjective stance (my thoughts and feelings are the primary reality), arguing instead that it is impossible for one to exist without the other. The interpreter does not exist independently: existence is interpretation, and interpretation is existence. Prejudice is not a condition in which the subject is led to interpret the world falsely, but is the necessary condition of a background for interpretation (hence Being). [25]

Heidegger's and Schon's ideas offer a counterpoint to the obsession with rationality and logical, heuristic knowledge representation which the early proponents of AI and ES believed to be the exclusive building blocks of intelligent computing. Most of them now realize that they have to take seriously behaviours that inform action and lead to solutions but which are not so easy to model using rule-only systems. Understanding how tacit knowledge comes about, how it is acquired and its role in solving problems and informing action is one challenge. Exploring information and knowledge discovery that arises out of engagement with the action itself rather than from independent meditation, and studying that knowledge, which is often explicable only in retrospect, is another. Scarrott [2] identified the limitations of the mathematical culture that excluded this kind of 'primitive judgement' from the rule-based computer approaches of AI:

> In living organisms the brain has been evolved to carry out the judgment process by taking into account against a background of experience, observations from several organs simultaneously, for example sight, scent and hearing, in order to make an appreciation of the situation appropriate to guide action. This process may be termed 'Primitive Judgement' since it is common to many species. Mankind also uses primitive judgement on a grand scale in daily life, but as a byproduct of the evolution of natural language the technique of logical argument based on the abstract concept of certainty has been added comparatively recently to our human judgement skills. Computers are essentially logical argument machines and they are of great value for assisting or undertaking any judgement that can be resolved into logical argument; but since primitive judgement preceded logical argument in the evolution of human information handling skills the widely held belief that every judgement must be describable in logical terms is ill-founded.

Many computer scientists have taken these criticisms on board and have switched from modelling mental processes that were good for emulating high levels of rule-based reasoning to emulating the kind of pattern recognition facilitated by the connection-making motors in the human brain. Although exciting work is being done by computer scientists in these areas, a lay observer would still be confused as to what is being modelled and why. I am not sure that the following quotation from Marvin Minsky, one of the leading inheritors of Turing's vision in the US, would help them very much:

> One of the problems of Artificial Intelligence is that when we do think we're able to make smart machines maybe the first hundred or so of them will be insane. [21]

When insanity abounds so prolifically in nature, investing in machine constructions of insanity seems a less than effective transfer of our intelligence! Identifying discrete properties of the mind or specific processes of the human memory is simple, compared to the complex chemistry of the brain, but modelling such properties in silicon and plastic does not approximate to anything we would recognize as a real human brain, and it may take decades to discover precisely how the brain works. We may even have to admit that some of it might remain unknowable for all time. Rose [26] is concerned that the complexity of behavioural phenomenology and the task of creating an acceptable language to translate chemical phenomena into human behaviour is not oversimplified by the modelspeak of the computer scientist:

> If, then, modelling brain function is intended to develop models which help us understand that function better as it is incarnated in real brains, the task is best seen as the discovery of those translation rules that enable us to convert between the language of cellular neurobiology and those of behaviour (Rose 1987). To decipher such rules requires that we locate a type of Rosetta stone – a phenomenon which we can simultaneously study in the two languages.

He goes on to suggest that such code-breaking will require a common language to more accurately locate the links between chemical changes within the brain and subsequent changes in behaviour. Pinpointing the changes in cellular states that correspond precisely with changes in behaviour could provide the translation service needed.

Such a language could aid the construction of more credible models of the brain and the role of memory within it. The sequence might look something like this:

1. A particular experience or sensation gives rise to new information being absorbed into the brain.

2. This new information or learning is stored in memory by a measurable chemical change as certain synaptic connections are strengthened.

3. This results in measurable changes in behaviour.

A key issue will be the level of confidence that researchers can have in the validity of any rules that might seem to govern both chemical and subsequent behavioural changes. Proving the credibility of any rules between (2) and (3) will be necessary to prove the validity of any new models that emerge from breaking the code. The proponents of neural computers see their capacity to learn from assemblies of patterns, analogous to the 'experience' acquisition in (1), as a major breakthrough in the search for truly effective electronic minds. Using a training algorithm, a device undergoes a kind of supervised training exercise not very dissimilar to that often offered to humans.

Neural computing

Researchers see this as the most likely pathway to a credible breed of 'intelligent' computers. Dating back to work done at the University of Chicago during the 1940s and by Windrow at Stanford University in the 1950s, neural computing (NC) has witnessed a tremendous upsurge in popularity. Regarded by some as the father of neural networks, Windrow developed a neural program for weather forecasting in 1963 which achieved an accuracy of about 83 per cent compared to the 65 per cent achieved by meteorologists [2]. Conventional computers have to be explicitly programmed. Someone has to analyse the problem in depth, describe it in a particular kind of code and construct an explicit set of step-by-step instructions which the computer must follow in order to solve it. The problem usually has an associated set of data in a defined structure that has to be manipulated as directed by the program. In these classic systems information can only be stored as patterns of on/off switches, operated by an algorithm that moves the information back and forth between the memory store and the central processor. NC does not require an explicit description of how the problem is to be solved; instead, the computer is 'trained' by being fed examples of similar problems, often with a desired solution to each. After sufficient training, the neural computer is able to relate the problem data to the 'learnt' solutions and offer a viable solution to a similar but new problem. It can thus be trained to carry out specific functions without the need for a detailed understanding of the underlying reasoning process and without the prior requirement to develop a complex program. The NC system operates via a number of elementary processing units called neurons (the number can vary from ten to thousands), connected together into a 'neural network'. The neurons are usually arranged in layers (known as the network topology), with the input data being fed via the input layer, through the network to the output layer, to provide the solution. Each neuron takes one or more inputs and produces an output: every input has an associated 'weight' and the neuron simply adds together all the inputs and calculates an output to be passed on. During the initial training process the values of the 'weights' within the network are adjusted, taking note of the 'error value' or discrepancy between a given input and its expected output. This continual tweaking of the weights by working backwards from output to input layer eventually brings the whole network closer to the desired solution. As this process proceeds the connections that lead to the correct answers are strengthened and the incorrect connections are weakened, in much the same way as we believe the neural connections in the brain are strengthened or weakened. By modifying the interconnecting weights according to a particular learning rule the network begins to take responsibility for its own internal programming, i.e. it 'learns'. When it has 'learnt' enough during the training period to achieve the correct output for every input case presented to it, the 'weights' are frozen.

When new input data are presented to the network the system determines the optimum solution on the basis of the training it has received. Neural networks are particularly effective at solving problems whose solutions are difficult, if not impossible, to define. They are thought to be more robust than their conventional counterparts and they cope better with 'fuzzy' data. Because data and processing are distributed rather than centralized the network can be very tolerant of faults, unlike conventional systems, where the failure of one component often means the failure of the entire system, and because the processing units all operate on the same problem neural networks are usually faster.

NCs are particularly useful to help control complex industrial plants where managers seek improved products, higher levels of safety, more consistent quality, savings in energy, reduced wastage and shorter downtimes. British Nuclear Fuels (BNFL) uses a neural network controller developed by Logica in the UK to help achieve greater accuracy in its batch distillation control than was possible by using experienced human judgement. Batch distillation is a method of separating a mixture of liquids by exploiting their different boiling points and latent evaporation heats. The results taken from a number of previous runs of the distillation column are used to 'teach' the controller how to manage the distillation process via a fast simulator. This involved running through the training data about 2000 times (it can take as many as 100 000 times), varying the parameters between their minimum and maximum values in a number of steps and in a variety of combinations. The results at BNFL have exceeded all expectations, with the neural controller achieving a level of accuracy that has easily surpassed control by other means. NCs clearly have a significant role to play in integrated control and condition monitoring systems within industrial environments, particularly those hostile to humans. Such systems are also characterized by the automatic generation of large volumes of data, thus producing the suitably large data sets needed to facilitate the 'training' that is the key to NC. Often interfacing with traditional control methods and knowledge-based systems, some of the most successful neural solutions have been those that operate in conjunction with conventional computer programs. NCs are also increasingly being used in many forms of pattern recognition, e.g. signature verification, face and fingerprint recognition and credit card processing; in intelligent data management, e.g. multiple-sensor analysis and fault and trend detection; in real-time data analysis, e.g. vibration analysis for machine health monitoring, signal analysis for error correction and noisy data processing; and in activities where some kind of prediction about future volumes is required, e.g. the stock market, crop yields and aircraft scheduling. Car fleet management, mailshot targeting, medical diagnosis and oil exploration are also areas where NCs are being used or developed. NC is now thought to be so versatile and important that the British government, via the Department of Trade, has recently set up a modest two-year 'NeuroData' technology-transfer initiative. Funded at $c£600\ 000$ a year, it hopes to help generate a better understanding of NCs in the UK and to secure better exploitation of NC techniques by British companies. NCs are clearly more analogous to human neural processing than conventional computers; by learning basic connections and then building on this knowledge to learn more sophisticated rules, NCs are getting close to taking 'responsibility' for their own programming, and by setting and resetting the weights given to particular connections in order to improve their performance, they are close to simulating the modifications in the strengths of synaptic ties that are believed to strengthen and weaken neural connections in biological systems.

Humans seek and process information to help them build meaning into life. In this chapter we have explored something of this process. We have seen how some information and knowledge acquisition can be attributed to straightforward, step-by-step building and how some of it may not be so readily explained; we have also seen how these processes can be helped and hindered by human memory. We have noted how recall, interference and information overload can have an effect, and how design and simplicity in conveying information is now a critical factor in human endeavour. We have seen how the location of memory, how it works and its exact role in the brain, is still one of the great unsolved mysteries of science, although we do know that it is extremely plastic, reconstituting and reforming itself as we work on it. Whatever its strengths and deficiencies human memory is one of the most precious parts of our information processing capability: losing the ability to remember is ultimately about losing track of who we are. We respect the brain as the most complex human organ because it is the most indeterminate. Although we can transfer our knowledge to electronic devices we have not yet been able to emulate the sheer versatility of the human brain.

This is particularly true of machine approaches to non-specific clue recognition. Information stored in the brain is often retrieved after stimulation by only the vaguest or most ambiguous of clues. Even the most successful NCs need 'training' by repeated exposure to thousands of unambiguous patterns, any of which, together or in isolation, could help form the answer. An NC fed only snippets from a data set, or eccentric patterns not acquired during the learning process, would require an almost infinite set of categorization retrieval rules before it could respond with anything like the success rate of a human mind. The study of artificial intelligence is still in its infancy as regards the emulation of information and knowledge connectivity, particularly in relation to modelling the role of tacit knowledge. The heuristic search models of AI programs and the classic von Neumann computer architecture that they were designed for both became prisoners of the limitations of logical information processing. Expert systems accepted these limitations and confined the knowledge base to very well defined and specialist domains. These, although comprehensive enough to proffer an accurate diagnosis or a manageable selection of options, nearly always leave the operator with the final say: the last link in the application of the specialist knowledge is still human.

Despite the promise of neural computing, the higher mental processes of information acquisition still reside most effectively in humans. Imperfect, fallible and infuriating, these exceptionally creative 'primitive skills' have yet to be transferred successfully to machines. It is these same humans who receive and process the 'information moments' that are explored in Chapter 2, who create the 'knowledge surpluses' of Chapter 3, who organize the societies examined in Chapter 4, and who both control and receive the outputs of the media discussed in Chapter 5, and it is important that we never lose sight of this. It is human ingenuity that fashions and improves technology, that takes it on to the next stage and which, if we are so disposed, can always pull the plug on it.

References

1. Strathern, M. (1993) Society in drag. *Times Higher Education Supplement*, 2 April
2. Stonier, T. (1990) *Information and the Internal Structure of the Universe*. London: Springer-Verlag
3. Eliot, T.S. (1944) *East Coker, The Four Quartets*. London: Faber
4. Rose, S. (1992) *The Making of Memory: From Molecules to Minds*. London: Bantam Books

5.   Rose, S. (1993) Interview with Tim Bradford. *The Guardian*, 27 May

6.   Rosenfield, I. (1988) *The Invention of Memory*. New York: Basic Books. Quoted in Stonier, T. (1992) *Beyond Information: The Natural History of Intelligence*. London: Springer-Verlag, pp. 140–141

7.   Meadows, J. (1989) *Info-Technology: Changing the Way We Communicate*. London: Cassell

8.   BBC 2, 'Tomorrow's World', Wednesday 31 March 1993

9.   Greene, R. (1992) *Human Memory: Paradigms and Paradoxes*. Hillsdale, NJ: Lawrence Erlbaum

10. Fonotov, G. (1967) The libraries of the USSR during the last fifty years. *Unesco Bulletin for Libraries*, **XXI**(5), 240–248

11. Campbell, D. (1993) Intellectual joyriders jailed. *The Guardian*, 22 May

12. 'An evening with Victoria Wood', Symphony Hall, Birmingham, April 1993

13. McCrone, J. (1994) Don't forget your memory aide. *New Scientist*, 5 February, 32–36

14. Lynch, B. P. (1989) Collections and the library user. RTSD Midwest Collection Management and Development Institute, University of Illinois at Chicago, 17 August

15. Ford, D.F. (1982) *Three Mile Island, Thirty Minutes to Meltdown*. New York: Viking Press

16. Burns, C. (1985) Three Mile Island: the information meltdown. *Information Management Review*, **1**(1), 19–25

17. Cronin, B. (ed) (1985) *Information Management: From Strategies to Action*. London: Aslib

18. Collingridge, D. and Douglas, J. (1984) Three models of policy-making: expert advice in the control of environmental lead. *Social Studies of Science*, **14**(3), 343–370

19. Spender, J. C. (1989) Meeting Mintzberg and thinking again about management education. *European Management Journal*, **7**(3), 254–266

20. Moore-Ede, M. (1993) *The Twenty Four Hour Society*. London: Piatkus Books

21. Turing, A. (1912—1954) quoted in 'Electronic Frontiers', Channel 4, Horizon, 7 June 1993

22. Polanyi, M. (1967) *The Tacit Dimension*. New York: Doubleday

23. Schon, D. A. (1983) *The Reflective Practitioner: How Professionals Think in Action*. New York: Basic Books

24. Lewins, H. (1991) Teachers and knowledge. In *Knowledge and Communication*, ed A. J. Meadows. London: Library Association

25. Winograd, T. and Flores, F. (1986) *Understanding Computers and Cognition: A New Foundation for Design*. New York: Addison-Wesley

26. Rose, S. (1989) Can memory be the brain's Rosetta Stone? In *Models of Brain Function*, ed R. M. J. Cotterill. Cambridge: Cambridge University Press

Chapter 2

Information moments

The whereabouts of the sabre-toothed tiger at any one time must have been a critical piece of information for Pleistocene *homo erectus*. There must have been a lucky first time when, too close for comfort but far enough away to be able to make his escape, he distinguished between the noise made by this and other big predators, and the sounds made by smaller, more welcome creatures. The unidentified noise (data) became information when he discovered, via a 'near miss' or as a witness to a neighbour's more immediate contact, why the originator of such a noise would eventually be called 'sabre-toothed'. There must also have been a first time when, out for a Pleistocene stroll, someone recognized a place or a physical feature that reminded him of previous tiger activity, and advised others, by whatever means advice was transmitted, that they should go this way rather than that, so as to avoid the 'big one'. Over time, information about the significance of particular animal noises and the likely location of big predators would have been remembered and passed on to others, to help reduce anxiety and improve longevity, much as the modern day visitor is advised to be wary of pedestrian crossings in Taipei.

These early life-preserving acts of information acquisition, and subsequent remembrance, constitute the first 'information moments', moments during which people acquired new information, stored it away in memory, added new information to it over time and eventually refined it to a point where it became knowledge. This knowledge then gave rise to a state of confidence which could later be converted into action or a plan of action. It is interesting to conjecture how and when early man learnt to transfer information acquired from a particular experience to another experience or activity. East Africa 100 000 years ago was a melting pot in which the first human minds wrestled with the problems of survival via hunting and gathering. Focusing on the relentless energy-to-gain-food-to-support-more-energy-to-gain-more-food efficiency chain, ancient humans developed many functionally specific skills. Although displaying advanced learning in many domains of behaviour, the skills of the first hominids tended to be acquired within quite narrow domains, with little or no transferability between them. Mithen [2], in seeking to refine the catch-all notion that 'our modern skulls house [100 000-year-old] hunter-gatherer minds' articulated by Cosmides and Tooby [1], has suggested that there was something of a major transition in the behaviour of ancient hominids around 50 000 years ago:

> The magnitude of the behavioural change at this time involving the appearance of art, the colonization of extreme environments and a dramatic increase in behavioural flexibility, suggests that their origin lies in a fundamental change in human cognition. The most parsimonious explanation of this change is the transition from a highly domain specific intelligence . . . to one in which cognitive mechanisms are coopted for use in behavioural domains other than for those for which they had evolved. We might refer to this as 'domain sharing' rather than a 'domain specific' intelligence or rationality. [2]

At this time particular skills deeply associated with specific actions and materials, for example the fracturing of stone to make tools, began to be transferred to work with new materials such as antler, wood and ivory. Also, the emergence of art in the form of cave paintings and stylistic messages on stone tools suggests the successful integration of a range of mental processes drawn from the compartmentalized tasks of hunting and gathering. The convergence of an emergent 'domain sharing' intelligence and the first appearance of language could have been the motor by which information moments became part of a social rather than a private intelligence. Mithen suspects that such a convergence did occur, accelerating the development of higher-order mental behaviour during the later stages of cognitive evolution:

> These may be related as the appearance of fully modern language or consciousness may have enabled deep introspection, allowing one to become aware of one's own cognitive processes so that they may be used in new behavioural domains. [2]

The human ability for tool making, plant control, the domesticating and rearing of animals, conducting war and developing communities grew out of ancient minds that had learnt to transfer information and experience between domains. Using tools to reduce the daily effort needed for basic survival, they created time to reflect on, and to make connections between, the specialized cognitive processes which had evolved to address functionally specific tasks. They were beginning to grow new knowledge.

In transferring information gained from one domain-specific activity to another, these early hominids were introducing themselves to the mysteries of both Heidegger's 'ready to hand' (see Chapter 1) and Karl Popper's 'three worlds'. World 1 is the material things that they accessed through their senses, the world of trees, hills and animals, hot and cold, light and darkness, earth and water, dampness and dryness. Sometimes harsh and frightening, sometimes pliant and welcoming, much of early life would have been taken up by gathering information about this world and reacting to it. World 2 exists in our heads and is a mental analogue of the first, where the first reflections-in-action, evaluation, interpretation and conversations-with-situations were taking place. World 2 is where the physical elements of World 1 are reconstructed, ranging from cautious and slow reflection, where knowing and exploring how we know is constantly being re-evaluated, to the instant action–reflection–action information moments that so fascinate Schon and Heidegger. This is the world where the qualities of everyday items are translated into abstract ideas. World 3 is the continuing interaction between the first two, a world where theories, ideas and problems are constructed and where we consider transferring abstract ideas to domains other than the one which initially inspired them. World 3 is also where information begins to inform our social relations and where we share, record and store World 2 conclusions about World 1. McGarry [3] has noted how much of the philosophical debate about the relationship between Worlds 1 and 2 has been occupied with the nature and impact of the filters that mediate the process of transfer from one to the other:

> Others take the view that we do not perceive the physical world in its pristine state at all. We perceive or see it through a screen (as it were) of symbols, particularly through our language and social customs. There is no 'immaculate perception' and different people from different social and cultural groups perceive the physical world in noticeably different ways. If knowledge is what somebody knows, then without a knower, knowledge is an absurdity. The knower, however knowledgeable, is a contingent social creature related to and influenced by other human beings - all knowledge of its very nature has a social and cultural basis looking backwards and forwards in time.

It is interesting to reflect on how close the early hominids might have been to an 'immaculate perception', given that the filters of language, culture and social customs would have been absent, or present in only the most rudimentary of forms. It is just as likely, given the small size of early hominid groupings, that as many acts of 'domain sharing' were explored by individuals alone as in social settings; sharing could always be undertaken later. Like middle managers in modern organizations, some early hominids would have anticipated the benefits of holding on to information for personal use, anticipating by 50 000 years the competitive-edge imperative so common today.

One of the great questions of social anthropology concerns the nature of the social information processing that occurs among primates such as chimpanzees and baboons, and the evolutionary links between these and the first hominids. The chimpanzee's use of similar tools for simple breaking and opening tasks constitutes something of a shared knowledge base, while the individual members within baboon groups seem to carry out different roles in initiating group movement, the timing of departures and the eventual direction of travel. Although none of the primates ever entered Popper's World 3, of generating artefacts to store knowledge, this preverbal conventionalization of knowledge suggests that there may be a strong continuity between them and the processes that began to characterize early hominid behaviour. Quiatt and Reynolds [4] distinguish between 'social knowledge', i.e. knowledge about others and their actions, such as is acquired by observation and what we would call learning, and 'knowledge in the social domain', which operates at a supra-individual level. This latter would include the prelinguistic knowledge that was stored externally, as in crude pictures or graphics. It would also include the non-linguistic knowledge which was distributed in the minds of a particular social group, for example the way they cooperated to share the tasks involved in the tracking and killing of an animal, or the labour-dividing cooperation that they might have used to minimize the physical effort involved in gathering food. Whether inspired by information processed by a group or by the individual internalization of experience that was not necessarily shared, there can be no doubt about the force of language as a key facilitator in aiding 'domain-sharing' processes. Language is the key to understanding human culture. It is also unique in the way that it makes possible, and helps solidify, the prescriptive rules that constrain, as well as liberate, humans as compared to other animals. It is via language that humans create publicly recognizable institutions to regulate their behaviour and relationships. It is language that enables Popper's World 3. By developing and refining language as a flexible conduit between the mental, natural and social worlds, humans made possible the individual construction of shared experience. The discrete information moment was coming of age.

Speech and language

The effective communication of information gained from recalled experience was only made possible by the emergence of the human ability to modulate sound, articulate speech and develop language. We are not overestimating the importance of language to note that its acquisition by humans, and humans alone, caused an explosion of culture fundamentally different from that found in the rest of the animal kingdom. So far, humans have continued to be the sole custodians of its secret. Despite several well publicized projects it has proved impossible to teach other animals, including our closest relation the chimpanzee, to use language. Stonier [5] has noted the debt owed by all human collective intelligence to man's ability to speak. This phenomenon was to form the basis of a major discontinuity in the evolution of intelligence:

> The depth of its impact can be fathomed by looking at its effect: human speech allowed communication across generations so that a store of collective wisdom could be built up much more rapidly than by other means (such as learning by imitation). Cultural evolution now became more important than biological evolution; the meme superseded the gene. In fact, it is likely that the great increase in brain size of the later hominids represented the highly selective value placed on those of our proto-human ancestors who could learn and remember words, then articulate phrases and sentences. It was a time when the poet ascended over the brute.

Here Stonier is building on Dawkins' concept of 'memes', i.e. selectively retained ideas and beliefs that are transmitted down through the centuries in much the same way that successful genes are selected and transmitted in biological systems. Strong memes carry over because they arise '. . . internally from a goal-orientated intelligent system (human culture) attempting to master its environment' [6]. The more successful the act of exploitation the more likely that cultural transmission will occur, and the more tenacious the information moment the greater the ability to enhance survival. Pinker [7], in a new and persuasive ode to language as an instinctive tendency directly attributable to natural selection, notes the improbability of random forces playing any significant role in human language development:

> . . . there is an obvious adaptive benefit in being able to convey an infinite number of precisely structured thoughts merely by modulating exhaled breath. Considering the adaptive value of language and the precise micro-circuitry needed to learn and arrange words, not to mention the changes in the human vocal tract and auditory system needed to utter and compre-

hend them, natural selection is the most plausible explanation for its emergence in our species. . . . .Selection is the only natural force capable of evolving 'adaptive complexity'. . . .. Complex organs are simply too improbable to have arisen from random forces like genetic drift or by-products.

Given order by rules, speech as language facilitated the precise repetition of common sounds and allowed for the clear association of these with people, things and ideas. Interestingly, despite considerable research in many locations around the world, the nature of human language acquisition is still not completely understood. Modern studies of the way children acquire their language skills, for instance, are still torn between a number of theories, most of which can be placed in one of two groups, innateness and imitation, or cognition and input.

Innateness

The theory of 'innateness', largely developed and modified by Chomsky, promotes the idea that a child's brain has a built-in capacity for language development. In 1965 Chomsky posed the question 'What are the initial assumptions concerning the nature of language that the child brings to language learning, and how detailed and specific is the innate scheme?' [8]. At that time, simply suggesting that a child brought any initial assumptions at all to language acquisition about the nature of language was something of a breakthrough. Up until then the orthodox view had been that the human mind was an information-free blank slate, empty of content until written over by the hand of experience. Chomsky went on to suggest that when children are exposed to speech the brain is ready and waiting for it, and that certain general principles for discovering or structuring language automatically spring into action. He labelled this the child's 'language acquisition device' (LAD). Equipped with this a child begins to make sense of the utterances it hears around it. Over the next 20-odd years Chomsky, still vexed by questions of learnability, the poor clues and information sources available to young children and the nature of the triggers that switched a child on to a particular language, frequently revisited his original ideas. He concluded that his earlier approach was probably too simple and that he had underestimated the amount of prior information necessary to trigger a particular language route. He developed his ideas further by exploring the concept of an information-rich innateness akin to a 'universal grammar'. This was part of a separate language component of the mind quite distinct from general intelligence.

Richer and more tightly structured than his old ideas of 'innate universals', universal grammar modules were to language what the individual instruments in an orchestra are to a symphony:

Within each module, there are sets of principles. Each principle is fairly straightforward when considered in isolation. The principles become complex when they interact with those from other modules. ... Chomsky's major concern therefore, is in specifying the principles operating within each module, and showing how they interact. ... There are option points within the modules, with switches that can be set to a fixed number of positions, most probably two. Children know in advance what the available options are. This is pre-programmed and part of a human's genetic endowment. A child can therefore scan the data available to him or her, and on the basis of a limited amount of evidence will know which way to throw the switch. [9]

Thus from the observation platform of its highchair the child will set up the parameters of its own 'core language' system. He is then set up to assimilate more detailed information about the specific rules that govern the grammar and sentence construction of a particular language. The largely untestable credibility of Chomsky's theories arises out of:

1. The remarkable speed with which children learn to speak using grammatical patterns that are similar in nature across all children and in all languages.

2. The fact that language emerges at more or less the same time in all children, irrespective of where they live or the language they use.

3. The way in which children acquire the rules of a language, despite the variable qualities of their environments, sometimes rich, sometimes poor. That they generally succeed irrespective of their surrounding conditions, often operating on the minimum of triggering clues, strongly suggests facilitation by some powerful preprogramming.

4. Language being found to exist separately from general intelligence, and appearing to use dedicated neural systems. In some neurological disorders language capability might be impaired despite intelligence remaining intact, or language can be intact despite impaired intelligence. [7]

The idea of a built-in processor waiting to manipulate the language that a child is exposed to would go some way towards accounting for the rapid progress of language acquisition and its worldwide uniformity. Most commentators agree that these two features of language maturation could not arise simply from imitating the complex and sometimes disorganized use of language that children are exposed to. Nonetheless, however persuasive the built-in LAD and universal grammar theories may be, they are still hotly contested by the advocates of other theories.

Imitation

It was long thought that children learned to speak simply by copying the utterances heard around them and that their responses were gradually strengthened by the repetitions, corrections and other reactions that the adults close to them would usually provide. However, this is contradicted by children's regular conversion of irregular past tense forms and plural forms into words which they would rarely hear from adult conversation. Children assume that grammatical usage is regular and they try, via a form of analogy, to work out for themselves how words should sound. 'Went' and 'took' get converted to 'wented' and 'tooked', 'mouse' and 'sheep' to 'mouses' and 'sheeps'. Children also seem to be unable to imitate adult grammatical constructions exactly, even when these are repeated over and over. This experience suggests that the acquisition of language is more a matter of maturation than imitation, i.e. that there is a quite specific time in the language processing experience of a child when it can get it right.

Cognition and input

The Swiss psychologist Jean Piaget argued that successful language acquisition can only follow on from established cognitive discoveries. For example, before being able to articulate big, small or medium, a child must first have developed the conceptual ability to make relative judgements on size. These ideas suggest that a linguistic status for anything always follows intellectual understanding, that linguistic skills always shadow non-linguistic learning.

Piaget portrayed the growing child as an active, information-seeking being, one that is constantly conducting experiments on the world to see what happens. Although revolutionizing thought on child development by formalizing four key stages in a child's cognitive progress, Piaget's research tended to stress the progress of the individual child as a lone explorer in and around its own physical space. The growth of studies in 'social cognition' from the 1960s onwards has challenged the value of knowledge growth as a purely individual activity. The development of language skills as part of early social engagement, how we learn from each other in groups, how learning in groups helps both the weakest and the strongest participants, and how the total knowledge acquired by individuals often seems greater when they work in groups, are all issues that affect the richness of the language available to absorb. The rise of the importance of care-giver language or 'motherese' since the 1970s, in part as an antidote to the ideas of innateness, stressed the importance of family input during a child's acquisition of language skills, particularly maternal input. These theories suggest that parents do take the trouble to adapt and simplify their conversation when in contact with young children, that the information available to a child is often much more than the minimum suggested by Chomsky, and that mothers in particular devote a great deal of time to giving out language clues and absorbing feedback. This is done via the use of simpler words, shorter sentences, slower speaking, heavy repetition, the expressive use of special words and very clear contexts for the description of concrete things [10]:

> Adults tend to speak in shorter sentences and make fewer mistakes when they address children. There is a considerable difference between the way a mother talks to another adult and the way she talks to her child. One researcher recorded a mother talking to an adult friend.
>
> Her sentences were on average fourteen to fifteen words long . . . But when she spoke to her child the same mother used five-or-six word sentences. The words were shorter, and referred to things the child could see or do.

To a lay person it would seem that all the following might play a part in aiding the progress of language acquisition:

1. That we do all arrive in the world somehow wired for language acquisition and that a biological clock activates this at a certain time. A baby able to utter more than 50 words before 18 months would be a very rare baby indeed!

2. That a state of language readiness encompassing both biological maturation and a growing store of general intelligence begins to develop quite rapidly at around two years old, when dramatic increases in vocabulary start to take place.

3. That language acquisition is both natural and artificial.

4. That maternal input, especially during the first three years of life, is an important part of a child's exposure to language.

5. That nature sets us all up as hospitable receivers but that this hospitality has to be nurtured within a rich language environment for us to reach our full potential. Deficiencies in either our natural equipment or the richness of the environment will inhibit our progress.

6. That children do not learn language simply by repetition and practice.

7. That correction and imitation can sometimes be a hindrance to language acquisition.

There is still a tremendous amount of work to be done before we can confidently establish the real impact of all or any of these factors, either as independent motors or in varying degrees of association. The process of language acquisition and refinement is no less important in the modern world as it was when the early protohuman speakers were being selected. It is still a skill, the levels of attainment of which determine serious social and economic differentiation within both information-rich and information-poor communities.

Writing

One very early form of communication, which developed independently of language, was picture-writing. These very personal representations depicted people, events and physical features in simple drawings which, taken together, often look as though they might provide some sort of narrative. It has proved difficult for modern scholars to read these pictograms with any degree of precision, due to their subjective nature and the inevitable lack of knowledge about the context of their creation.

Ideographic writing represented a development of the pictographic type by compressing the images into even simpler shorthand forms often no longer recognizable as pictorial representations. Ideographic symbols began to represent ideas and notions as well as things, allowing for the representation of more complex connections between thought and the physical environment. Despite some ideograms evolving into representations of sounds or words, pictographic and ideographic forms generally developed independently of language. The Egyptian hieroglyphic script contained a mixture of pictograms, ideograms and linguistic or phonographic elements, as did the early scripts of the Sumerians and the Hittites, while Chinese script remains ideographic to this day. However, it would be wrong to assume that there was a common thread running from pictographic through ideographic to the phonological alphabetic writing systems with which most of us are familiar. It is generally agreed that several sound or phonetic writing systems evolved independently of each other at different times, e.g. in Mesopotamia, China and Central America, with little evidence of any common origin. Phonetic writing, although less ambiguous and composed of fewer elements than ideographic forms, was a complex construction:

> An idea has to be translated into the sounds of a particular word or sentence in a particular language, then those sounds have to be made visible in the form of engraved, painted or incised signs on the surface of a definite object, signs which more often than not bear no relation to the content of the original thought. In order to consult the information (and ultimately the whole purpose of information storage is

communication) these visual signs have to be translated back into the sounds of the same language, and from this the word, the sentence and the original idea have to be reconstructed in the mind of the reader. And this is in fact exactly how primitive people without any writing of their own view the process. [11]

Despite this complexity, phonetic scripts, particularly alphabetic scripts, have developed to serve successfully the many social, political and economic needs of most societies:

> In comparison to the 50 000 (or at least 2000) Chinese characters, or the 700 or so Egyptian hieroglyphs, syllabic, consonantal and alphabetic scripts can manage with 20–60 signs. Information storage becomes thus more economic, less labour intensive in relation to the time taken to learn, read and write the script, and information can be stored in less space. In short, phonetic scripts are generally more cost-effective. [11]

One of the earliest forms of writing still remains undeciphered. Known from fewer than 400 inscriptions and yet used for around 250 years between 1700 and 1450 BC, the syllabic script known as Linear A was used by the palace bureaucrats of the Minoan civilization at Knossos on the island of Crete to record inventories on clay tablets. Linear A seems to have evolved from an older, part pictographic/part ideographic script that was further developed and adapted by the invading Mycenaeans from 1450 to 1400 BC. This latter adaptation is known as Linear B, and was eventually deciphered in 1952 by the British architect and scholar Michael Ventris who, noting that versions of it had been discovered inscribed on tablets found on the Greek mainland, pronounced it to be an early form of Greek.

It was the mainland Greeks who, by putting back the vowels into the earlier 'contextual' consonantal alphabet developed by the Semitic peoples of Palestine and Syria around 1700 BC, eventually made writing more accessible. The Greeks took the Phoenician version of the Semitic alphabet and added new letters for vowels to make it their own. This extended Greek form then became the foundation, at around 800 BC, for the Etruscan alphabet, from which, via ancient Roman, all subsequent western alphabets were derived [10]. Schement and Stout [12] note that throughout their chronology various peoples were engaged in extending the advantages of writing, with no century passing by without some refinement or improvement in this form of recording and storing knowledge:

> . . . until the sixth century BC, all efforts focused on inventing systems of writing, counting, or representing time. Their profound significance is evident when one considers the break with tradition required by such

levels of abstraction as the map and the calendar. Furthermore, early farmers considered counting the seasons of such great importance, that calendars were invented at numerous places and times, representing the first direct application of mathematics. These earliest information technologies formed the basis for all that follows. The Sumerians stand out as inventors of the library and of the library catalogue. In terms of information technology, they were the first to experience the necessity for a social institution devoted to storing information, and for a technology of retrieval. . . .

Some civilizations bypassed writing as a means of conveying messages and storing information. The Yoruba nation in Nigeria, for instance, used cowrie shells to convey messages about attraction and repulsion: two shells together suggested 'let us get together' or 'let us meet', while one shell conveyed a message of 'defiance' or to 'stay away'. Many non-written forms of information storage drew their inspiration from long-established devices used to store numerical data, such as wooden sticks with marks or notches cut into them, or different-sized beads strung out along a line. Gaur [11] notes the ubiquity of the knotted cord as an information storage device:

> The use of knotted cords was equally widespread. Though normally a means of enumeration, a memory aid for keeping statistical records, knotted cords have also been cited in connection with the development of writing. In this context they are supposed to have been used in ancient China, Tibet, Japan, Siberia, Africa, California and the Polynesian Islands. In Hawaii they played an important role in the gathering of taxes; and in the Solomon Islands strings with knots and loops are still used for the exchange of news. The best known and most accomplished version of the knotted cord is the quipu of ancient Peru. Quipus were a highly efficient means of information storage, and Inca administration greatly depended on them. They may also have been adapted, at least in part, to the sounds of the Inca language.

Effective communication around the 3250-mile road system of the Inca empire was fundamental to the smooth running of the complex bureaucracy that kept the ruling elite informed and the taxes coming in. The quipus conveyed information via:

> . . . the type and number of knots (from one to nine), the position of each knot (decimal place value), the colour and ply of each string and the position of a string along the main cord. It is generally believed that a special type of interpreter called a quipumaster (quipu-camayoc) read and interpreted the strings, often in conjunction with abacus-like boards . . . [11]

As transactions within and between societies grew in complexity so the means of communicating between them required devices that were more subtle than knots or tallies. Writing, with its capacity for representing so many ideas and connections between ideas, transformed human communication, facilitated administration and provided the instant recognition of terms and conditions required for trade and exchange. Gaur [11] notes how, once a community begins to place a high value on property, it needs to set out terms for its legalized exchange and transfer in a simple, unambiguous and safe form. A small number of easily learned signs which can be set down and read quickly offers the kind of exactness that a society, accumulating and transferring surpluses of capital, requires for confident dealing. Writing also allowed humans to look back and reflect on their first thoughts and ideas, change or modify them and keep them under review. Revisiting experiences was no longer entirely dependent on the vagaries of memory, but writing could still carry over the deficiencies of imprecise recall. Inexact recollections might thus gain status and even greater power to mislead simply by being permanent. The often heard cry of 'Don't believe everything that you read in the newspapers' is a direct descendant of the status that humans have come to bestow on the written word.

Writing has been a powerful means of passing on information over time, but its value to us as distant receivers can often be deceptive. Via the interpretations of scholars written representations of the living and immediate world of one generation can assume the status of fixed and frozen testimony for another. Whatever the original writers thought they were recording, posterity may corrupt in the search for a different meaning. Thus filtered, the writings of the past often acquire an unwitting meaning because there are few, if any, objective witnesses to the circumstances of their construction. This eventually becomes a conundrum. If there were written witness to the creation of a particular piece of writing, how would we validate its assumed objectivity? How would this testimony in itself avoid becoming endowed with new meaning due to our own processes of interpretation?

The papyrus and leather manuscripts found stored in earthenware jars in various caves in the Qumran valley on the north west shore of the Dead Sea in Jordan between 1947 and 1958 are an outstanding example of such post-creation endowment, in this case even by many who have never seen them. The Jordanian government's original decision in 1952 to allow a largely Catholic team of only eight international scholars, later expanded to fifteen, to work on the scrolls, and not to let any Jews work on them, has repeatedly given rise to accusations of scholarly hoarding, racism, elitism and manipulation.

Each of the designated scholars was given exclusive access and rights to the translation, interpretation and publication of a particular group of manuscripts. The largely non-controversial portion of the manuscripts relating to the Old Testament were accordingly translated and transcribed by this group within 13 years of the original discovery. However, the other, often miniscule extracts, some of which are suspected of contradicting long-held Christian and Jewish beliefs have still not been officially released. This has prompted a number of scholars excluded from the 'club' to develop novel techniques for analysing these extracts, the originals of which they still cannot see. Via reconstructions, using a computer program to build on a published concordance and other devices, a number of unofficial interpretations of the Dead Sea Scrolls appeared in 1991 and 1992.

The rivalry and secrecy that has surrounded these documents, some of the most important written sources of information on the foundations of the Christian religion, highlights the vital role played by mediation in assessing written testimony as communal memory. By restricting the mediation of these fragments to such a small group, wider confidence in their interpretation has been jeopardized, and the comments and views of a whole generation of scholars have been lost. In praising the role of writing in democratizing access to information as it is transmitted across the ages, it is interesting to reflect on who holds the copyright of intellectual property produced nearly 2000 years ago and found in a cave by a bedouin shepherd known as 'Mohammed the Wolf'. From this now notorious example of the human mediation of ancient texts we can see how questions of significance, interpretation, access, legitimacy, validation and responsibility become a serious part of the discovered permanence of past stores of communal information.

Modern interpretations of old documents apart, we know that writing allowed for the construction of more complex ideas and connections. It enabled the development of longitudinal themes and made durable multiple inputs, the origin of which would inevitably have been lost in purely speech-based exchanges. The 'information moment' had found a home. Stored, relatively secure and endowed with a new status it could now lie in wait to have a further impact. Future moments would be added to it. Almost as the laying down of old materials creates new and distinctive rock formations, so new layers of information and meaning could grow out of the recorded past. The major difference is that information moments inevitably become merged, the distinct layers are now rarely visible, the moment itself no longer recognizable as a discrete entity. Writing brought about the democratization of information: a person could now 'share' in experiences that they could not possibly have for themselves, and perhaps more importantly, could now gain access to ideas formed and developed outside the boundaries of their own culture; ideas which they might be equipped to understand, but which might have taken many years to emerge from within their own cultural framework.

The concomitant of this was that writers and readers were likely to be remote from each other. A reader on his own could not interact with the author, as in oral communication. The original thoughts and ideas might well have changed or been refined during the time that it took to acquire the document, but it was not always easy for the reader to confirm its current status. Given that many early texts were devoted to exploring religious and philosophical issues, and that such ideas on the whole changed slowly, this was not the problem that it is in our own 'date it or junk it' time. However, humans have always been interested in what might have happened since a known point in time, and thus the seeds of concerns about the up-to-dateness and reliability of written information were being sown. It is a concern that is still with us, and one that many electronic information sources seek to eliminate.

It was also true that any questions arising out of reflection on written ideas often had to remain unanswered, other than via long drawn-out and cumbersome communication systems. The letters written to and by the Dutch scholar Erasmus during the late 15th and early 16th centuries are unusual, if valuable, examples of this. McGarry [3] has emphasized how the advent of literacy changed both the availability and the status of knowledge:

> What is collectively known by the group is externalized and fixed in space and time. This collective knowledge is externalized literally 'outside the body' or is known as 'exosomatic' knowledge in the technical terminology of the anthropologist. This externalization has an important consequence for human reasoning processes. There is a greater separation between the knower and the known and, because text is linear, the structure of recorded thought becomes more amenable to logical analysis. In the words of Walter Ong, 'writing restructures thought': literate societies take a different view of the world – and of knowledge.

While there can be no doubt about the paradigm shift brought about by the advent of writing and reading, it is interesting how, even as we approach the 21st century, many of us still rate the up-to-dateness of information obtained face-to-face as superior to that in written form. Hearing it 'from the horse's mouth' is still something that we are willing to go out of our way to secure, or to pay a premium for. The successful marketing of much modern communications technology is based on the continuing human preference to bridge the gap between the knower and the known by seeing, or at least hearing, it for ourselves.

Although spoken and written forms of communication have now been around for over 4000 years, we still have a lot to learn about the way we actually process the signs and symbols of both. Harris [13] poses some of the key questions that psycholinguists are still struggling to define as they study the mental processes involved in word recognition (lexical access):

> One major difficulty for psychologists has been to decide how information about words and their meaning is stored in memory. Is every individual word stored – for example, run, running, ran, re-run – or only the main stem, and do polysemic words – such as bank – which have two distinct and unrelated meanings also have two separate entries in the mental lexicon?

Recent research [14] supports the theory that although both main stems and derived words have separate entries in memory, polysemic words are only represented once. Despite evidence that the human brain has an enormous capacity for some kinds of memory storage, and that '. . . children, in the years between infancy and late teens, acquire a word-recognition capability of 80 000 words, learning to recognize, on average, more than ten new words per day' [5], it has clearly evolved space-saving mechanisms to cope with the heavy demands that modern lexical access can impose. Meadows [15], reflecting on how the concentration of different meanings around single words in many of the world's languages can tax memory capacity, notes that:

> Since our short-term memory is limited, as much meaning as possible has to be crammed into a small number of words, and the shorter those words are the better. Interestingly, the most used words in all cultures are usually the shortest. Indeed, when something that is initially rare becomes common, its name is often abbreviated. 'Television' has become 'TV', aeroplanes became 'planes', and 'telephone' was reduced to 'phone'.

The picturing of words in memory, truncated or otherwise, is an ability we acquire as a result of repeated exposure to word and phrase patterns. In literate societies the written word is the most frequent vehicle of information transfer; it is also supported by educational systems that are almost entirely built on expediting its recognition. As well as exporting their language, religion, administrative systems and sports, the colonial powers of old also tended to export their own ideas about literacy. Understandable as it was to those involved, to civilize by sharing access to their language, they may have set about redefining communication too narrowly for those cultures exposed to it. By setting aside local traditions of discourse, storytelling and pictorial representation, they set parameters around the future development of their colonies which continue to prove a serious shock for the majority of their indigenous citizens. However, where the 15th century psalter failed to impress, the 20th century's television and radio signals, transmitted by satellite and microwave, may now succeed!

Paper and printing

The invention of printing during the 15th century in Europe dramatically increased the number of copies of documents that could be made available. There was already a general demand for multiple copies of texts, which legions of scribes and copyists in university towns all over Europe strove to satisfy. These reams of tortuously inscribed manuscripts could now be replaced by easily duplicatable volumes which would all look the same.

For the Indo-European languages of western Europe, with their simple alphabet and simple numerical system, printing was a technology just waiting to happen. Governments, scholars, engineers, civil servants, and most of all the merchants and traders of western Europe, were hungry for a more efficient way of duplicating information. But before they could get print there had to be paper. Held as a secret state monopoly for almost 600 years, the Chinese invention of paper and the skill of rubbing off positive impressions on it from a negative-relief wood-block, can be dated as early as 594 AD. Spreading along the caravan trading routes, paper reached Samarkand in 751 AD, and hence to Sicily and western Europe via the Arab papermakers of north Africa, by about 1100 AD [16]. In the haste to celebrate the more recent electronic information technologies, the influence of paper in enabling the recording and communication of information should not be forgotten. Piles of it gather dust in every office and workplace in the land, and for all the advances in paper-replacing technology most people still prefer it. Paper is the stuff on which all the world's universities are built. Despite it being eminently feasible now for students to complete their essays or assignments on a computer and send them to their tutor's workstation, this seldom happens: both students and staff prefer to use printers. Add this to the ongoing academic love-affair with the photo-copier and paper looks set to coexist with the microchip for a very long time. As we move towards the end of the 20th century, despite the promise of a 'paperless information society' we seem to get more and more attached to this old Chinese technology, in something more akin to an 'informationless paper society':

> The influence of paper on western civilization has been enormous. The quick spread of printing, the popularization of education, our whole industrial society depending on administration not only at government but at office level, is in retrospect unthinkable without easy access to almost unlimited quantities of cheap paper. By the beginning of the 20th century nobody would have been in any doubt that paper was here to stay, that it was the most important, efficient and totally irreplaceable medium of modern information storage. [11]

In 1450, when he had perfected his printing press to a stage where he could exploit it commercially, Gutenberg would have been very familiar with the technology of both paper and the negative-relief wood-block. Like so many inventors, Gutenberg built solidly on existing ideas and traditions, bringing together a number of existing technologies in a synthesis that created a new one. His key achievement was in replacing the fixed and static form of a wooden block with the individually formed letters of metal type which could be combined and rearranged at will. This breakthrough, allied with a new use for the old principles of the Roman wine-press, and inks that could adhere to metal rather than wood, fulfilled the need of the age for more and cheaper reading matter by substituting machinery for handicraft. Accelerated by the overwhelming desire in all spheres of life to share and disseminate information, and by the easy replication of the technology, printing presses spread through Europe like wildfire. Within fifteen years of Gutenberg's death in 1468, printing presses had been set up in nearly every country of western Europe, giving teachers the opportunity of teaching by rote (read and repeat, read and repeat), religions the capacity to spread thousands of 'approved' versions of the word and scientific societies the ability to produce and disseminate the learned papers which have become the hallmark of the modern information explosion. Mediated by the urgency of wars and the restless search for profit, printing encouraged and accelerated literacy. The information moments of scientists and artists, soldiers and merchants, craftsmen and engineers could now travel the tracks and byways of Europe in uniform, compact packages that would not look unfamiliar to a modern-day reader. A Scottish shepherd with his paperback stuffed in his coat, far away from any source of electricity, is the modern inheritor of this still highly convenient information technology.

Each of these stages – the development of speech and then language, the evolution of writing and the invention of printing – contributed to putting information moments into convenient, collectable and sharable form. They could now be experienced second- and third-hand, and individual observation could be checked or validated against the published experience of others. These collective-memory technologies enabled a new kind of information build-up, but one that always had its origin in the very personal circumstances of the individual information moment. Handy [17] has noted how:

> . . . the social paradigm seems to change when a new technology coincides with a shift in values or priorities. The new paradigm then needs its articulate exponent to spell out and legitimize the new assumptions on

which we can begin to build an new era of continuous change. . . . Could it be that a new technology of information will combine with a new value system to give us a new paradigm, a paradigm only awaiting its prophet?

As we saw in Chapter 1 in relation to expert systems and neural networks, our imaginations are indeed beginning to fashion technologies for storing, processing and disseminating information that will transform its role and value in society. These technologies, allied with 'shifts in values [and] priorities' will also transform and multiply the moment of discovery, making it even more difficult to identify as a discrete event. We now know, and indeed expect, that each new technology will have its 'articulate exponents', its 'prophets' and its persuaders. However, I am not sure what kind of 'new values' Handy expects to emerge from the changing technology of information. However it works, and whatever it looks like, current and future technology will continue to freeze, amalgamate and distribute information drawn from the cumulative information moments of humans who subscribe to widely differing value systems and beliefs. The centreless Internet may be less controlled and more chaotic than the international telephone network, but in the end its main function is to facilitate the sending and leaving of messages. News on demand may bring events to us closer to the time when they occurred, but it is still news. I would guess that speed of delivery and the high monetary value with which timeliness can now endow some kinds of information will continue to transform economic values, and that the phenomenal copyability of everything that can be digitized will transform the way in which information distributed for profit will be managed in the future.

Some of these developments will affect the way in which information moments are used and valued. Technological change always coincides with something. Currently it may be the cult of the individual, the enterprise culture, hands-off government and the celebration given to personal economic success. The new and lonely monasticism of life before a screen might well coincide with and accelerate some of these underlying trends, but major shifts in the values and priorities of peoples are still social. Their most important information moments may still never involve a piece of paper or any kind of machine. We can still recognize that such moments derive from one or a mixture of three main circumstances: accident, trial and error, and structured learning.

Accident

As in Walpole's 'Three Princes of Serendip' [18] who were always making happy and unexpected discoveries by accident, a portion of all information is gained unexpectedly. This is where the potent and subtle connectivity of the human brain interfaces with its environment to the greatest effect. Browsing in libraries, flicking through newspapers and magazines, switching between television channels or talking with friends and colleagues, we pick up information that we were not looking for but which we recognize at once as being valuable. Sometimes it astonishes, even frightens, us by its sudden importance: how can something so valuable have been there all the time and yet not apparent to us? Sometimes we linger over it long enough to lodge it in our long-term memory, sometimes it is in and out of our short-term memory within seconds. It has to be said that regular illumination via serendipity is as much a measure of human inquisitiveness as of being in the right place at the right time: those people restless for discovery, inquisitive and open to new experience almost put themselves in the way of it. Almost planning for the unplanned, they seem to stand out as being particularly hospitable recipients of new information.

Electronic minds and memories are not yet very hospitable to the 'happy accident'. Browsing in a library, a book shop or a museum may be a tactile pleasure; browsing through information stored in a computer is rarely very satisfying, but as computers become more user friendly searches will undoubtedly get easier and become more fun.

There is generally nothing efficient about serendipity, no Boolean strategy, no application of a prior search logic and no conscious search costs. Commercial organizations seeking to surround themselves with relevant information want information retrieval to be cheap, efficient and targeted. They want to hold and store just enough of it to fuel the key 'moment': a 'just-in-time' approach rather than 'just-in-case'. The dilemma of what to provide to prompt the magic circumstances of the 'happy accident' component of innovation, is one constantly faced by enterprises of all kinds. Given the great range of information sources now available to us, the pure happy accident is becoming more difficult to isolate. There are now probably more occasions when serendipity has been set up or informed by some unconscious rule of thumb, or by a very personal heuristic. For instance, a decision to be in a particularly information-rich environment could make the probability of an accidental discovery more likely. This is analogous to an 'epiphany' a word of Greek origin meaning 'a manifestation or a showing-forth'. An epiphany can be regarded as a serious information moment which, although not planned for, does occur within a context of possibility. Artists of all kinds are likely to recognize and remember these kinds of 'happy accidents' more often than the rest of us, as they generally take the trouble to record them as part of their journey towards the completion of a novel, a poem or a painting. The novelist James Joyce is reputed to have infuriated his friends by suddenly taking his leave of them during conversations to make notes on some idea or insight that they had unconsciously provided him with. He called these jottings his 'epiphanies'. Though apparently trivial, obscure and unconnected to anyone else, such unexpected ideas may become charged with meaning on recall, providing the building blocks for a fuller treatment later on, perhaps even forming the basis for a complete narrative. Such revelatory moments are often brief and the time interval between the happening and the recall so cluttered that they would easily be forgotten if someone had not taken the time and trouble to record them. An epiphany, in this context, has been described as:

'a sudden spiritual manifestation', a flash of significance, yet also 'delicate', 'evanescent'. In other words, its objective existence is unremarkable, and its importance lies in the meaning the novelist finds in it . . . to prompt him to invent a situation where such a conversation might provide a clinching – a revelatory – moment. . . . The underlying idea of an apparently trivial gesture, event, conversation, description, being suddenly charged with significance, suddenly standing away from its context as the revealing episode, is a valuable clue in reading Joyce. [19]

Serendipity can be all these things. Given the existence of previous information stores, desirable information picked up via serendipity can be integrated with previous information moments, at once extending knowledge and choice. The common thread is spontaneity. A further dimension to this is the issue of catalysis, i.e. what kind of information stores might more effectively tap a predisposition towards serendipity? Can we provide environments where serendipity is more likely to occur, and if we can what might they look like in the future? As individual curiosity levels are different, it is important to realize that the impact of technology will always be different from person to person with regard to its facilitation of successful and repeated serendipity.

Trial and error

Trial and error has become a natural way of doing things. We use it to make things and to solve problems. Unlike serendipity, the imperative is clearly to reach a destination via experiment, although the role or function of each stage may not be entirely clear at the start. Today we would call this activity 'research', and the process generally begins with the formulation of an idea about how something might work, i.e. the establishment of a hypothesis, which is then tested to discover whether it is true or not. The idea can be quite vague; indeed, it may be so vague that the process looks more like an intelligent setting where some hoped-for serendipity can occur, rather than a methodical research project.

At various stages of the exploration we would pick up new information, process it into knowledge and use it to move on towards our goal. If it was not instantly relevant to the present task we might store it, consciously or unconsciously, for retrieval during some future problem-solving activity. Obviously there is a lot of scope for serendipity during any trial and error process, the only difference being that the 'happy discoveries' would derive from a conscious search for new information or a solution to a particular problem. However, in serious defiance of the perceived predominance of logic and objectivity, Wolpert [20] gives examples of the interesting mixtures of passion, prejudice and the stubborn holding-on to a basic idea that really do accompany modern scientific research. In the same piece, and particularly in the case of Epstein's search for a viral aetiology for a human tumour, he underscores the unpredictable nature of the insightful 'information moment' [20]:

1. A chance encounter with the notice advertising a lecture to be given by a doctor from Uganda.

2. Attending the lecture and making a connection between geographical factors and a biological cause of tumour formation.

3. Obtaining funding to drop everything else and work on this 'hunch'.

4. Overcoming the political problems in getting tumour samples delivered from Uganda.

5. Dealing with repeated incidents of tumour contamination in transit.

6. Living with the repeated failure of the techniques and recipes he had been using to try and grow samples of tissue culture over nearly three years.

7. Almost casually, one afternoon, deciding not to throw away a seemingly contaminated sample but to have a look at it through the microscope.

8. Noticing single cells floating in a way he remembered from the work of researchers, years before, at Yale University.

9. Realizing that he had been on the wrong track in following the standard procedure (i.e. trying to grow little lumps of tumour), and that breaking them up and allowing them to grow as single cells might work better.

10. Succeeding in growing enough of the culture to examine by electron microscopy.

11. Identifying the first cell with 'unequivocal virus particles in it', three years after hearing the original lecture.

This was a journey with a clear goal, supported by an established set of scientific procedures, but in the end the key factors in achieving success were a determination to prove that an important link existed between geographical factors and biological causation; an almost accidental viewing of a 'contaminated' sample; and a remembrance of a similar splitting-up of cells by workers in another country, years before. A story of success via determination, accident and the reawakening of unconsciously stored information due to a repetition of similar patterns. Sir Alexander Fleming's 1928 observations on the mould *Penicillium notatum*, as it destroyed the bacteria it was contaminating on a dish he had set aside to discard, and the still controversial journey of Watson and Crick in identifying the molecular structure of DNA in 1953, involved similar mixtures of structure and accident. The history of most inventions – the safety razor, the sewing machine, the supermarket trolley, nylon, false teeth, Coca-Cola and dynamite – all involved similar treks of structured and unstructured discovery. Sometimes it was a lucky observation quickly and profitably followed up; sometimes, as with Goodyear's tortuous experiments to perfect vulcanized rubber, it was dogged hard work and persistence, with little in the way of recognition or reward. These mixtures are still being repeated wherever the inventor's spirit is alive, and wherever original research is being carried out. In a much less spectacuiar way, such processes engage each and every one of us as we build up the information moments that inform our own more modest, day-to-day discoveries.

Although investing in research and trial and error, discovery generally has a high status and credibility within most developed and developing societies, there are some aspects that are beginning to look questionable. Many people are asking serious questions about the value of publicly funded research, as practised and institutionalized within universities. The following list raises some of the still very valid questions raised by Sykes [21], together with some that I have added myself:

1. How much of the research that is actually carried out in academic and associated institutions actually makes a contribution to the enlargement of human knowledge?

2. What proportion of it is just institutionalized humbug, whose dominant theme is academic careerism (most of it unread and unreadable)?

3. Does not the academic system tend to reward conservatism and conformity rather than originality and challenging insight?

4. Are not researchers who seek to explore interdisciplinary connections often hampered by the high level of academic compartmentalism still prevalent among assessors and examiners?

5. Does not the race to win tenure in the US and recognition in the UK force young academics to simulate new discoveries every few months in order to turn out the requisite number of articles in learned journals?

6. Does not this same race inhibit young researchers from working on real problems that would take several years to evaluate and publish, which they see as too long to wait to get the recognition that they need to make further progress?

Armstrong [22] suggests that research cultures are more often about 'what not to do' rather than a free and exciting opening up of the unknown, and concludes that professors who wish to be published in the academic press must not pick an important problem; must not challenge existing beliefs; must not obtain surprising results; must not use simple methods; must not provide full disclosure of methodology, sources and findings; and must not write clearly.

Barzun [23] has described the assumption that every college teacher can write a book that will contribute to knowledge as 'preposterism'. Because one trained mind investigates a subject and the subsequent publication is regarded as having made a real contribution to knowledge, the culture assumes that all aspiring professors can do the same. It is, of course, difficult to generalize about the information-gathering behaviour of academic researchers. Scholarly work is as much a prisoner of discipline and individual domain culture and their restrictive practices as any other activity. Indeed, the custodians of research cultures have built up some strong totems and beliefs concerning the way they should operate and the issues they should explore. This can give rise to the kind of narrowness, conservatism and conformity so robustly condemned by Sykes and others.

It can also give rise to a perceived hierarchy of value within and between disciplines that is often not liberal, and not necessarily in the best interests of the community. That there is little fraternity between different research domains and no automatic equality of opportunity in the treatment of research within academic institutions may not be surprising; that it wastes time and resources on unprofitable rivalry may not be so easy to forgive. However, much of the 'research' carried out in universities is privately funded and many part-time students pay for research experiences which are about enjoying knowledge for its own sake and taking their information handling and presentation skills to a higher level. Universities have a key role in celebrating and extending the richness and diversity of communal knowledge and in facilitating access to it at a range of levels. This function needs cherishing and protecting in its own right without shackling it to the often ridiculous publish-or-die culture prevalent in so many western universities.

The issue of how research feeds into and enriches information moments in classrooms is one that communities definitely do care about. It is one that has occupied educationalists from time immemorial, but it is one still more honoured in the breach than in the execution.

Structured learning

The key difference between the structured approach to information acquisition and the others is that time is deliberately set aside for the sole purpose of transferring information and knowledge from one person to another. In developed societies this has been institutionalized and refined into something we call 'education', and since the late 19th century it has formed a key element of community-based social control. Under this system children are sent to school for specific periods to be taught by professional teachers, who share with their pupils a set plan which we call the curriculum. The quality and vigour of this experience is perceived, generally correctly, to be a major factor in determining future material and spiritual opportunities, and teachers, parents and politicians hotly debate the content of the curriculum that children should be taught. However, there is no uniformity among developed economies on what should constitute a minimum or balanced curriculum. Developing economies, particularly those around the Pacific Rim, have on the whole adopted western styles of education and expectation without much investigation into just how relevant these might be to their own deeply ingrained value systems and learning traditions. Indeed, conscious of the ground that they have to make up in securing their place on the world stage, these nations often endow education with an urgency that is now almost unknown in the west. They also endow it with certainty, whereas we in the west have come to appreciate the great uncertainties that bedevil accumulated knowledge. We believe it is important that knowledge should always be open to question and critical examination, but scholarly scepticism is not the norm in southeast Asia. Education in Singapore and Japan is still very much about imparting facts, about the existence of precise solutions and correct answers, while developing skills in argument and debate is often regarded as improper, rude or even slightly decadent. Knowing and repeating what you know is the preferred route to academic success, and if cramming is necessary to achieve this then so be it. It is common in Tokyo to hear stories of children leaving school in the late afternoon, going straight to cramming classes in the early evening and then continuing with two or three hours of homework before they go to bed. Defining young people's information journeys in this rigid and exclusive way may be good for economies but only at the cost of denying large numbers of children what still passes for the more carefree information moments of childhood.

All governments profess to see educational opportunity as the key factor in developing their human capital, both in terms of a preparation for responsible citizenship and to ensure a workforce that can produce high-quality competitive goods and services. Education is also the route whereby the governed seek to learn how to govern. In a brief description of the preparations for his book *The Scramble For Africa*, Pakenham [24] notes:

> I think 1980 was the nadir for post-colonial Africa. The powers had left most states wretchedly ill-prepared for independence. Education was rudimentary, technical training rare, graduates non-existent in some countries. There were no deep-rooted traditions of democracy; the white men had proved the power of autocracy, the whip and the gun.

The idea that a state should have to be 'prepared' for independence, and that preparation should take the form of education, technical training and a goodly supply of something called graduates, is very much founded in a western idea of what education is and what its aims are. The theory is that organization and administration require a formally educated elite who own the knowledge necessary to govern and develop a society, and who have access to the information to improve and refine that knowledge. The patrician families of ancient Rome would have been at home with this approach. They set a high value on teachers and philosophers, and male children were often placed in the house of a well connected friend to learn how public life was conducted. Girls were expected to learn from their mothers. The idea of sending aristocratic young men away from their home environment to look and learn has been popular with many societies at many different times in history and the still flourishing English public school system probably owes its origins to this 'away from home is best' idea. Many civil officers of the British government are still recruited from the public schools, often via undergraduate studies spent in the collegiate halls of Oxford and Cambridge. The one-to-one tutorial system of 'Oxbridge', proud inheritor of the ancient mentor idea, is still alive and well, albeit struggling to defy the blandishments of a more cost-efficient educational culture. After 'learning and looking' the Roman way of continuing education was to expose young men to a rigid and formulaic involvement in civil and military service. Any deficiency in part of this meant that one was not completely 'educated', and thus not acceptable as a candidate for some of the higher civil or military honours on offer. Post-Republican emperors, such as Tiberius, might, for instance, calculatingly deny access to active military service as one way of limiting the experiential development of a potential rival.

With the growth in importance of trade and commerce in Europe from the 12th century onward, came the organization of crafts and trades within a system of guilds, which defined, nurtured and protected specific crafts and groups of crafts within towns. They regulated conditions of employment, upheld standards and controlled quality, they oversaw training and they set down strict rules of production. Again, going away from home to learn as an apprentice, as often as not living on the job, was the route to gaining proficiency in the requisite technical knowledge. Apprenticeships within a guild could last anything between seven and ten years, and this was a deliberately slow and difficult way to gain entry into a craft. Having a relative on the inside could speed up the process considerably. The five-year engineering apprenticeship schemes that still operate in Germany and, until recently, in Britain, derive from these old guild apprenticeship schemes.

Since the late 19th century information and knowledge has been transferred to young people at distinctly identified levels and phases, within a variety of formal educational systems, replacing the old one-to-one tutorial arrangements by teaching the same material to large groups at different times. Under these systems a certain number of years are set aside to provide time for a minimum level of transfer to take place, e.g. 16 years in the UK from primary school until graduation with a first degree from a university or college – roughly 22 per cent of an average male life! Since the second world war the most popular issues for debate concerning education have been:

1. The balance between theory and practice in all subjects.

2. Government involvement in curriculum design.

3. The perceived value of studying a subject which is clearly related to a future job role, i.e. vocational studies, against studying purely academic subjects such as linguistics, philosophy, sociology, politics, English, history and economics.

4. The ratio of teachers to students.

Other themes have also been important, e.g. the training and competence of teachers, the duration of programmes, the cost of education, the politicization of the curriculum etc., but these four issues have occupied the most prominent place in the ongoing debate about education.

The issue of theory versus experience within education arises, in one form or another, nearly every day in classrooms and laboratories all around the world. Interestingly, in ancient Rome there would have been no obvious status difference between 'academic' and 'vocational' activity: the great writer Cicero, as well as being a scholar and orator, was also a respected general and an active politician. At some time in the history of our educational systems we began separating out these two streams, compartmentalizing them and eventually linking them with a notional hierarchy of value. Narrow started to become beautiful, and the academic degree became a symbol of achievement that somehow distanced itself from a more practical education. The different degrees to which practical and theoretical elements reside in a subject have also given rise to powerful hierarchies of perceived value. It is still true in the UK, for instance, that the largely academic subjects of English, history, sociology, philosophy, economics and psychology are generally believed to endow a student with qualities of understanding, reasoning and critical awareness which are somehow denied to students of accountancy, nursing, engineering or computer science. So strong is this perception, in Britain at least, that it is now an unalterable truth within the national psyche, as any analysis of applications to British undergraduate programmes will testify, although some success has attended the piloting of vocational 'A' levels during 1993/1994. The recent announcement of plans to extend vocational subjects into the range of GCSEs on offer to 14–16-year-olds represents the first real attempt in the UK to offer a progression of credible vocational qualifications to parallel the established academic routes. The Chairman of the School Curriculum and Assessment Authority, Sir Ron Dearing [25], in announcing the piloting of some five or so vocational courses attempted some dilution of the 'sheep' and 'goats' perception which, despite so many denials, is still so prevalent in the UK:

> It is not a matter of academically inclined children going one route, and others the other. . . . The choice of some vocational content should be there for all . . . if within the framework of a primarily academic education, an element of vocational education is to prosper, it is essential that it should achieve esteem in its own right.

Such initiatives will need the active support of all those in higher education to ensure their success. Nowhere are the old prejudices and academic preferences so rife as in the older British universities. Never quick to adapt to change, they will continue to rate the narrow comfort of academic routes more highly than vocational ones for as long as they can, seeing it as their duty both as custodians of standards and as guardians of an increasingly archaic tradition. So far they have proved to be intractable.

Although more and more students are going to university in the UK, the proportion of them studying science is getting smaller. Even the dropout rate is higher, with 1 in 5 science students and 1 in 4 engineering students dropping out of their studies before completion, compared to the 1 in 7 who drop out of the arts and humanities, and so far the government has been unable to redress the balance. The educational history of British government ministers and senior civil servants has probably not helped, as few representatives of vocational disciplines have ever been represented in a British Cabinet. Not all countries share this narrow theology. Large numbers of students in the US, France, Germany, Sweden and Japan study science and engineering. They are rewarded with well paid jobs, high status and a sense of doing something that is both clever and important. They also see the fruits of their endeavours exported to the accountant-rich countries that no longer celebrate the information and knowledge base necessary to successfully engineer their environment. For such endeavours to be rated highly within a society, science and engineering must have the status of noble and respected professions, enjoying the same rewards as diplomacy, law or finance. More than any other group it is the scientists and engineers who discover what is possible and what else might be achieved. Not many people would contest this idea but it is a component of the information–knowledge chain that many information-economy, postindustrial society commentators still seriously underestimate. Edward De Bono [26], in a letter to *The Guardian* in March 1993, highlighted just how entrenched the patronizing British view of manufacturing is, and how difficult it still is for young people to exercize their curiosity and information acquisition around the exploration of things and the creation of new value from them:

> Nowhere in basic education are youngsters exposed to the fascination and joy of creating value through putting things together and making decisions. The endless emphasis on knowledge, description and analysis does not encourage the needed skills of 'making things happen'. The only exposure youngsters have to business is in playing Monopoly, a game which emphasizes all the very worst features of capitalism: greed, luck, exploitation, speculation and the rentier attitude.

In his Inaugural Address as President of The Institution of Electrical Engineers in February 1992 Brian Manley [27] drew attention to the circumstances that have taken Britain from being a nation of great engineers (e.g. Robert Stephenson, Isambard Kingdom Brunel and Joseph Lock, all of whom died in 1859) to being one that has come to romanticize everything except engineering. He notes the British government's startling lack of interest in the Paris International Electrical Exhibition in 1881, and the lack of a tradition, in England at least, of valuing education as a means of social and economic advancement. He charts a growing antipathy towards industry by the new middle classes, who also controlled the forms and content of primary and secondary education. By the end of the 19th century, due largely to a growing celebration of, and nostalgia for, the pre-industrial English idyll of the cottage craft, the UK's future as a nation of non-engineers was cast. Informed by this history and from his perspective at the beginning of the 1990s, Manley was not optimistic about the UK's ability to recover its position as a well educated and technically advanced manufacturing nation. Any progress would require a massive shift in the current status and priorities given to vocational as opposed to academic disciplines, both in schools and in universities. It would be a long haul:

> Measures to improve vocational training will be fruitless without corre-sponding developments in the schooling system. As Forster had recog-nized in 1870, it is not feasible to train uneducated people. We must recognize, however, that a problem that has developed and taken root over 150 years will not be solved overnight. We have so ingrained the educational disparities in our society that education itself is not valued by much of that society. One generation educates the next, so changing those values will be the work of many years. [27]

This is not meant to decry or devalue the richness of the arts as motors of enlightenment and fulfilment. Rather it is a plea for some parity of esteem, for less snobbery, for more integration, more open-ness and more understanding of how the information and knowledge of both strands can inform and delight. The great liberal arts tradition of US undergraduate education has never stopped their industrialists and inventors pushing forward much of the technology which we now take for granted. Societies need both streams: neither should be celebrated over the other. It is the search for a more renaissance-like approach to integrating them within our curricula and our lives that is the big challenge.

Most nations still see their educational systems as important links in the chain of social control, teaching the values of the society and establishing patterns of behaviour that conform to those expected of good citizens. Traditional education also plays a significant part in encouraging individual competitiveness, through sport, prizes and examinations that exhibit clear winners and losers. Despite contem-porary rhetoric about teamwork and group assessment, the overriding tendency within western educational systems is still to celebrate the achievement of individuals. Conformity in behaviour, competitiveness and individual achievement are the sometimes incompatible, and often stressful, contradictions that continue to mark the success or failure of students in both developed and developing countries. Most publicly financed education systems have to assume that we all start from roughly the same point, with no major differences or discontinuities in our information journeys. Just how likely is this? Nowadays, at home, children will probably have access to the same television images, the same popular music and the same radio programmes, but the context of their access to information will in many cases be as different, and as unequal, in the 1990s as it would have been in the 1950s. This will be manifest in differential access to material conduits of information provision, e.g. television sets, video players, computers, software, books, newspapers and magazines, opportunities for travel etc. It will also, and just as importantly, be manifest in their access to the shared experience and beliefs of the domestic group with which they come into contact. From this group they will assimilate ideas about the value of learning and knowledge, ideas about inquisitiveness and ideas about the use of their leisure time. These ideas will eventually orchestrate the value and the time that a child is inclined to give to information-gathering activities. The changing structure and shape of family life in many western countries [28] must be affecting access to information in the home. Lower birth rates mean smaller family units and thus fewer opportunities for interaction and experiment with sympathetic peers. More single-parent families and the often greater distances between the scattered members of a modern family group could mean less access to a normal distribution of older wisdoms, both to learn from and to disagree with.

All of us can map the important and distinctly personal 'information moments' that have brought us to where we are today. Like the layers of geological strata, they represent the incremental changes that altered the direction of our lives. None of this happened evenly or equally, nor was the information that we acquired and retained in any way evenly balanced between school and home. Some of us grew up in environments where there was little in the way of access to information sources, and where parental knowledge about further educational opportunities was limited or non-existent. Others grew up in places that were rich in information sources and in people willing to share and develop the habits of curiosity and inquisitiveness necessary to access them. These capricious journeys in and out of highly variable information habitats have brought us all to where we are today. And how serendipitous much of it was! The teacher who took a particular interest, the brother or sister who brought home a prospectus from a local college, the theatre visit that kindled a love of drama, the casual generosity of the man who owned the second-hand bookshop around the corner. Opportunity-information comes in many guises, the most important of which is still access to further, continuing and higher education. Unfortunately it is still the case, even in the most educationally developed nations, that the language of access to education and the routes by which it is attained, still bypass the social and domestic settings of many people. The construction of information moments that illuminate educational possibilities among groups where it is not part of the everyday culture continues to be a major challenge to those charged with bridging this gap.

In the UK two surveys, both published in March 1994, provided some insight into the success of both formal (school) and informal (home and social) channels of information acquisition among young adults and secondary school children. The first, published by the Adult Literacy and Basic Skills Unit (ALBSU), explored levels of understanding and literacy among 21-year-olds. The results were surprisingly bad. A quarter of those surveyed could not understand a video recorder instruction manual, six out of ten of them could not add up four prices, nine out of ten could not work out the difference between two discounted prices, and more than six out of ten could not understand the arguments put in favour of hunting by summing up the points from a short text. Only 12 per cent of those surveyed had reached the literacy levels expected of a bright 16-year-old who had been following the national curriculum. Not surprisingly, given the importance of informal information acquisition, 60 per cent of those with low literacy scores came from unskilled backgrounds, but interestingly, many of the survey subjects, when asked for a self-assessment, believed that their literacy and numeracy skills were much better than they in fact were. This suggests that they manage to hide the real level of their skills during day-to-day transactions, that they are not often tested to what we would call normal levels of adult understanding, or that they were too embarrassed to declare the true level of their skills. On a more practical, and again unsurprising, economic note the survey found a direct correlation between joblessness and poor levels of literacy. Unemployed young adults with low literacy scores had been, on average, jobless five times as long as those with high scores: ten months compared to two for men and five months compared to two for women [29]. As if this were not bad enough, earlier research among a group of UK 23-year-olds born during one week in 1970, carried out during 1993 by the Institute of Manpower Services, also for ALBSU, found that up to 10 per cent of young adults in the UK have literacy skills more akin to those expected of children aged between 7 and 9 [30]. Both these surveys warn of the continuing existence of an underclass of people who are reaching adulthood without acquiring quite basic levels of literacy, numeracy or oral communication, and this in a developed society which has had formal education systems in place since the late 19th century.

The second major survey, of 29 000 children aged 11–16, was carried out by the Schools Health Education Unit and was aimed at discovering how secondary school children acquired their information on a range of sex and health matters. It also sought to ascertain their behaviour with regard to alcohol, smoking, drugs and personal expenditure. Although the survey confirmed that most children, after reaching 11 or 12 years of age, rely on their friends more than school lessons and parents for information about sex, over half thought that their parents should have been the main source of the information. It discovered a widespread ignorance of the birth control services available locally, including how and where to get condoms free of charge. More than 90 per cent of the 14-year-olds surveyed correctly identified needle-sharing as a way of passing on HIV, and an overwhelming majority cited unprotected sexual intercourse – either heterosexual or homosexual – as the other main route. In testament to the media's coverage of the few cases of AIDS caught from blood transfusions, one in five of the pupils surveyed believed that AIDS can be contracted by donated blood. About 45 per cent of them considered that having to have a blood transfusion would put them at serious risk of contracting AIDS. One of the most surprising results of this survey was that nearly 60 per cent of boys and girls in their GCSE year were working more than six hours a week, with nearly one in five boys working between 11 and 20 hours per week. It is hard to believe that such a commitment to economic independence would not conflict with their school work [31]. These surveys, with all their imperfections, highlight serious discrepancies in knowledge and information handling skills between children and between young adults.

Although no-one would be sanguine enough to expect there to be no differences in attainment between economic groups with differential access to social and educational opportunities, the size of the differences is still surprising. Since the Second World War most UK governments, irrespective of political hue, have agreed that education is a key factor in drawing out the nation's human capital and in forging more equality of opportunity. Something, perhaps the old British disease of low expectations, has come between the declarations and the reality, as both the formal and informal domains of information acquisition seem to be failing in a number of ways. One critical factor may be the willingness of teachers to act as guides to information acquisition, and their competence at so doing. Lewins [32] has described what she regards as a crisis of confidence within the UK teaching profession, in regard to both the definition and the boundaries of its role. It has long been understood that classroom education was more than listening to a teacher, and that this important element should be integrated with other, more student-centred, activities:

> We see teaching as an attempt to create opportunities for encounters between curiosity on the one hand and, on the other, information that is granted the status of knowledge only through critical reflection and analysis. These encounters are structured through tasks that seek to maximize understanding by helping pupils to relate what they come across to their past experience of living and learning, and to adjust their frameworks for comprehending experience in the light of new insights. [33]

Creating opportunities for encounters between curiosity and information and relating these to children's other experiences of living and learning seems an excellent way to introduce them to the connectivity that exists between information and knowledge. However, student-centred learning is not cheap. It needs time, well stocked and well managed libraries, field trips, up-to-date laboratories and opportunities for pupil exchanges between regions and countries. It also needs resourceful teachers skilled in directing their students to information sources and in helping them to map out their enquiries within what they find. In addition to inculcating good search strategies, teachers also need to be capable of passing on the very best in research methods and of organizing and evaluating accumulated knowledge, however it is sourced or packaged. The omens for this latter requirement have not been good. Two surveys of teachers as information users [34, 35] suggested that many were often strangers to primary sources and had little motivation to seek much information on recent trends and developments in educational practice. Teachers also cited lack of time and, astonishingly, lack of advice on the location of relevant information sources, as other obstacles to their information gathering. Most also rated the experience of other practitioners and one-to-one conversations with other teachers as much more valuable than the information available in specialist journals or research reports:

> Only one-third of the teachers reported having made an enquiry for specific information relating to their work in the recent past; however, most were satisfied with the result. The largest number of enquiries was concerned with resources to assist the teaching of specific topics. The enquiries were pursued in a variety of ways, the most common being through various types of library. The lack of available information, delays in receiving information and ignorance of where to find the answer to enquiries, were the most often cited problems encountered. [32]

How to ensure that the student is central to any academic learning process is one of the great dilemmas faced by all educational systems. Teachers inevitably see themselves as central to processes in which they set the daily agendas. That academic learning should proceed more like a conversation between the two is still, in higher education at any rate, the exception rather than the rule. Such conversations first require a confident exposition by the teacher, setting out his or her views, followed by the student setting out their descriptions, priorities and perceptions of the way things are. Given the extent to which the two views differ, the teacher can then identify tasks for the student that highlight or minimize the differences, designed to enable the student to explore both the strengths and the weaknesses of their own ideas. Both teacher and student can then revisit their own descriptions in the light of the conversation and continue the process. All this requires great skill and confidence. Engaging is always more stressful than declaring, but now may be the time to nurture a few more exponents of the former.

In the UK, school teachers and university lecturers are under increasing pressure to deliver more and more with fewer resources. Paradoxically, at a time when all would agree that it was imperative for students to develop effective information seeking and handling skills, the burden and variety of teacher responsibilities may be conspiring to preclude the development of a serious information curriculum. In higher education, despite its often-proclaimed adherence to a more student-centred approach, little in the way of information handling skills is imparted to students apart from the library 'tour' and a few 'finding your way around the library' seminars. The old university ethos that fumbling around the library for a year or two before you find something really useful is good for you and all part of the great journey of learning, is still very much alive. Indeed, many academic staff cheerfully burden themselves with the narrowest view of their discipline, simply to ensure that it precludes much in the way of further exploration. Information poverty seems to be a chosen way of life for some academics: they have chosen a shutdown date for the latest information they are prepared to hold, and the idea of teaching information skills to students in order to facilitate their owning more recent information is not really on their agenda. Indeed, it sometimes seems to pose a threat! One of the little-known qualities of acquired expertise is how blinkered it can make us, how resistant to lateral thought and how naked and insecure it can leave us if we are unexpectedly surrounded by broader or wider perspectives. Despite being its assumed natural home, academe can be as hostile as any other group to the unexpected impact of new information.

Gender benders

As well as affecting all children differentially, it is clear that the information moments available to girls are still quite different from those accessible to boys. As a result the collective information moments that each group brings to the classroom are also quite different. Unfortunately, these home-based inequalities are often exacerbated by a continuation of differential access to certain kinds of information in the classroom, where time and support preference is often concentrated on boys. This seems to be particularly true with regard to the predominantly male orientation that computers and computer technology often assume. Although there is no logical reason for this, computer clubs and the less formally timetabled access to computers in schools are nearly always dominated by boys. Paradoxically this is not how it started: much anecdotal evidence suggests that in the early 1950s and 1960s women made up over half the number of programmers and systems analysts employed in the UK. In 1975 over 25 per cent of the applicants for computer science courses in the UK were women [36], but by 1993 this had dwindled to around 17 per cent. Thus, over the 20-year period that saw the birth and consolidation of the women's movement, the place and role of women in computer science, instead of getting stronger, got weaker. On reflection we can see that the early celebration of what computers are inside rather than what they can do in the world continued to feed well established 'science for boys and boys for science' attitudes. Excluding girls from this concentration on the physical technology meant they were eventually excluded from the equally exciting domains of potential uses and applications:

> . . . its roots lie in the popular idea that IT is a purely 'technical subject'. This misconception feeds into one of our strongest cultural stereotypes and creates exclusion from early childhood. Computer games have not been geared towards girls – just look at the name Gameboy – and as girls go into IT classes in schools computing is firmly fixed in many minds as 'nerdy', with computers seen as 'toys for the boys'. [36]

Once the computers acquired by schools fell into the hands of science and maths teachers their exclusivity was confirmed and, other than in single-sex schools, access for girls almost automatically reduced.

The misplaced reinforcement of such 'macho-tech' stereotypes has long inhibited girls from participating in science, engineering and technology programmes, other than in small numbers. The information that feeds restrictions and barriers like these, built up within cultures and reinforced by their institutions, is some of the most powerful and destructive that humans have to cope with. Deeply embedded and controlled, it resists change over centuries rather than just a decade or two. In developed nations women who have not had the opportunity of a formal post-secondary education have to overcome all kinds of prejudicial obstacles before they can even make first base. For a long time they stand on the sidelines looking in, believing that those on the inside have a secret they will never share; they are right: the secret is access to information, and perhaps some help and encouragement to use it. Even women on the inside can suffer disproportionately from lack of information, excluded by male-priority information networks. The North American university system of requiring academic staff to seek tenure via a six-year assessment of their work can just as often be a vehicle for the exercize of male prejudice as an objective survey of achievement. During discussions in North America between late 1988 and early 1989, about the academic environments in which future library and information science curricula might develop, I saw and heard much about low levels of confidence in the system among junior female faculty [37]. Despite operating in a domain populated by more women than men, many female academics still felt that the inherent masculinity of the main information conduits within universities – male presidents, male-dominated committees, informal networks and processes that always seemed to be populated by more men than women – all seriously disadvantaged their chances of gaining tenure. Dorothy Zinberg [38] recently reported the problems that a successful woman engineer experienced in securing tenure at a mid-western university in the US. She had achieved it only after:

> . . . a bizarre episode where her male colleague, the very one who had recruited her, changed the locks on the laboratory doors so that she was unable to carry out her research. It seems that as she matured intellectually and became independent, he resented losing 'what he had thought would be a slave, a super-post-doc.' She was on the verge of resigning after other male colleagues sympathetically told her it would be impossible to go up against the system.

A series of chance encounters with other women, both inside and outside the university, encouraged her to fight on and she duly achieved her tenure just before the case came before the courts.

Even in information-rich communities information sharing by men among women is still often something that is more spoken about than carried out. There would be no problem in celebrating the rich plurality of a 'woman's' or a 'man's' world if the store of information held by the latter was not so exclusive or so powerful in hindering women's progress. Over 2000 years, and led by a Judaeo-Christian emphasis that has always placed men before women, European culture has encouraged, often by legal means, the accumulation of male-exclusive forms of knowledge and information holding. These have given rise to what many western women now refer to as the 'glass ceiling'. Despite gains at the lower levels of information-intensive employment, women still look unlikely to improve much on the current 8 per cent of senior executive positions that they hold in the UK. Gregg and Machin's recent UK study [39] for the National Institute for Economic and Social Research found:

> . . . that even when women are more numerous in lower management levels, they still find that younger men leapfrog them to maintain male domination at higher levels of the hierarchy. In many cases male bosses promote younger men because they will be keener to work longer hours to further their careers, and that they are less likely to interrupt their progress up the greasy pole to care for children.

The study concluded that although women may be making some advances in professional jobs that require very specific individual skills, e.g. some parts of the law, medicine and teaching, they are still not making much headway in the kinds of managerial jobs that involve direct control over resources and staff. Where women do win management jobs in bigger organizations, it is often in areas such as personnel, finance and sales, which call for precise professional quali-fications rather than general management skills and decision-making ability. In the developed world suble forms of gender segregation and subconscious selectivity keep the glass in the glass ceiling thick enough to prevent the majority of qualified women breaking through it. Shifts in employment patterns from manufacturing to service industries should improve opportunities for women, but only a major pro-gramme of demasculinization of the instruments of job control and definition will really begin to even things up. As Goethe [40] suggests:

> . . . if you treat people as they are, you will be instrumental in keeping them as they are. If you treat them as they could be, you will help them become what they ought to be.

Gender discrimination has its origins in a male-based elitism which, by sustaining ancient role definitions and stereotypes and by maintaining so many different barriers to inclusion, keeps women info-poor. This is particularly true of women in developing countries: always with little or no economic status (The Gambia is the only country in Africa where women can claim a title to land), often the carers of children and the elderly, nearly always the providers of real income for the family, they also, via their work on cash crops, make the major contribution to a nation's foreign currency earnings. Where women are the main wage-earners, and to the extent that most governments tax wages, the social and economic returns from invest-ing in women are likely to be greater than from investing in men. The males in such communities continue to gain comfort and convenience from their old-established roles as hunters and gatherers, despite having little or nothing to hunt or gather: though their tasks are redundant they have no intention of changing their role. Ruthlessly exploited by the information embedded in ancient customs and behaviours, women are the worst victims of information poverty, despite a growing core of evidence suggesting that quite small investments in education, knowledge and skills development for girls and women brings back economic and social benefits many, many times greater than the original cost. Such a view is even becoming the conventional wisdom within institutions as conservative as the World Bank. In January 1993, its chief economist noted that:

> . . . recent research and concrete calculations show that educating females yields far-reaching benefits for girls and women themselves, their families and the societies in which they live. Indeed during my tenure as chief economist of the World Bank, I have become convinced that once all the benefits are recognized investment in the education of girls may well be the highest-return investment available in the developing world. [41]

Add in the improved confidence, self-esteem, self-value and dignity that would flow from the full integration of women into a nation's social and economic life, and it is astonishing that millions of women still live lives more akin to those of slaves than modern citizens. In 1993, 900 million people worldwide were still illiterate; 540 million of these were women who, more than any other group, could positively influence new approaches to feeding, child-rearing and sanitation if only they could read and write, but more than for any other group 'time is the enemy' when it comes to finding some of it for women to participate in literacy programmes. Fatigue, frequent pregnancies, caring for children and the elderly, the requirements of seasonal agricultural work and the increasing demands of both formal and informal employment are among the many demands that crowd out the opportunity for female education. The burden of these heavy workloads is often reflected in the high rate of female absenteeism and drop-out from literacy activities. Long distances to travel, often without any help from public transport, to the schools and centres where literacy programmes may operate, is another obvious hurdle that tired women may just not be able to overcome. The high literacy rate in the state of Kerala, southwest India, owes its success to a unique community which has had a long tradition of empowering women. Tropical, beautiful and poor, Kerala is India's most densely populated state, with little by way of industry or mineral resources. By involving women at every level of literacy, education and health, Kerala has a significantly lower infant mortality rate than the rest of India. It also enjoys better general health care, better educational opportunities, a high awareness of the benefits of family planning and wide acceptance of smaller families. A number of special factors came together in Kerala. One was an old tradition of matriliny, where women were always guaranteed a share of the family inheritance and were thus less dependent on potential husbands. Another was that a long-standing and relatively stable socialist coalition, committed to ensuring that all basic community services were met, had governed the state for the last 30 years. More interestingly, a local tradition dating back to the 1920s, of young girls leaving the state to train as nurses, eventually returning to encourage their own daughters to seek and achieve education, particularly in the medical sciences, had led to girls attending school in much larger numbers than was typical in other parts of India [42]. Heartwarming as this example is, it is a remarkable exception in what is otherwise a bleak landscape of opportunity for women in most developing economies, particularly those of sub-Saharan Africa.

In reality, all types of information acquisition and processing activity take place simultaneously within the experience of individuals. These moments cumulate in rich and varied information acquisition journeys, which in turn inform actions. The simple taxonomy of accident, trial and error and structured learning is designed to identify the building blocks that continuously slot together during human information acquisition. Whether our modern minds still hold some threads of the information moments that guided the hunter–gatherer of old, or whether our modern attitudes to cheating, sharing or improper behaviour during food acquisition and distribution really were etched and embedded by experiences 100 000 years ago, it is clear that some circumstances and some kinds of behaviour result in information moments that are richer, and that travel far better, than others. The challenge for any society that seeks to help each of its citizens reach their full potential is how to preserve and then shower the benefits of both its ancient and modern information moments so that they are accessible to all.

References

1. Cosmides, L. and Tooby, J. (1993) The lords of many domains. *The Times Higher Education Supplement*, 25 June

2. Mithen, S. (1993) Pictures in the mind. *The Times Higher Education Supplement*, 9 July

3. McGarry, K. (1991) Epilogue: differing views of knowledge. In *Knowledge and Communication, Essays on the Information Chain*, ed. A. J. Meadows. London: Library Association

4. Quiatt, D. and Reynolds, V. (1994) *Primate Behaviour: Information, Social Knowledge, and the Evolution of Culture.* Cambridge: Cambridge University Press

5. Stonier, T. (1992) *Beyond Information: the Natural History of Intelligence.* London: Springer Verlag

6. Dawkins, R. (1976) Memes and the evolution of culture. *New Scientist*, 72, 208–210

7. Pinker, S. (1993) The language instinct. *The Times Higher Education Supplement*, 25 June

8. Chomsky, N. (1965) *Aspects of the Theory of Syntax.* Cambridge, Mass: MIT Press

9. Aitchison, J. (1989) *The Articulate Mammal*, 3rd edn. London: Unwin Hyman

10. Crystal, D. (1987) *The Cambridge Encyclopedia of Language.* Cambridge: Cambridge University Press, pp.234–235

11. Gaur, A. (1984) *A History of Writing.* New York: Cross River Press

12. Schement, J. R. and Stout, D. (1988/89) A time-line of information technology. (Preprint given to the author by J.R. Schement in 1989)

13. Harris, M. (1993) Entries in the mental lexicon. *The Times Higher Education Supplement*, 2 April

14. Caron, J. (1992) *An Introduction to Psycholinguistics.* London: Harvester Wheatsheaf

15. Meadows, J. (1989) *Info-Technology: Changing the Way We Communicate.* London: Cassell

16. Steinberg, S.H. (1979) *Five Hundred Years of Printing*, 3rd edn. Harmondsworth: Penguin Books

17. Handy, C. (1989) *The Age of Unreason.* Business Books

18. Walpole, H. (1754) *The Three Princes of Serendip: a Fairy Tale.*

19. Martin, G. (1973) *James Joyce, The Nineteenth-Century Novel and its Legacy.* Unit 31, A302, Arts: A Third-Level Course. Milton Keynes: Open University

20. Wolpert, L. (1988) Science and myth information. In *New Horizons for the Information Profession*, ed. H. Dyer and G. Tseng. London: Taylor Graham

21. Sykes, C. J. (1988) *Profscam: Professors and the Demise of Higher Education.* Washington DC: Regernery Gateway

22. Armstrong, S. J. (1982) Barriers to scientific contributions: the author's formula. *Behavioural and Brain Sciences*, p.197.

23. Barzun, J. (1968) *The American University.* New York: Harper and Row

24. Pakenham, T. (1991) *The Scramble For Africa.* London: Weidenfeld and Nicolson

25. Dearing, R. (1994) Secondary Heads Association Conference, Bournemouth, 19 March; quoted in *The Guardian*, 21 March

26. de Bono, E. (1993) Major and the manufacturers. Letter. *The Guardian*, 6 March

27. Manley, B. W. (1992) Learning our lessons: the future of education and training in Britain. Inaugural address as President of the Institution of Electrical Engineers,

28. Hite, S. (1993) *The Independent Magazine*, 6 February, p.164

29. Adult Literacy and Basic Skills Unit (1994) *The Basic Skills of Young Adults*. London: ALBSU

30. Melkie, J. (1993) *The Guardian*, 27 April

31. Schools Health Education Unit Survey 1994

32. Lewins, H. (1991) Teachers and knowledge. In *Knowledge and Communication*, ed. A. J. Meadows. London: Library Association

33. Hopkins, D. (1987) *Knowledge, Information Skills and the Curriculum*. London: British Library

34. Line, M. B. *et al.* (1971) *Information Requirements of College of Education Lecturers and School Teachers*. Bath: University of Bath Library

35. Hounsell, D. *et al.* (1980) *Education, Information and the Teacher*. London: British Library Research and Development Report 5505

36. Buchanan, K. (1994) The IT girls. *The Guardian*, 3 May

37. Haywood, T. (1991) *Changing Faculty Environments*. London: British Library Research and Development Report 6052

38. Zinberg, D. S. (1994) True grit with feelings. *The Times Higher Education Supplement*, 1 April

39. Gregg and Machin (1994) *Is the Glass Ceiling Cracking? Gender Compensation Differentials and Access to Promotion Among UK Executives*. London: National Institute for Economic and Social Research

40. Goethe, J. W. Von (1749–1832) quoted by Cooper, Cary S. in her review of 'Masculinity and the British Organisation Man Since 1945' by Michael Roper, OUP, 1994, in *The Times Higher Educational Supplement*, May 13th 1994

41. Summers, L. H. (1993) *Women's Education in Developing Countries: Barriers, Benefits and Policies*. Johns Hopkins University Press for the World Bank

42. BBC 2 'Lessons From Kerala', 2 October 1993, an Open University programme made in 1992

Chapter 3

The knowledge surplus

If information moments define who we are and what we can do, the stock of information held by communities and nations at any one time now tends to define their place in the hierarchy of world wealth and power. The geographic proximity of some nations to important raw materials, e.g. the oil reserves in the Middle East, the timber of the Amazon Basin, the coffee of Kenya, the raw jute of Bangladesh or the copper and cobalt of Zaire, still endows them with a fluctuating source of wealth and economic power, but their customers increasingly pay in currencies earned by selling information, knowledge and intelligence, whether this is high-level value-added services or embedded in high-technology manufactured products. The continuing capacity to innovate and to create distinctive stocks of information is what now gives one nation an advantage over another. What I call the 'knowledge surplus' is the ability to give away or trade information in the complete confidence that you retain a sufficient stock of core competencies and intellectual capital to stay ahead of the competition. Exchanging your knowledge surplus may take the form of building manufacturing capacity in other countries; giving aid to developing countries; registering new patents and subsequently licensing them out to others; renting out copyrights; and offering distinctive consultancy services in the more advanced aspects of applied technology, e.g. railway construction, civil engineering, mining, chemical processing or pollution control.

Nations build up important knowledge surpluses by investing in ongoing programmes of pure and applied research, funded by both public and private investment or partnerships of both. Pure research is time-consuming and carries few guarantees of success. Except in a few fields, such as pharmaceuticals, where the returns can produce significant profits, this kind of research requires serious national support through universities, specially funded research centres or research councils, who are often given public funds to promote research in particular disciplines. The great military research centres funded by the US, the former USSR and other governments often consumed the bulk of 'superpower' investment in 'blue skies' research. One often proclaimed expectation of the post-cold-war 'peace dividend' is that these national resources might now be channelled into more community-friendly research and development.

The perception of where the greatest advantage lies in terms of research investment varies considerably around the world. In the UK the government tends to concentrate on funding pure research, seeing it as the responsibility of the private sector to convert and add value to this with near-market research and development. Until quite recently the Japanese government took the quite opposite view that the greatest advantage lay in developing and refining ideas generated elsewhere to higher levels of quality, utility and convenience. Its virtual monopoly of the fabrication of integrated circuits, a technology first pioneered in the US, is an example of how a dogged determination to continually refine one area of applied technology helped it to keep a distinctive edge on the rest of the world.

In the US the much more pragmatic tradition of corporations getting back some of their taxes through military and other contracts nicely blurs the line between private and public funding, and between pure and applied research. The recent Pentagon suggestion that it and the Department of Energy should pump US$1 billion into the development and manufacturing of a strong, home-based LCD, flat-screen capacity is a good example of this. Japanese firms like Sharp and NEC are well ahead in the bright, sharp and fast-reacting 'active matrix' versions of this technology, so vital to laptop computers, and currently supply 95 per cent of world demand. However, they have so far shown scant regard for the Pentagon's needs in relation to flat-panelled displays for military use, and the Pentagon does not want to be left outside this particular knowledge domain. It is clear that durable knowledge surpluses now require continuing and increasing levels of investment in research of all kinds if they are to remain relevant and avoid rapid decomposition. The US microchip maker Intel had a US$1.1 billion product development budget for 1994, in addition to the US$2.4 billion that it planned to spend on new plant and equipment. Intel's business, the design and fabrication of microprocessors and microcontrollers which now comprise the logic centres of all computer-driven devices, is truly information rich and commands a healthy knowledge surplus over its competitors. Siemens, the German multinational with core businesses in telecommunications, power generation and distribution, electronic communications and industrial systems, medical technology and transportation, spends £3 billion a year or 9 per cent of its income from worldwide sales on research and development. Merck, the US drugs company, now invests around US$1 billion per year in research, and estimates that it costs US$359 million and takes ten years just to bring one new drug formulation to the market. Advanced pharmaceutical knowledge is increasingly becoming isolated within four or five companies. Their accumulation of information gives them a surplus which new entrants to the business would have to risk many years and many millions of dollars to emulate.

Like corporations, fast-growing nations such as those around the Pacific Rim are also seeking to control key information moments that will help them move on to the next level of knowledge generation. Japan has begun shifting resources to support the less predictable outcomes of pure research, while Taiwan and the People's Republic of China are actively seeking partnership deals with western companies that not only manufacture goods on their soil but also speed up the transfer of technology to their local populations. South Korea, a relatively new entrant to this arena, believes that it must now invest a good deal of money in pure research to build up its own information and knowledge base in order to remain competitive. To do this, the South-Korean government intends to pump US$46 billion into research and development in 14 key industrial sectors until 2001, via its Highly Advanced National (HAN) programme, launched in 1992. Earmarked projects include a 256-megabit semiconductor chip, high-definition television, electric cars, bioengineering and the development of an advanced telecommunications network.

Like other Pacific Rim nations South Korea desires self-sufficiency, i.e. major knowledge surpluses, in at least some of the most advanced technologies. Up until now Korean companies have tended to fund expansion rather than research, and the HAN programme is designed to get them to cooperate and work together on ground-breaking technology. Industrialists in South Korea may require a lot of convincing; they are not known for their cooperative spirit and many will disagree with the government over what the key research priorities should be, as well as recoiling from the kind of command economy in which the state tries to pick winners and avoid losers. Undeterred, and using Switzerland as a model, South Korea aims to 'steer' towards certain niche technologies, possibly forming alliances with other countries. Its biggest electronics company, Samsung, already leads the world in digital video-disc recorders, but in semiconductors and flat-screen technology they still lag behind the Japanese. Like South Korea Malaysia has set a 'visionary' date, the year 2020, by which it hopes to have achieved the status of a fully developed and technologically proficient nation, exhibiting a thoroughly modern export-orientated manufacturing base. It also has set out some domains where it intends to achieve a high degree of capability. These include advanced materials, automated manufacturing, biotechnology, microelectronics, information technology and energy technology. Learning all the time from direct foreign investment, Malaysia's official plans call for a doubling of the percentage GDP devoted to research and development between 1990 and 1995. Its aim is to progress to the complete design and manufacture of the kind of sophisticated products that it currently assembles for foreign investors.

Measures of knowledge surpluses that grow out of research are often contradictory. Britain has won over 60 Nobel Prizes for science this century against Japan's three, but the exploitation of ideas by Japan, via patent registration, easily outstrips Britain, whose own level of patent registration was outstripped by Germany many years ago.

In order to trade a knowledge surplus confidently there has to be a considerable differential between the lowest and highest levels of achievement that a nation or a firm can offer. Japanese, American and British companies, for instance, all build advanced manufacturing operations in many countries, but they nearly always retain the higher levels of research and development knowledge at corporate headquarters. The width and depth of information embedded in different levels of achievement becomes a critical factor in the ability to trade. Customers pay more of a premium as they get closer to the latest information on offer, although cutting-edge information is rarely on the table as it is exclusive access to this, particularly during the vital 'novelty' period of the information or product lifecycle, that ensures the continuance of a healthy knowledge surplus.

The information that supports a knowledge surplus can of course flow into and out of a particular community. Nations drift into and out of all kinds of knowledge creation as they react to both local and global trends. The capacity to innovate is always volatile, intelligent people are increasingly mobile and the decomposition of what once might have been quite stable information chains can now occur much faster, as one industry disappears altogether or gives way to another that is more profitable. The nations of western Europe, via a mixture of colonization and technological advantage have, since the late 15th century, set standards of economic and social development that other nations have come to aspire to and, ironically, compete with. It is against western European, and since the late 19th century North American, achievements that we have come to measure the success of other nations and to categorize them as undeveloped, developing or developed. This latter state we recognize as the fulfilment of a high standard of economic and social achievement within stable political structures. Such countries are regarded as 'nations whose time has come', hence the popularity of setting dates for the achievement of certain levels of development. By such dates they hope that their stock of information and knowledge, in alliance with their own brand of cultural energy and determinism, will have grown to exhibit the kind of differentials between the highest and lowest levels of their achievement, exhibited by those economies which were most developed at the time of starting their own programme.

Some nations build up their knowledge surplus and accelerate their development at the expense of others; some will wait in vain to achieve any kind of non-commodity-based advantage at all. The latter are destined to receive carefully apportioned slices from the surpluses of others at prices that they can ill-afford, and in currencies that they have to starve half of their populations to generate. At times they will get some minimum levels of knowledge and technology doled out to them as long-term aid, but no one is rushing to give them membership cards to the upper school.

That information, and the knowledge and intelligence that it feeds, is increasingly a factor in the competitive advantage of nations and a key motor of their continued wealth creation has become a generally accepted truth. What is not so clear is where it comes from. Is it just a matter of financial investment by companies and countries of the kind noted above, i.e. funding for information? Is it important that a nation be still engaged in inventing and making things at the cutting edge of science and engineering? Is it a mixture of these plus the spreading of non-profit-purposeful information among a nation's citizens who, by being better informed become more effective thinkers and innovators in more visible wealth-creating domains?

The first of these possibilities is now clearly understood, although levels of investment vary significantly between companies and between different business activities. Funding for future information moments within commercial enterprises is clearly a function of both the timescale of potential returns and the belief systems that inform enterprise within a particular culture. The enterprise culture in the UK is often criticized for its endemic short-termism, whereby fund managers and shareholders tend to hold and sell shares for quick returns, rather than to see the enterprise prosper as part of a wider social contract. UK banks also have a reputation for hesitation when it comes to supporting innovation and long-term planning, and many companies would still rather pay their managers more and disperse higher profits to shareholders than invest in continued innovation.

The second possibility suffers in parts of the older developed world from schools of thought that see little or no relationship between a continuing capacity to engineer their environment and a capacity to generate wealth from information. Another view, and one that I share, sees it as vital to the continuation of a healthy knowledge surplus that a nation operate at the cutting edge of at least some engineering domains, thus retaining links with the critical information moments of experiment and discovery. Such a nation also displays levels of confidence in its core competences that give it credibility with both its customers and its competitors. As well as keeping their stocks of problem-solving information relevant and high, the knowledge surpluses generated can also be used to develop whole new families of products or services which continue to look credible to consumers and which come to the marketplace faster than their competitors' products.

The third possibility, always difficult to measure in terms of inputs and outputs, ebbs and flows as the prosperity of nations ebbs and flows. It is often more enthusiastically accept'd as a necessary investment by a nation when the workforces of competitor nations are seen to be better informed or better educated. Britain's seeking parity with what it perceives as a better informed and educated German population is a good, if not very successful, example of this phenomenon. The acceptance of the power of literacy as an agent for lifting undeveloped nations into higher levels of economic activity, and the undoubted reverence for information and education in all fast-developing economies, are other examples.

Second-class information

As all economists know, human wants are virtually unlimited despite the resources available, even within seemingly rich communities. A central issue of economics is therefore that of scarcity: at any one time the world can only produce a limited amount of goods and services from the production factors available to it. These have traditionally been described as:

1. Labour, or human resources. This is limited both in number and in skills.

2. The natural and finite resources of land and raw materials.

3. Capital, made up of all those inputs that themselves have had to be produced in the first place, e.g. factories, machines, engines, the means of transportation etc. The productivity of capital is of course always limited by the state of technology.

Scarcity can therefore be defined as the excess of human wants over what can actually be produced, and is what necessitates choice. It is difficult to define information in these terms, and economists have on the whole fought shy of recognizing information as a serious factor in the reduction or creation of scarcity. They have even more trouble recognizing information as a resource equivalent to labour, land and capital, the availability or scarcity of which might be critical to economic activity.

As well as scarcity, economists have always been much engaged by the issue of public and private goods and the issues of 'rival', 'excludable' and 'non-excludable' that arise as limits or opportunities within them. Information can be both a private or a public good, and many of the debates concerning access to it hinge on which of these factors should condition its use. All governments intervene in the market to provide 'merit' goods. These are the goods and services which a government believes everyone ought to have access to, regardless of whether they are wanted, and which, if left to an unrestricted market, would fail to materialize in sufficient quality or quantity to satisfy the .reasonable needs of a population. One important characteristic of merit goods is that they are not very easy to divide up and sell in small units, e.g. £10 worth of clean air or £12 worth of defence.

As we know, there can be considerable variation in what governments regard as their duty to provide as public goods, i.e. those which ostensibly benefit everyone. Indeed, as societies evolve and change we would expect the definition of this to change. In 1944 the British government issued a White Paper on employment which made it clear that they accepted '. . . as one of their primary aims and responsibilities the maintenance of a high and stable level of employment' [1]. Fifty years later the UK government is still expected to intervene in the market to support this pledge, but other issues have moved to the top of the political agenda, e.g. the curbing of inflation (success in which, it is claimed, will also help reduce unemployment) and the impact of economic activity on the environment.

Other examples of public goods are the water supply, education, health care, street lighting, public parks, museums, art galleries and public libraries. These are always non-rival but may exhibit varying degrees of excludability, i.e. the consultation with the doctor may be free but you may have to pay for the medication prescribed. The great benefit of investing in public goods is that they can be used by growing populations at no additional cost. Thus once a lighthouse has been built any number of ships can benefit from it without excluding others from the same benefit [2]. Information is very much like the beam from a lighthouse: if I use a reference book in my public library I have not diluted the value of the information for anyone else; indeed, it might be used for a hundred different reasons, and remains intact for as long as the paper and binding will stand. However, information is often 'excludable', i.e. a charge may be levied to gain access to where it resides, whether this be on video, an electronic highway, in a book, or in a building where different kinds of information packages are stored.

The economics of information are complicated in that its impact or output can rarely be represented using easily measurable criteria. Even recognizing its eventual utility is almost impossible, as it acquires value only after a complex process of human filtering, which we still do not fully understand. Full, partial or non-use is thus not easily measured or predicted, and thus information takes on the characteristics of a hidden-property good. Its properties or benefits may take a long time before they are realized and, in orthodox economic terms, they may never be realized. The fragments of information that one day coalesce into a profitable insight or action are not easily weighed or measured. Information has to be acquired and processed before it can be used, and this is largely a private and invisible process, which poses tremendous problems for those who would promote the cause of information as a public good, particularly those who perceive access to it as a kind of fourth right of citizenship after food, clothing and housing. Governments are often told that easy and cheap access to information results in important economic benefits for individuals and the wider community, but this is difficult to prove and therefore government-funded agencies such as public libraries, law centres and Citizens Advice Bureaux frequently find that their resources threaten to dry up at any time. Information to improve, enhance and develop non-profit-purposeful citizenship is being given lower priority by the year.

Fewer and fewer policy makers believe that public investment in information services is worthwhile; that those who work to provide these services believe they change people's lives, sometimes dramatically for the better, is no longer enough: the benefits need to become more obvious, the changes more measurable. In many developed economies providing access to information as a public good is now perceived as being marginal to economic and social wellbeing. Competing demands for public funds and government policies which favour market responsibility are increasingly squeezing the resources that might have been available for public information provision. Proving that the 'information moment' is still as important as street lighting or defence seems likely to become much harder. The developed economies of Europe seem to be at a major turning point in the evolution of the balance between providing public and private goods, and the provision of easy and cheap access points to information will not escape these waves. While some countries are still enthusiastically providing new public libraries and other forms of public information provision, many others, including the UK, are closing them down.

Doyal and Gough [2] promote the idea of 'need satisfiers' as an anti-dote to the orthodox economists' equation of welfare with subjective wants, rather than objective needs. They note how:

> . . . the hard pressed adjust their wants downwards to cope with life; the affluent have new wants created for them. Want satisfaction cannot provide a metric to compare the welfare of different societies.

After testing a set of needs indicators, in association with economic, social and political variables for 128 rich and poor countries with a population of over one million during 1990, Doyal and Gough discovered that only those countries with regulated (i.e. not entirely free-market) capitalist structures were associated with the highest need-satisfaction levels:

> Two extreme forms of economy fare badly. Free market capitalism has no system for identifying common human needs (as opposed to wants) and provides no way of granting people the need satisfiers they require. It encounters market failures and cannot foster community-based forms of provision. [2]

They suggest that needs-based welfare is clearly provided at a higher level when associated with a socially regulated form of capitalism. To me this sounds very much like the old mixed-economy approach, now so reviled in much of Europe, which dominated political and economic thought in the UK during the 30 years following the Second World War. Those who have legitimate 'needs', i.e. a proper diet, good physical and mental health, housing, the development of cognitive skills and a social life offering both recreation and opportunities, will need access to information to enable them to discover where these benefits are and how they work. They will then need more information to help them make the most of them. As individuals progress from needs to wants, and as they move up from one economic level to another, they will want access to different kinds of information and, most importantly, the cognitive skills to be able to use it.

During 1988 the US state of California took a lead in exploring some of the broader social, economic and political issues associated with information showering when it considered setting up a 'Commission of the Information Age'. Prompted initially by the liberalization of telecommunications in the US, and the subsequent regulatory vacuum that this created, its agenda extended far beyond access to telephony by including the following concerns:

(a) the conditions that will promote continued development of a viable information industry in California that is based on the application of information and telecommunication systems.

(b) the public's need for information, the structure of the information economy, and the contribution of information to productivity and quality of work-life and leisure.

(c) questions of equity related to the proliferation of electronic systems of information collection, manipulation, storage and distribution.

(d) the requirements for citizens to be active participants in the information industry, as entrepreneurs, and workers, including their educational and cultural preparation.

(e) California's place in the global information economy, with a special emphasis on how the state can attain and maintain a position of competitive advantage in the global information economy. [3]

While sections (a) and (e) correspond to the kinds of issues that would dominate many modern 'information charters', such as those in Singapore or Japan, sections (b), (c) and (d) suggest a concern to explore the less immediately measurable role of information for citizenship which would have been political anathema in the UK at that time, or at any time since.

First-class information

The decline of information as a public good has seen a parallel rise in its perceived value as a private commodity, and its status as a powerful replacement for the old economic factors of labour, natural resources and capital has been increasingly celebrated. Indeed, there is a widespread belief among many western commentators that the developed economies of the world will eventually come to depend almost entirely on marketing and selling information and knowledge:

> We will only be able to make our living in the future literally by selling our knowledge. [4]

This is part of a growing belief fuelled by a long line of surveys and observations, such as those made in 1962 by Malchup [5], in 1973 by Bell [6], in 1977 by Porat [7] and in 1985 by Strassmann [8], that information handling and the production of knowledge is replacing labour as the main ingredient of all work, and that it has become the key motor for all future economic success. Despite some attempts to assess the size and growth of information industries, the size and extent of the new wealth created by information itself has proved difficult to measure:

> A major difficulty is that the aggregated data homogenize very disparate economic activities. Information economists' enthusiasm to put a price tag on everything has the unfortunate consequence of failing to convey the really valuable dimensions of the information sector. [9]

There is, however, a lot of evidence to show that certain kinds of information, knowledge and intelligence-rich activity are seriously disturbing the old economic paradigms of capital, plant and labour. Microsoft's market value passed that of General Motors in January 1992 and its earnings topped US$3.75 billion in 1993, and although seemingly in the business of hi-tech manufacture, the US firm Texas Instruments made more than half its turnover in 1992 from licensing its existing patents and intellectual property.

The 1994 merger of Novell and WordPerfect created a US$1.9 billion turnover company, while Larry Ellison's Oracle company, specializing in the relational databases that IBM saw no future for, and which now look set to handle all the chores used to manage interactive television, turned over US$1.5 billion in 1993. The world market for computer games, hardware and software, despite some overstocking problems in 1994, stood at more than US$4 billion. Intel, the world's largest maker of microchips, recorded US$2.3 billion in net profits in 1993, more than the rest of the top US semiconductor manufacturers combined. The annual UK spend on information technology has been estimated at around £12.4 billion, a third of which is located in the travel and tourism business. The worldwide market for biotechnology products is expected to reach US$40 billion by the end of the decade, and worldwide spending on television programming in 1993 was estimated to be double this figure, at US$80 billion, and expected to rise by 10 per cent per year. Clearly, such signs herald major shifts in the values that will be attributed to both human and capital assets.

Two different kinds of information 'software' will dominate the new economics, one designed by humans to emulate humans, i.e. intellectual property in all its forms, and one increasingly refined by years of intellectual testing and development contained within humans. The portable relational databases of the latter, often infuriating with their unpredictable mixture of intelligence, insight, creativity and imagination, have always taken us forward. That humans can now transfer the memories of so many information moments to electronic devices, together with some of the intelligence that they use to make new knowledge, is what is meant by the information revolution. However, as yet, it is not something that many institutions, including those in the business of lending money, feel comfortable with or know how to put a value on.

This is a particular problem for those seeking finance for information-intensive enterprises. Many businesses that offer services rooted in intellectual property, e.g. translating, systems design, programming, consultancy, patent searching etc., find that their lack of the traditional ingredients of buildings and plant makes it difficult for them to raise money. The potential lender has only a documented history of their intelligence and their skills at using it as collateral, and this often does not seem substantial enough to justify handing over the money. This is ironic, given the serious losses that many banks have made in recent years on loans to those who did have material assets to offer as security. It also contradicts the widely promoted wisdom that the collateral of our future lies in the added value that will come from information intensity rather than investment in manufacturing. If the finance to support the build-up of competitive intelligence requires the kind of collateral that a heavy engineering company might have offered, some parts of the information revolution are never going to get off the ground and those that do could be short-lived. The world of entertainment recognizes talent as a resource that often has a high premium, and so it should come as no surprise to us that paying for a unique, finite talent will be expensive. Describing the information embedded within the people and systems of a large organization as the 'talent' of the enterprise may be a more understandable way of identifying information as a corporate resource with a critical economic function. Coming as it does with people, rather than a place or a building, talent is always difficult to manage. Floating and unpredictable, it offers poor stability at a high cost: the carriers of the corporate knowledge surplus are highly mobile and can become even more so when tempted by the blandishments of competitors. The property of proven superior intelligence undoubtedly carries a premium in so many more areas of expertise than it once did. Once it was the old-established professional groups who tended to take their 'intelligence' and hence their customers with them when they moved on; now it can be market researchers, management consultants, financial advisers, designers, bio-engineers, systems analysts and creative teams in areas as diverse as fashion, advertising, electronics, acoustic design and pharmaceutical research.

Without diminishing the value of information, knowledge and intelligence, it is important to keep some sense of balance between ideas and action, between information and the actual delivery of the goods that result from its use. There was a time, during the 1980s, when the dimensions of the 'information economy' looked set to embrace everybody. Serious academic thought was being given to whether a gas fitter's work was purely informational in character or just information intensive; whether a postman is someone who delivers letters or a batch-processing multidestinational information conduit; whether Marilyn Monroe was really a charismatic beauty or just a set of data that arrived in a popular and photogenic configuration. The premise for this novel occupational analysis (some of it almost as wild as my examples) was the expected shift in developed economies away from the kind of low-skill-based industrial and manufacturing occupations that characterized the first industrial revolution, to the more highly skilled knowledge and information-based occupations that supposedly characterize the new information revolution. These booming non-industrial occupations are predominantly, but not entirely, service-based activities in areas like local government, design, leisure, tourism, marketing, advertising, entertainment, media, communications, management and technical consultancy, insurance, finance, all forms of health care, education and training. A significant value-added component has also grown up in support of manufacturing in areas such as network design, computer programming, systems analysis and design, robotics and control. In the enthusiasm for widening the taxonomy of the information economy, just about anyone who handled information was being renamed and their principal function subsumed in favour of the newly identified information component of their work. The change from 'white collar worker' to 'information worker' in the US Bureau of Labor's table of occupational classifications during the mid 1980s is indicative of the impact that 'information' branding was having at that time.

Of the 90 new departments of economics and business administration set up in Japanese universities since 1990, more than a third were named the 'department of business administration and information' [10]. 'Information' has now joined 'international' and 'environment' in Japan as the most popular label for new university programmes and departments. However, this tells us nothing about the level of the work being done, nothing about the status-conscious hierarchies that still operate and nothing about the power and influence being exercized by these new information workers. The spread of technology is also often regarded as another indicator of information intensity, but again, just counting the sale of units is not enough: such figures may be saying more about the dimensions of past utility rather than current or active value. Also, concentrating on the numbers of computer 'boxes' delivered tells us nothing about the quality of use. Perhaps they are just speeding up basic data-processing functions, adding little of value and stimulating nothing in the way of creativity or innovation.

The distribution of technology is often disparate and there may be serious differentials in access to it even between the regions of a small developed economy such as the UK. New technologies may simply overlay deep structural disparities which they do nothing to improve. Connors [11] explores a number of factors that might contribute to the different information densities of different nations. He suggests that this is not simply a function of the abstract or cerebral activity that a population might be engaged in, but rather the levels of sophistication at which these abstractions operate:

> The opposite case – that of the low abstraction society – is characterized
> by relatively few occupational categories, concentrated mainly in primary

and simple secondary production, and a relatively narrow range of issues with which the population at large typically concerns itself. There are fewer aromatherapists and interior designers in Botswana than in California, with correspondingly fewer related professional associations, magazines, conferences, expenses claims and endowments.

Despite the undoubted rise in the number of aromatherapists and interior designers in the old, rich economies of the west, the promise of information-rich high-abstraction employment has been an empty one for many people in both Europe and in the US. It has more often been a cloak for work which neither pays a living wage nor survives very long; work which is often part-time and exploits those – generally women – who are trapped by poverty and other circumstances which both inflate their desire for any kind of work and invariably reduce their asking price. This is not to romanticize the harshness and drudgery that has always characterized manual, heavy or unskilled work; nor is it to underestimate the tedious and boring routines that have been removed from so many workplaces by developments in technology; it is rather a plea for some old-fashioned balance in assessing the value and durability of 'new' work in the harshly competitive world of global business. The uncritical optimism that assumes that technology always enriches life, that it always offers new opportunities and that it always stimulates more liberal economic and social regimes is as harmful as the unthinking Luddism that would suppress its advantages. Technology is, after all, the 'information moment' in action. Getting it to work for us rather than allowing it to dictate its own pace and direction has always been the challenge, but it is one that we should be able to address without mindless surrender. In 1982 Jones [12] predicted the emergence of what he termed a 'post-service' society in the 1990s which would pose serious problems of cultural absorption for the currently rich, developed economies of the west:

> Advanced economies have now moved into a post-industrial era, in which services such as welfare, education, administration and the transfer of information dominate employment. The displacement of agriculture by manufacturing as the dominant employer was the first of two major 'cross-overs' in economic history. The second was the displacement of manufacturing (industrial) employment by service (post-industrial) employment. The post-industrial era will be of short duration: the technological revolution of the 1980s will bring about a third major transition – to a 'post-service' society in which routine and repetitive service employment will be significantly reduced, or eliminated. This change will raise unprecedented human problems: the whole relationship of people to time use, personal goals, economics, politics and culture must be re-examined.

Despite Jones's suggestion that the post-industrial era will be of short duration, it is interesting to note that, halfway through the 1990s, the old industrial economies of the west still derive their wealth from a mix of familiar, if highly variable, industrial and post-industrial activities. Employment in both manufacturing and service areas is a complex weave that often defies separation. Indeed their tenacious grip on survival is undoubtedly derived in no small part from the bonding that this invisible mixture of the material and the abstract builds. Inside these bonds manufacturing is spinning off information-intensive surpluses, which in turn spin off new demands for more sophisticated manufactured devices. A highly developed industrial enterprise currently practising the Japanese-inspired 'lean' production approach to its manufacture of artefacts might be expected to exhibit a high level of post-service tendencies. Such a company might be experimenting with a 'lights-out' manufacturing and testing environment, such as the one at Fujitsu's telephone switching plant at Oyama, north of Tokyo. Here, robots linked to automated sensors and control devices exchange components and information about components in an eerie dumb show, without human presence. However, slightly apart from them humans still sit at small, magnifying-glass equipped workstations waiting to check the errors the machines have identified. The machines invariably reject components which are perfectly acceptable but which their sensors and mathematically rigorous checking processes are not 100 per cent happy about. The humans confirm that nine out of ten of the rejects do in fact meet the required standard, and stamp them 'passed'. Having shared their intelligence with the robots they then turn the lights out, go home and wait for the machines to discard another batch of perfectly good units overnight. Europe's top 30 international companies with headquarters in the EU, ranked by the size of their workforce [13], would still include Daimler Benz (2nd), Siemens (3rd), Phillips (5th), Fiat (7th), Volkswagen (8th), British Telecom (9th), French Railways (10th), Bayer (12th), Hoechst (13th), Peugeot (14th), Thyssen, Iron and Steel (19th), ICI (22nd), British Aerospace (23rd), Mannesmann, machinery (24th) and Michelin (25th). These industries may be using the latest available technologies to better use information to add more value, thus improving both the efficiency of their operations and the quality of their products, but they could not be described as post-industrial. The one purely 'information' business that would be included in this particular top 30 is Barclays Bank, ranked at 28th.

There may be some edging towards a 'post-service' trend in some sectors of some economies, but too many people still 'go out to work' for this to form the bulk of employment opportunities in most developed nations. Major shifts in the foundations of successful economic activity do not lend themselves to very precise crossover times: these are usually allocated to them in retrospect, with terms like 'age', 'era' and 'revolution'. Data signalling the relative decline of manufacturing industry as a proportion of a nation's GDP are usually cited as further evidence in support of the trend towards a world information economy. In early 1993 The Economist [14] noted the decline of manufacturing as a percentage of GDP (a drop of between 5 per cent and 13 per cent over a 21-year period) in three major economies:

> In Japan 36 per cent in 1970 down to 29 per cent in 1991, a fall of 7 per cent;
>
> In Germany 41 per cent in 1970 down to 28 per cent in 1991, a fall of 13 per cent;
>
> In the US 26 per cent in 1970 down to 21 per cent in 1991, a fall of 5 per cent.

Of course this is not a measure of actual manufacturing output, which undoubtedly rose in all three countries during these years; it is rather an indicator of the size of this sector relative to that of the growing service sector.

Like many other well established industrial centres, the West Midlands region of England, once the melting pot of British industrial inventiveness and entrepreneurism, has seen similar structural changes over the last decade. In 1981 this region supported 800 000 jobs in manufacturing industry. Between 1981 and 1992 one-quarter, i.e. 200 000 of these jobs, were lost, whereas 120 000 jobs were gained in the service sector. The data from the UK Labour Force Survey, previously only available as national and regional figures, can now be disaggregated at the city level. The data for Birmingham, which related to employment patterns between June and August 1993, showed that the city still employed 26 per cent of its labour force in manufacturing, some 5 per cent more than the national percentage and with almost 6 per cent more plant and machine operatives working locally than were found nationally. However, the city lagged 4 per cent behind the rest of the country in hotel, catering and distribution industries [15]. Perhaps in an attempt to rectify this, and to make the most of both its business and geographic strengths, Birmingham City Council has adopted an objective of developing 'business tourism' as a key employment strategy for the future.

Birmingham is widely regarded as having shown considerable foresight in its use of European funds to help revitalize the 'rust bowl' spaces left behind as each set of factory gates closed for the last time. The move to replace industry with a 'tourist industry', although understood and welcomed by most of those directly affected by de-industrialization, is still often perceived as a light and insubstantial replacement for old-style wealth creation. For some it seems demeaning to become a tourist attraction. Such a view no doubt lay behind the harsh satire of Auberon Waugh [16]:

> . . . since our future is plainly not as a manufacturing nation, but as a provider of services, particularly tourist services, we should make a positive virtue of these slums. Scandinavians, Germans and Japanese, tired of their well-ordered existence, might well thrill to see a druggie catch AIDS with his shared needle, to count the rats in our public wards, etc. etc.

but given the massive negative equity currently facing the inhabitants of nearly every type of building in Tokyo, the economic trauma still haunting German reunification and the slashing of public-sector funding in all areas of Scandinavian social policy, the citizens of these countries may well be too busy building virtues from their own dilemmas to seek them elsewhere.

Jones's book [12] was an important pointer, a warning that structural changes were afoot which, if not planned for, could seriously destabilize the fabric of many states. Our history has been one of incrementally reducing the need to invest in and use human labour. The first industrial revolution produced machines that either replaced or extended human capacity and produced surpluses of wealth that stimulated the desire to be served, e.g. by tradesmen or household servants. Many modern service occupations often require little in the way of intelligence or skill from their employees, many of whom seem to be required simply to be 'in attendance'. The adding up, the stock control, the logistical calculations, the design of systems or spaces has been or is being done remotely by intelligent workers who design the software, keep it up to date and transmit the results wherever they are needed. Railway signalmen, bank clerks, motorcycle messengers, postal workers, meter readers, typists and shop assistants have all lost work to 'central control', whether this be a computer program or a smaller number of people supplementing a computer program. This is the ongoing reduction in routine and repetitive service work that Jones predicted would soon disappear altogether, i.e. the elimination of the market for unskilled time.

Leaving predictions and deadlines aside, it is clear that more and more electronic devices are coping with unskilled routines and that this trend will continue as more intelligence can be transferred to machines. These developments coincide with increasing global competition from nations whose minimalist regulatory cultures can assimilate new technology and new investment even faster than we can in the west. Their economic systems accommodate low wages, low taxes and low levels of social and welfare support. Their political systems, often low on ideology and 'softly' or 'firmly' authoritarian, worry less about human rights, relying on economic growth to bring peace, prosperity and, eventually, equality to the majority of their citizens. These are business governments who see technology as a vital agent in raising the incomes of their peoples quickly to levels that satisfy material desires rather than inspiring political unrest and agitation. Such countries seek the material riches of the west within less than half the 100 years that it took a country starting out to modernize in the early 19th century. For them democracy is a fractious sideshow using up valuable energy that could be better invested in improving GDP. Speaking in 1993 about the first change of government in Japan for two generations, the senior Singaporean statesman Lee Kuan Yew sought to reassure his Asian colleagues that nothing seriously untoward was in the air:

> They [the Japanese] want growth and they want to get on with life. They are not interested in ideology as such, or in the theory of good government. They just know a good government and want a good government. Americans believe that out of contention, out of the clash of different ideals, you get good government. That view is not shared in Asia. [17]

This probably holds true so long as a government delivers the economic growth that ties up most of its people in racing the rest of the world. But as Asian countries move towards rich-world income levels they will also find time for western fractiousness. Thailand, despite its circa 8.6 per cent annual growth rate since 1985 and its strong military control of radio and television, has had its fair share of political disruption already, with no fewer than 17 coups since 1932 [11]. A rising middle class, more time, more education, the space to develop more critical views on information access and information freedom and cheaper satellite dishes, will all contribute to strong desires for more influence over more events. Stirrings of political opposition are even being seen in repressive Burma. Changes are already afoot in Japan and South Korea, and something akin to a political opposition is even beginning to emerge in Taiwan. Even the 'orderly' citizens of Singapore might sacrifice a dollar or two for some real political debate now and then.

In the meantime, intense global competition combined with the replacement of many simple, information-intensive jobs by low-maintenance technology suggests nothing short of economic catastrophe for the west. It raises the prospect of as many as 40 per cent or 50 per cent of working-age populations never finding work in the sense that we understand it. The most obvious signs that Europeans have seen this and are trying to do something about it are the now regular exhortations urging workforces to be more flexible. Communities are being drip-fed the news that they should be prepared to retrain and reskill, perhaps three or four times in a lifetime, and that they should expect only the minimum of state support when they are not working. It is an attempt to Americanize, or even Asianize, Europe's economic system but without 500 years to spare to change the culture.

Flexibility and poverty: Europe, America and Asia

In coincidence with the growth of low-level low-paid information work, workers throughout the world are now expected to move more often and change jobs more regularly; in short, they are expected to become more sensitive to changing employer needs. This is not the flexibility of pragmatism and compromise that has often characterized workforce responses to economic change, but rather the resurgence of 19th century market-efficient 'insecurity', where employers cheerfully adjusted wages and jobs with little or no consideration for humanitarian or social impacts. The assumption that this kind of flexibility offers only gains at no cost is short-sighted. The social and economic costs of despair, mental distress and uncertainty that arise from such a philosophy are never considered, and hiding information about these costs is becoming an increasingly addictive habit of western governments and their agencies. Any hint that such costs are exceeding the bounds of what should be acceptable in a 'civilized' community is nearly always met by 'we have statistics that prove it was worse in 1934' responses. The doorway sleepers in London's Strand and around the White House in Washington, most of them born a long time after 1934, live the 1990s reality. The great paradox here is that despite the almost daily rhetoric espousing unhindered laissez-faire economics among western nations, the state is still expected to pay for an increasing number of such casualties while demanding less and less in taxes with which to do so. The US has always been a flexible market-driven economy. Levels of job security have always been lower than those in Europe and hence wages easier to hold down:

> Yet blue-collar workers in the United States have seen falls in their real wages of up to 20 per cent over the last 15 years. Meanwhile, surveys of US workers show that 20 per cent expect to lose their jobs within 12 months and another 20 per cent expect to be temporarily laid off. 'Flexibility' is as much the result of the new trends as their solution. [18]

Viewed from a European perspective the US has always seemed better at creating new jobs and thus at holding down aggregate unemployment than the countries of the European Union (EU). The impact of US unemployment also tends to be more widely distributed, resulting in shorter periods out of work, e.g. nearly half of America's unemployed find work within a month, while only around 5 per cent of unemployed Europeans are so lucky. In 1973 roughly 65 per cent of the working-age population in both Europe and America were in work; by the early 1990s this was 72 per cent in US but had fallen to 62 per cent in Europe [19].

In the US it is both easier to lose your job and to get a new one that is poorly paid. Wages in the lowest decile tend to be around 38 per cent of the median, while in Europe wages in the lower decile approximate to nearer 68 per cent of national median pay. Low-income Europeans currently earn around 44 per cent more per hour than low-income Americans, and low-income Germans earn more than twice as much [19]:

> America's labour market delivers more employment and, therefore more output and higher average living standards than Europe's; but the price is worse poverty in and out of work, and greater economic insecurity. This is not an accidental conjunction. America's harsh benefits system, which threatens the unemployed with poverty and then delivers on the threat, is a crucial reason why America suffers less from unemployment in general, and from long-term unemployment in particular. In a labour market in which wages can fall to whatever level is needed to match supply and demand, an impressive rate of job creation is to be expected.

US job creation schemes, like those in the UK, seem to have shifted the poor into low-paid highly volatile low-tech jobs, while in the higher echelons of information and knowledge intensity fewer and fewer people work longer and longer hours for higher and higher pay. It is these latter heroines and heroes of the information age who will form the core of the new tradeable competencies in information handling and processing necessary to produce the knowledge surpluses needed to fuel a nation's ongoing competitive advantage. These are the people that Reich calls the symbolic analysts, those of the top 20 per cent of his three categories of US worker as outlined by Handy [20]:

> . . . those who deal with numbers and ideas, problems and words. They are the journalists, the financial analysts, the consultants, architects, lawyers, doctors, managers, all those whose intelligence is their source of power and influence . . . It is the symbolic analysts, the knowledge workers, the professionals and the managers who are the real beneficiaries of the information age because they own the new property.

To get there they will have used their previous 'information moments' well. They will have exploited all the information available on seeking and securing higher education, and they will leave it seeking intelligent, mind-enriching work associated with the latest technology. They will want to develop, interpret, repackage and market information-based products and services to a waiting world. That they will have been funded by the 70 per cent of parents whose children did not make it into higher education is not something that they will worry too much about. They will worry about the progress of their own children, though. They will take every care to ensure that they too grow up to be a part of the symbolic analyst 20 per cent.

By replacing land and capital with intelligence we will have created a new aristocracy, and there is so far no evidence to suggest that they will be any more generous, less inward-looking and conservative than the one they replace. The information-rich will become a smaller and smaller group within those economies that retain anything approaching a serious knowledge surplus. They will demand more and more for the knowledge surpluses they generate, and will want to contribute less and less of their income to the old safety-nets that have 'civilized' economic conditions in Europe since the Second World War. This new social and economic Darwinism will be no different from the normal disparities that exist between the rich and the poor of all nations, except that both the numerical ratios and the economic differentials will be much more marked. The social price of generating and keeping future knowledge surpluses will be high, as will the percentage of individual wealth that is spent on security systems. This will be a double blow for the UK; its refusal to invest in the kind of well-educated workforce that gives the edge to its main competitors in Europe and the US has already left it technologically poor. Concentrating on less demanding products at the lower end of the market, being too easily satisfied with less advanced machine tools, tolerating high levels of machine downtime, limping along with poor production planning and materials management in association with high levels of indirect labour, the UK has grown complacent and its once favoured status with its customers has gone elsewhere. Indeed, by drifting to the lower end of so many markets it has become the unfortunate competitor of low-wage countries with low-margin products [21]. Perhaps as a result of this poor performance it is not surprising that, of all the developed economies, the UK has been the most enthusiastic to move out of manufacturing and into the tertiary sector. However, even the generally optimistic Connors [11] sees that, without a more diverse base, this can become unsatisfactory:

> However productive workers in the tertiary sector may be, the services which they provide are less tradeable internationally than are goods which can be put into boxes and loaded onto ships and aeroplanes. Tertiary sector people and those in the information and control sectors in particular, are highly paid and the demand which they generate tends to draw in imports of physical goods. It is no coincidence that it is those developed countries in which the concept of the post-industrial state is most strongly established which tend to have chronic balance of trade

deficits or that rapid growth of the tertiary sectors in those countries has often coincided with the problem becoming entrenched.

By 1995 unemployment will become the old world's biggest problem. By that time some 20 million people are expected to be unemployed throughout Europe and a quarter of these will be aged between 18 and 25. The social fabric of the EU, once protected by high social security benefits and a culture of minimum entitlements for everyone, will begin to unravel. European nations currently spend around 22 per cent of their GDP on social protection plans, compared with less than 15 per cent in the USA. Privatization, so loudly pioneered by the UK, will ruthlessly prune thousands of European jobs, and the restructuring of all kinds of businesses to cut costs and improve competitiveness will inevitably do the same. Across the EU nearly one-fifth of the labour force consists of public-sector employees. Shrinking this part of European GDP will not be easy, given the proportion of voters who would be directly affected. The international competition that requires changes to these old structures will not go away, just as the problems of poverty, homelessness, violence, crime and political instability that the changes will produce will not go away. This is an economic time-bomb which European politicians seem, currently at least, impotent to handle. Nonetheless, the pressure for Europe to emulate US social and economic approaches is building up:

> Between 1970 and 1990 the US economy created 38 million jobs against just 10 million in Europe. Real wages in the more flexible US market grew by less than half a percent each year; Europe's real wage growth was three times as fast. Between 1970 and 1992 the EU created 3 million new private sector jobs, compared with 7 million in the public sector. In the same 22 years the US saw 32.8 million new private sector jobs and only 6 million in the public sector. [22]

Given that the EU is still made up of sovereign governments who have to face regular re-election, and given that short-term political imperatives are always a severe brake on structural change, the Americanization of economic policy in Europe faces an uphill struggle. Although it makes some sense for Europe to look to the US for comparisons between their respective approaches to employment, unemployment, social security benefits and job creation, it is in Asia and to a lesser extent eastern Europe that most west European and American unemployment will be created. Despite their export emphasis often being promoted at the expense of the current welfare of the majority of their populations, the hourly manufacturing wages paid in South Korea (£3), Hungary (£1.20) and the People's Republic of China (30p) ensure the continued migration of many millions of G7 jobs to anywhere in the world but Europe and America. Interestingly, Krugman and Lawrence, two economists from the Massachusetts Institute of Technology and Harvard University respectively, have suggested that foreign low-wage competition is marginal in terms of the decline of the US manufacturing base and the reduction of US blue-collar wages and jobs. While noting that the wages of the average American worker, which doubled between the end of the Second World War and the early 1970s, have risen by only 6 per cent since 1973, and that only highly educated workers have seen real salary rises during that time, they believe that this often-cited scapegoat seriously misleads the American public. Their thesis rests on the premise that home-based manufacturing productivity has done so well that Americans now have to spend a smaller fraction of their incomes on manufactured goods than they did 20 years ago, because they get all they need for a lot less money:

> Between 1970 and 1990 the price of goods relative to services fell 22.9 per cent. The physical ratio of goods to services purchased remained almost constant during that period. Goods have become cheaper primarily because productivity in manufacturing has grown much faster than in services. This growth has been passed on in lower consumer prices. [23]

Americans now spend just over 53 per cent on services, compared to around 41 per cent on goods. Given this shift it is hardly surprising that manufacturing has become a less important part of the economy, and as nearly all services are home-produced 'buying American' is much easier to do!

As people buy fewer goods manufacturing employment falls, companies replace people with machines and they make more efficient use of the people they keep. Less skilled workers see their wages decline and their opportunities diminish because a high-technology economy has less and less demand for their services [23].

A Mintel survey of consumer habits published in 1994, exploring lifestyle trends over the last 20 years, also confirmed that spending in the UK had shifted away from goods towards services. As well as predicting further growth in services such as life assurance, personal pensions, health insurance and leisure activities, the survey also noted a strong reaffirmation of the home as the principal centre of many leisure activities. Future growth areas identified included cable and interactive TV, home shopping, computer games and other home computing, as well as the inevitable home and personal security services needed to protect these and other home-based investments [24].

In their work Krugman and Lawrence also explore the idea of added value in manufacturing and how the raw value of national trade deficits often overstates its actual effect on the manufacturing sector.

Using a measure of 'value-added' that deducts from total sales the cost of raw materials and other inputs that a company might buy in from other firms, they noted that:

> In 1950 value-added in the manufacturing sector accounted for 29.6 percent of gross domestic product (GDP) and 34.2 percent of employment; in 1970 the shares were 25.0 and 27.3 percent respectively; by 1990 manufacturing had fallen to 18.4 percent of GDP and 17.4 percent of employment. [23]

Although trade figures measure sales, Krugman and Lawrence draw attention to the need to differentiate between the mix of elements that make up the official statistics. Thus when foreign imports displace a dollar of domestic manufacturing sales, a substantial fraction of that dollar – in the US they estimate around 40 cents – would have been spent on inputs from the service sector, which are not part of manufacturing's contribution to GDP. Reducing the manufacturing sector's contribution to GDP to 60 cents significantly modifies both the steepness of manufacturing's decline in the US and the real impact of imports on manufacturing GDP [20]. Persuasive as this argument is, I am not sure that it can be extrapolated to other industrial countries. The US does, after all, have one of the richest home markets in the world. However, I would concur with them in wanting to draw attention to the importance of the service sector as a part of all manufacturing effort, and caution against oversimplifying the difference between what we identify as 'manufacturing' and what we identify as 'service'.

Many of the information-intensive activities that were once part of the total economy of a manufacturing unit are now bought in from outside or, in modern parlance, outsourced. Thus finance, accounting, payroll, computer services, legal advice and personnel services are often no longer integrated with the unit, but they clearly depend on the success of such units for their own existence and success. Just because the links between the two are now more subtle and not always obvious, it does not mean that they do not exist, or that they do not depend on one another, or that the economics of their survival are not deeply intertwined.

The shipbuilder's tale

From ships to Lloyds: long-term knowledge migration

One issue which must be of deep concern to policy makers in the old industrialized economies of the world, but one that does not seem to have been given much serious attention so far, is the on-going relationship between their older established manufacturing industries and their evolving information-centred businesses. Where there is a strong manufacturing base does this help to feed and foster the development of new information-rich activities? Conversely, where the manufacturing base of a nation is run down and ceases to operate at the cutting edge of a particular technology, when it loses its core competence in areas in which it had been supreme, do these losses adversely affect its potential as a future supplier of information-based products and services? For instance, we know that the UK merchant marine declined from around 75 per cent of the world share of shipping to around 2 per cent since 1975, although worldwide shipping fleets increased by 22 per cent. In the wake of this decline considerable reductions in shipbuilding and heavy engineering capacity have taken place throughout Scotland and the northeast of England. This is a visible loss that all can understand, but even here some of the ripples are not instantly obvious, e.g. that due to the reduction in shipbuilding there is nowhere in the UK with the capacity to roll 2″ thick steel plate; that with the exception of a few steam turbine manufacturers (now almost entirely devoted to supplying power stations), Britain's largest combustion engine manufacturers now only build generators for ships; and that British Rail, the nation's second largest consumer of combustion engines, now have to import their locomotive engines from Germany.

But what about the knock-on effects that we do not see, that we do not, initially at least, associate with the loss of shipbuilding? It may be just a matter of time, perhaps 30, perhaps 40, perhaps even 50 years, before we lose the much more subtle stock of information and knowledge that used to make its way into important information/knowledge-rich businesses. We stop building ships and we have far fewer ships flying the UK flag. Our credibility as a maritime nation drops and the all-important concepts of confidence and reputation take a serious dive. What effects does this have on insurance, commodity exchange, shipping information, consultancy and education – all areas in which Britain was once well established and influential, and where its businesses set worldwide standards? We train fewer officers and engineers, and the colleges that once offered those training courses diversify into more attractive areas. The number of fully qualified ships' engineers drops and the number that are available to take early retirement declines. There are no longer enough engineers retiring from the merchant marine to join the insurance companies who once relied on them for assessing ships, advising on salvage, setting standards prior to insuring and confirming levels of seaworthiness.

All these knowledge-based activities seem a far cry from the noisy bustle of a shipyard. The line is indeed a long one, hence the almost unnoticed chronology prior to decline. The practical, hands-on engineering activity declines in one place and impoverishes the knowledge capital of another kind of business in another place half a century later, raising questions such as: Does the business of marine insurance, once the pride of the London insurance market, eventually migrate to where the most modern and up-to-date shipbuilding knowledge resides? Does insuring ships require access to a home-based engineering credibility that inspires confidence in customers? We know that the knowledge now resides in other places, where the words 'heavy industry' and 'engineering' still form a significant part of a manufacturing culture. It resides at Mitsubishi Heavy Industries, Kawasaki Heavy Industries, Sumitomo Heavy Industries and Ishikawajima-Harima in Japan; in the Daewoo shipyards of South Korea; and in the niche-specialist shipyards of Norway and Hamburg. In 1993 South Korea took a major lead over Japan in shipbuilding orders, capturing no less than 45 per cent of the world total. With Japanese shipbuilding quotes estimated to be running at around 30 per cent higher than those in South Korea, this 'half' of a country looks poised to be the world's biggest shipbuilder by the 21st century. How long will it be before these shipbuilding nations seek to be as good at insuring ships as they are at making them? Will the year 2010 see the final chapter in a journey which began with the closure of shipyards in the 1960s, as 'Insured in Japan' or 'Insured in South Korea' becomes the norm?

Many would say that there is a lot more to marine insurance than a knowledge of marine engineering; after all, we can always buy that in. They would say that the skill lies in cutting the deal, knowing the market, getting the balance right, 'knowing' what kind of risks to bear and how to share them out. True, these talents are important and will undoubtedly continue to retain confidence for a while, enabling firms to diversify into other areas of risk assessment; but eventually why should anyone buy insurance from a British insurer advised by German or South Korean engineers when they can buy it from a German or South Korean insurer advised by German or South Korean engineers?

Assessing a ship will always require knowledge and information about it: its engines, fuel system, fire hazards, the likelihood of its proposed cargoes suffering under different climatic conditions, its capacity to pollute should it founder, its value as salvage if seriously damaged. In short, it is a complex technical entity which requires complex technical knowledge to understand and assess: just knowing how to share out the risk is not enough. A little technical knowledge about the potential health hazards of asbestos packing in US buildings might have saved Lloyds of London a few heartaches! This example of the potential impact of a decomposing information chain highlights the simplistic nature of the polarization that has often characterized public debates in the UK about the respective merits of the service (information-intensive), and manufacturing (low information content) economies. So many of the skills in handling high abstractions rely on levels of confidence that draw their power from a continuing involvement in problem solving, and from information and knowledge gathering that can only be derived from engineering in action.

All engineering and manufacturing activity is information-intensive. Information is embedded in the design, in the knowledge and skill of workers, in the intelligence of the logistics that ensure the timely arrival of components and the delivery of finished products. As we look at each artefact we use, we are looking at a thing made up of materials moulded by information, knowledge and intelligence. These things are ingenious representations of advanced thought and creativity that owe their existence to one or more important information moments. To describe this process as something separate or different from information-intensive work that is not associated with engineering or manufacture is to misunderstand the intensity of information in action, and to relegate whole areas of human enterprise to second-class status. Every physical presence is a chunk of information, some parts of which may have their origins from halfway around the world. A Sony Walkman may be Japanese but its designers were born and educated in Britain. It is not an either/or situation, and yet so much western economic and political debate treats it as if it were.

One reason for such simplistic categorizations may be our propensity to assume that information processing in high-profile service domains can replace just about every other form of human endeavour. Nowhere is this more so than in the field of finance, which exponential gains in the transmission of time-critical information have turned into the darling of the information age. The vogue for describing the current phase of western economic development as the 'information revolution' has perhaps given a high status to even low-level information handling, which it clearly does not deserve, while at the same time denying the rich penetration of sophisticated knowledge and information that occurs in engineering and manufacture.

Such rhetoric nearly always underestimates the great differentials that exist between high and low levels of information intensity and the economic benefits that they bestow. Some of this stems from our growing obsession with the speed of information transfer. Time is undoubtedly a key element in the value of certain kinds of information, and the drive for faster and more sophisticated computer and communications facilities has often been directed at satisfying the seemingly insatiable desire to speed up access to it. This is particularly true of financial information, where the returns on research, development and capital investment generally come BBQ (big, bigger and quick!). In this sense it is certainly true that we have been experiencing a 'financial information revolution'. As a guide to the kind of explosion that this particular phenomenon has kindled, it is salutary to note that the average daily trading volume on the New York Stock Exchange in 1960 was around 3 million shares. On a typical day, this volume of buying and selling now takes place within the first six minutes of trading [25].

It is sometimes said that the technology of information collection and manipulation is changing not just the speed and nature of information processing, but the fundamental nature of the work itself. The images that accompany any contemporary description of work in the financial sector suggest that this is particularly true: we always see bright young things gazing at multiple screens, taking hectic decisions while talking to at least two people on the telephone, surrounded by incomprehensible waving and shouting. Compare these images with those associated with engineering and production, or even the bright young things quietly working away to design complex vehicles or gas turbines.

The equity trader's tale

Information about companies, interest rates, currency and share movements has become much more time-critical as a result of the growing desire to whizz it around the world in shorter and shorter timeframes in order to gain a competitive advantage. The speed has thus become embedded in the value of the service: a few seconds late can be too late! An equity trader trading shares matches the data in one of her 'windows' with the news unfolding in another 'window', much of it delivered in real time. She checks the equity trend information on another screen, matches this with other screen sources and, maybe within a few seconds, decides to advise one of her bigger clients to sell a particular equity. This may be a big sale but, for a short time at least, no-one else knows why the shares are being sold. Within seconds the new status of the shares is appearing on the screens of other traders all over the world; they too react quickly and advise their clients to sell or buy. The original trader's screens transmit the results of these responses to her original deal, perhaps illuminating a new set of options, and she in turn responds with almost instantaneous advice to the same or different clients, and so it goes on. The speed of these transactions is so fast that it eventually becomes difficult to disengage the technology from the action. Without the speed this kind of rapid response would be impossible, and the outcomes would be very different. The speed is both an enabler and a cause of the change.

The intelligence behind decisions like these derives at least in part from the conveyance of the information. This kind of trading behaviour was impossible when merchants had to rely on tea clippers to bring back news about trading conditions in different parts of the world. Then, timing was less important than the value of the trade itself, although the slowness of information acquisition would be regarded as something of a hindrance when it came to assessing the risk of certain kinds of investment, and no doubt the speed competitions of some of the tea clippers brought some competitive advantage to their owners. Even the outpourings of the 19th century ticker-tape machine needed a phone call to someone, who would usually have to call someone else, to register buying or selling decisions.

Our equity trader had the same information that was available to most of her competitors, but she converted it to a belief and, confident in that belief, she sold it on to her client. The sale of the shares could be interpreted in many ways, for instance a need for quick liquidity, but large sales are more often than not interpreted as a lack of confidence in the current value of the stock. In carrying the news of the sale the screens also carried a statement of her belief, triggering a new set of beliefs which in turn began to make further statements about confidence, or lack of it, in the particular stock and possibly even the wider economic sector of which the stock formed a part.

Compared to the kinds of remote database information that most academic researchers might use, these financial systems seem very expensive, although the returns easily justify the investment. The trader herself is also expensive. As a high-status, highly paid representative of a high-abstraction knowledge activity she sits at the summit of the current information economy. Yet the sophisticated connections that even she makes via her own neural networks and the knowledge and intelligence she owns that enable her to make those connections, may soon become cheaper, in non-human form. Since the late 1980s the big institutions (e.g. pension fund managers), as distinct from individual shareholders, have been taking a bigger slice of the equity market all over the world, and now account for something like 75 per cent of the total trading volume in US markets. One result of this is that they have begun to use their collective power to drive transaction costs down, creating pressure to move trading from the higher-cost exchanges to those with lower costs. Ten new electronic proprietary trading systems have been approved by the US Securities and Exchange Commission since 1987, mostly born out of the desire to cut trading costs by cutting out humans. The dramatic selling by so many automatic trading systems during October 1987 gave us perhaps the most visible example of the impact of automated transactions within 'virtual' financial marketplaces. Like the human traders that they replace, computer programs, so far at any rate, have some difficulty recognizing the wider economic and social impacts of a 'Black Monday'. By reducing all political, economic and social variables to a mathematical formula, computers have little need for the news services of CNN, Reuters or Datastream. Developing a way to get computers to understand and then keep up-to-date with the news, in order to recognize a new competitive opportunity when they hear one, could be the next big challenge.

There can be no doubt that computer technology has transformed the distribution and trading of financial information. That it will continue to accelerate speed competitiveness as a critical factor in profitability, is not a difficult prediction to make. Global networks such as NASDAQ and Instinet mean that being in a particular place at a particular time is no longer necessary, and future non-spatially dependent computer networks will increasingly trade among themselves within 'virtual' markets. Driven by pension fund managers, technology will continue to play a major part in reducing trading costs. Having stimulated the 'invention' of new and ever more risky financial instruments, the complexity of which can only be handled by computers, the evolving technology will undoubtedly give rise to new ways of making money.

The less customers knew about the differences between buying and selling prices, the more money traders made. Traders were thus, to a large extent, in the business of suppressing or withholding information in order to maximize their income, but the diffusion of real-time market information, now available to both fund managers and to individual investors via relatively inexpensive cable television services, has meant that lucrative spreads between bids and asking prices have largely evaporated. Armed with information that is now at least as good as their former advisers', and empowered by more liberal securities and investment laws in the US, clients can now bypass Wall Street. As information breeds confidence and as the technology makes the markets more transparent, middlemen become superfluous and, as has happened in many markets, they have responded by becoming involved in riskier strategies with poorer returns. It seems to be a new fact of the financial markets that, although technology always stimulates new ways of making money, each new generation of financial products rarely seems to match the profitability of those they replaced.

These trends are undeniably 'revolutionary' in their impact, changing the whole nature of financial markets. It is an interesting characteristic of information technology that new providers of information nearly always begin by delivering it, or the data with which to build it, to a select group, who quickly take on the role of valued intermediaries. They may be librarians or information brokers, consultants or analysts. Whatever their job title, this group take time to learn the mysteries of accessing the new technology in order to score more effective 'hits' than might be achieved by an occasional end-user. This includes mastering the various search logics, the little tricks that maximize useful responses, the codes which enable short-cuts through large databases and all the other techniques that deliver more information per dollar per minute. For a time they control the gateways to growing stocks of useful information, and through these may gain respect and kudos. But their days are inevitably numbered.

Over time, and in the search for higher and more regular returns, the information vendors simplify their pricing structures and search procedures and begin targeting their services at end-users. These may be the big clients of stockbrokers, academics, researchers or even doctors, all of whom wish to have access to information via their own terminals. The vendors' aim is to reduce the mystery and increase the number of consultations, and hence the financial returns. The intermediaries therefore either slowly become extinct or hone their skills to even higher levels of sophistication, to sell further up the information chain, where the opportunities are fewer and the expectations higher.

It is interesting to note that it was the unfriendliness of the original user interface that enabled an intermediary to justify a role and to charge for it. It is pleasing to see the priority now being given by software developers to the human–computer interface. It is their success here more than anything else that will accelerate real mass acceptance of the world of software, the Internet, CD-ROM and interactive television.

In flaunting its success in the highly lucrative areas of stock and financial trading, the kind of information technology used in these domains can delude us into believing that a nation could earn all or most of its living this way. Suggesting, as many politicians did during the 1980s, that the UK need never make things, that it could survive on abstractions that created wealth from wealth already created elsewhere, was a dangerous message and one that could inadvertently sound the death knell to the public provision of non-profit-making social and cultural information. Because mobilizing price-sensitive information can be such a dramatic facilitator of wealth creation, the technology and market forces that lie behind it are coming to be seen as capable of picking up the burden of public information provision. Thus the kind of market values and expectations that might accompany a subscription to one of Reuters news or financial services are now being used by politicians and civil servants to address the issue of support for information outside the corporate domain.

UK public libraries, once the embodiment of easy and free access to information for all, are now being seen as potential converts to market forces. Early in 1994 the government appointed management consultants KPMG to assist them in their plans for contracting out public library services to the private sector. Five pilot schemes have been approved, in the counties of Kent, Dorset, Hertfordshire, Hereford and Worcester and the London Borough of Brent. These schemes will involve either the operation of the whole service by a contractor, or franchising out just a part of the library operation. In Brent the whole library service will be operated by contract using business units, and one or more libraries will be 'market tested'; in Hereford and Worcester the libraries' cultural services will be contracted out, and in Hertfordshire a library franchise will be set up. KPMG expected to publish an initial assessment on the success of the pilot studies in the autumn of 1994. Whatever their conclusions the writing is on the wall for public libraries in the UK: either they behave more like businesses or they lose whatever public funding remains available to them. The values of the dealing room will have finally demolished what had taken half a dozen acts of parliament and over 140 years of liberal legislation to establish.

The chancellor's tale

Although amazing feats of speed and decision making might be normal within the electronic money markets of the world, not all financial information, even that deemed to be critical to a nation's financial stability, comes in as fast or as reliably. Governments seek to reduce uncertainty in their dealings with their own and other nations' currencies; they also seek information about the working of their own and other nations' economies. The person in the street still tends to think that governments have sensible tools and instruments in place to gather and transfer current information to help them govern more effectively. It was all the more chastening, then, to see an ex-Treasury mandarin cheerily announce that in 1986:

> Our perception of what was happening was just wrong and in that sense we may not have lost control over what we thought was happening, but we had lost control over what was actually happening'. ['A Brief Economic History of Our Time', Channel 4, February 1993]

During 1986 British industry was performing well and there was a major increase in the money supply as a result of industry taking up more credit. The official Treasury statistics, although noting this, failed to show any connection between this and industrial muscle flexing. Indeed, they were generally pessimistic about the performance of industry at that time, and this was the flavour of the information that the Chancellor of the Exchequer was allowed access to. As the pound went into free fall and inflation started to rise, Treasury statisticians continued to regard as insignificant any information gleaned from industry itself. Thus inadequate, incomplete and misleading information kept a British Chancellor of the Exchequer in the dark about the economic performance of the real world. This eventually prompted him to seek solace in solutions based on exchange rate policy rather than the internal money supply. Early in 1987, after the Louvre Accord, the semi-official policy of shadowing the Deutschmark at around 3 DM to the pound was initiated. This change of policy involved the British government in an almost suicidal attempt to buy up pounds in the foreign exchange markets, to make sure that its value stayed close to the magic 3 DM. The rest is history! Are we being naive in expecting that governments will have access to all the shades of information they need to make decisions on our behalf? This particular episode suggests that we are. Information transfer, even at the highest levels, can be hindered by ideology, in this case the ideology of Treasury statisticians who gave little or no credence to what was going on outside Whitehall. It would seem that academics have never had a monopoly on ivory towers!

The decomposing knowledge chain from ships to insurance, the equity traders whose tools have almost become impossible to disentangle from the decisions they take, a Chancellor of the Exchequer who is left largely in the dark about the true state of the economy, all represent different facets of the same problem: securing timely, accurate and manageable information and putting it to work effectively. The first is a cautionary tale. Do some important information and knowledge chains decompose when other core competencies disappear? If so, is the number of such decompositions, in aggregate and over time, serious enough to prompt the consideration of retaining at least a representative sample of core competences, and hence a potential knowledge surplus in these areas, perhaps via special development plans, tax incentives or subsidies of one kind or another? The second is an example of one of the high points in information intensity, where the technology has not only changed the job but has almost become the job, so much so that new levels of information transparency and acccumulating competitive pressures might render even the high-abstraction workers currently at the core of it redundant. The third example is just a reminder of the shambolic way in which much information is still collected and processed at even the highest levels of our social and political organization and of how snobbery, elitism and compartmentalism can still conspire to stop the very best and most comprehensive information getting through to the person who needs it.

That the use of technology is reducing labour costs in all kinds of work must now be beyond doubt. Human redundancy has always been one of the key imperatives behind investment in new technology, from the invention of the wheel onwards. Since the late 1960s the microchip has delivered hundreds of thousands of modern workers from their toil, in sectors as diverse as banking and telecommunications, carpet manufacture and bottling plants, stock-control and secretarial work. Optimistic commentators have always assumed that compensatory employment for these workers will come from new products and services developed from the technology itself, either in hi-tech manufacturing or from the creation of hitherto unheard-of services stimulated by its use. There is some evidence that in some places this has happened, e.g. the US, where entrepreneurial energy has always been encouraged to push new technology to its limits, and in Japan, Austria and Norway, who have always maintained sectors of the economy as employers of the last resort, and in Singapore, where central planning is tightly linked with business trends. Generally, however, those displaced rarely have the education or skills necessary to meet the requirements of the new forms of work that become available. This has been particularly true in Britain, where the decline of manufacturing has rarely been accompanied by the rise of hi-tech companies in the same locale. Indeed, in Britain there has been a marked shift in employment patterns between north and south, as most new hi-tech industries grew up in the south to be nearer the well developed and accessible infrastructures of London and the Thames Valley, to be closer to government and to Europe. As Goddard [26] noted in 1988:

> The technical and economic transformations are being superimposed on an already highly differentiated regional and institutional infrastructure. . . . The key question is whether the transformations will contribute to a widening or reduction in regional disparities.

Regional inequalities can be perpetuated or even exacerbated by the application of new technology. Goddard again:

> A crude approximation of the aggregate distribution of information occupations suggests that between 1979 and 1984 the south gained 800 000 information jobs while the rest of the country recorded a net loss. London is the hub of the UK computer networks, with 36 per cent of mainframe computers networked compared with only 19 per cent in the northern region.

Certain parts of the world, e.g. Ireland, the Bahamas and the Philippines, currently offer an attractive mixture of cheap labour, access to up-to-date communications technology, and sometimes more sunshine, as a magnet to information-intensive business. One low-level but nonetheless information-intensive type of work that can be easily accommodated within such countries is the comparatively new business of distributed data-input. Companies as diverse as

General Motors and American Airlines have been keen to take advantage of this kind of cheap information processing and transfer. Wages are lower, unionization is non-existent and, given a reasonable investment in cable, satellite and telephone lines that work more often than not, the data travel around as fast as they would at home. Naturally we can expect consumption expectations to rise in these countries, and wages will inevitably have to rise to meet them, causing even more temporary relationships between company and country. The multinational corporations who use the labour and facilities of these countries will always be looking out for the ever more elusive coincidence of high technology and low pay. They will grow adept at moving in and out of locations over quite short time periods. It is interesting how these geo-imperatives now bestow their benefits and their redundancies. For many corporations the UK is currently perceived as a low-wage economy (perhaps this was one of the attractions for BMW in their purchase of Rover in early 1994), and so some information-intensive work could well migrate there, temporarily at least.

It is salutary to note that during the recessionary years between 1989 and 1994 it has not only been the old-type manufacturing industries that have felt the pinch. To stay competitive, many hi-tech high-level information businesses have had to shed workers, some in very large numbers. British Telecom has shed 75 000 workers since 1984 and has plans to lose a lot more, National Westminster Bank has lost 23 000 jobs since 1989, Barclays Bank has cut 16 000 posts since 1990 and, since 1992, IBM has also been downsizing. The banking sector in the UK, an information business to its core, lost 100 000 jobs over the four years from 1989 to 1993, and many commentators believe that this 'cleansing' out of excess capacity still has some way to go. The 1 million-strong payroll of European insurance companies is also expected to shake out 300 000 more jobs in the next few years, as the competitive waves of the July 1994 EU Insurance Directive, extending the single market to insurance provision, come into effect.

Quite a mature technology is paying a big part in this shake-up in both insurance and banking. Telephone banking, epitomized by First Direct, a subsidiary of the Midland Bank in the UK, makes possible a low-cost round-the-clock service without the need for expensive branch facilities. Indeed, the 'branch' may soon become a thing of the past as the 'trunk' offers more and more customer services over the phone, or from electronic holes in the wall. In insurance, low-cost sellers of motor and household insurance, such as Britain's Direct Line, Guardian Direct and the Swiss-owned Churchill, are using direct telephone quotes and sales to undercut traditional suppliers by up to 30 per cent. The in-depth penetration of straightforward telephony in developed countries looks set to yield many more business opportunities, with or without interactive visual links. The wind of competition is also thinning out a few knowledge workers who operate right at the top of some information businesses. During 1994 both British Telecom and WH Smith announced plans to cut back on a large number of high-level management jobs. WH Smith scrapped around 950 management positions to save some £2.4 million a year, while BT dismissed 30, i.e. some 20 per cent, of its directors below board level. In the now popular search for 'flexibility' WH Smith plans to employ 400 part-time sales assistants, to put more staff in direct contact with their customers on the shop floor.

Relying on information-intensive economic activity to swallow up labour released from a declining industrial base would seem to be optimistic when set beside these examples of typical job losses in the information sector. The current recession can of course be blamed for the diminution of all kinds of economic activity, but as most economic indicators predict little real economic growth in the 'mature' economies of the west over the next five years, it would seem to make more sense for us to see where we are now as more of a norm than as one of the traditional dips in the economic cycle.

Irrespective of the capacity of a workforce to make the transition from, say, a traditional manufacturing base, it has to be accepted that information-intensive work, by its very nature, is highly susceptible to automation. Competitive pressures will always require more investment in labour-saving technology than in labour. Much of banking and insurance is not terribly complex: many of the workers are engaged in low-level checking and rechecking clerical work, with a status elevated more by its respectability than its complexity. As more and more of the intelligence associated with assessing risk and checking for creditworthiness is transferred to machines, large numbers of this labour force will be looking for employment elsewhere.

One area that is emerging as a growth industry is that of converting information collected by businesses for internal use to information that might have some value to a third party. Some of the most valuable information is that which employees produce in the course of conducting their core business. This would clearly be regarded as 'excludable', and 'commercial and in confidence' is the label often used to describe it. Such information could be the names and addresses or geographic distribution of their customers, their wages bill, the distribution of costs between various departments or statistical information on sales trends. This represents intelligence about the company, which, together with information gathered from the external environment, e.g. the behaviour of rivals, documented research on future markets, general economic and political news and demographic trends, represents a corporate resource the effective handling of which can become a potent weapon in the struggle to gain competitive advantage. Although often deeply compartmentalized and only capable of coordination via expensive systems, such information lies at the core of organizational self-knowledge.

Organizations that are growing and responding to changes in their external environments are, almost inadvertently, building up information that can help them to learn about themselves and to identify where they stand in relation to their competitors. When assisted by relevant and user-friendly computerization, this information can be manipulated to illuminate many different connections and relationships, helping a company to assess its strengths and weaknesses, highlighting opportunities and potential threats. The reworking of this information may facilitate the development of new products and services that have a potential value to external users. Information to support internal functions and processes can become a new trading asset, creating novel business opportunities for an enterprise which did not initially see itself as being in the 'information' business. If such an activity grows it can eventually be sold as a discrete service from a division within the holding company, perhaps set up as a wholly owned subsidiary, or sold off in its entirety to form a totally new enterprise. The commercial US online database that is now 'Dialog' began its life as an internal information system to support the Lockheed manufacturing operation; AT&T Istel in the UK started life as an information network to support information needs within British Leyland; McDonnell Information Systems was once part of the international information systems business of the McDonnell Douglas aerospace company, and now supplies computer solutions and development tools to worldwide healthcare markets, to UK police forces, to central government, to libraries and to the commercial, industrial and financial sectors.

One key resource held by many enterprises is a detailed list of customer names and addresses, held in computerized databases that can manipulate them by region, by post or zip code, by credit rating or, if they are other businesses, by size of turnover. This knowledge can be very lucrative. A database can be sold or rented out, in part or in total, to another party for an agreed use, thereby generating considerable revenues, often at higher margins than the core business. Peters [27], in an article exploring the value of customer relationships, noted how Blockbuster Entertainment in the US holds details of over 48 million people who use its video cards. This is just 9 million fewer than the total population of the UK, and 11 million more people than use American Express. On a smaller scale, Haymarket Direct in the UK, an enterprise spun off from Haymarket's core business of supplying magazines on subscription to niche markets in the business community, offers the names of over 110 000 targeted individuals at over 60 000 company sites in the UK and within 150 job categories. Telephone companies, cable and satellite providers, airlines, banks, insurance, mail-order and credit card companies also hold a tremendous amount of information about us. It can help them, or someone else, to target us for products and services other than the one that we signed up for. The small print warning of: 'Put a cross here if you do not want us to send you our or anyone else's promotional literature' on the application forms for many services is a growing testament to the power of the list as a relationship.

Info-poor, underdeveloped and likely to stay that way

For those who inhabit the poorest countries in the world such concerns are as moonshine. Their day-to-day priorities are as far away from the signs and signals of multiple screens as it is possible to get. They have no knowledge surplus that they can trade, and too often their objectives cannot be lifted above the demands of survival: how to feed a family, how to protect it from war and disease, how to get children to a school 20 miles away without transportation, how to retain access to clean water, how to get a loan to start a cash crop. Here is a real need for information. Most western countries would have to turn the clock back 1500 years to remember such a basic need.

The richer countries of the world go about helping these nations via disaster and development aid, often with strings attached. Religious groups and charities send helpers to work in villages and to support specific projects, individuals sponsor children and banks make them loans. All of these activities carry with them western or Eurocentric information. Sometimes, even with the best of intentions, we end up celebrating our own centrality, concentrating on ourselves as helpers and donors and relegating the other participants to passive receivers. In 1984 and 1985 Michael Buerk, reporting on the famine in Ethiopia for the BBC, drew the world's attention to the terrible conditions being endured by the people of that country, under which 3 million of them died. Amazingly the two television reports were given viewing times of six and eight minutes respectively – amazing because most western news reports on third-world issues get a maximum of two minutes. As well as instigating a massive leap in western awareness of the problems of Ethiopia, and by association many other stricken countries in sub-Saharan Africa, these two reports also confirmed some less than helpful stereotypes: although of the 108 Oxfam workers operating in Ethiopia 100 were from Ethiopia, by concentrating on images of European aid workers the reports tended to reinforce a picture of an Africa where there was little or no indigenous effort being made to solve their own problems. The overwhelming message was one of the white westerners operating as angels of mercy, filling the begging bowl of a black Africa that had no solidarity and no voice of its own. The compressed nature of all television news reporting often emphasizes one aspect of an issue or a crisis at the expense of another. From the point of view of developing countries the difference in degree and importance between 'emergency' aid and the longer-term and structurally more important 'development' aid is crucial. The immediate statistics of the dead and dying in an emergency always attract more viewers than a review which attempts to understand the 50-year decline in a nation's ability to feed itself. Although television has proved that it can encourage people to be concerned and generous, it has also shown that when the pictures go, for most of us at least, the problems go with them.

It is difficult for the west not to be paternalistic in our relations with developing nations. We cannot seem to orchestrate the help we give without passing on our views on poverty, the kind of governments they should have, the economic systems they should operate and the kind of world that they should be creating for themselves – preferably one that approximates to something like our own. Sometimes we carry our messages directly by offering the mixed blessing of our presence as tourists. At the Sarova Shaba hotel in Kenya's Shaba reserve:

> In one of the most parched regions of central Kenya, [a pure water spring] bubbles up from beside the lobby, runs under the reception area and re-emerges in a series of waterfalls and pools. A pipe runs from the spring into an enormous swimming pool, where tourists can drift beneath the Japanese bridge and around the rocky promontories. [28]

The bubbling spring was once the only reliable source of water for the Samburu tribe, whose cattle fed on the grazing lands now taken for an 'animals only' reserve that surrounds the hotel. Throughout Africa the idealized expectations of tourists, i.e. that nomadic hunters and gatherers and wild animals somehow never shared the same domain, have been realized by evicting local tribes from designated game reserves and national parks. This has meant shutting local populations out from some of the longest-inhabited places on earth, places where the soil was at its richest, where the game was most plentiful, where there was water and where, not surprisingly, the local people liked to settle. It has also meant that herds of animals that grow and thrive move out of the reserves to look for wider grazing. Thus groups of zebras may wander 50 or 100 kilometres from a reserve to areas where tribespeople now graze their cattle or grow crops;

predators such as lions follow, and people who have been moved on and deprived of their nomadic life find themselves endangered by the very animals that they were moved out to protect. The Shaba reserve in Kenya and other zones like it are deemed 'exclusive' in the name of foreign currency earnings, which often substitute luxury for some at the expense of basic necessities for others. This is raised to a good greater than any claims local people might make concerning ancestral habitat or current dependency, and it stands as a metaphor for much of what euphemistically passes for a relationship between rich and poor nations. Unfortunately, it also stands for the kind of income-generating activity that would gain credit with the all-powerful World Bank, the world's largest development aid agency.

Fifty years old in 1994, the World Bank is made up of two arms, the International Bank of Reconstruction and Development, which makes loans to the better-off of the developing countries at interest rates close to commercial ones, and the International Development Bank, which lends at minimal rates to the poorest countries. Since beginning its controversial structural adjustment programmes (SAPS) to help 'restructure' the economies of Africa, the World Bank has presided over a catastrophe the dimensions of which threaten every part of that beleaguered continent.

Thirty-six African countries have implemented SAPS on the lines laid down by the Bank. In order to receive aid, the recipient country would typically be required to privatize its economy, devalue its currency, remove all trade restrictions, cut all subsidies and severely reduce its spending on services such as health and education. Although the Bank regularly cites examples of African countries who have benefited from implementing SAPS, e.g. Ghana, Tanzania, The Gambia, Burkina Faso, Nigeria and Zimbabwe, many aid workers on the ground angrily dispute this, drawing attention to how the SAPS policy always hurts the poor. In declaring its 'best performing' countries in Africa even the Bank itself admits that many of them will not reduce poverty much over the next 30 years. Even in Ghana, the Bank's 'star' performer, the average poor man will not cross the poverty line much before the year 2045, and then only if things continue to go well, which, given the timescale and the domestic volatility of African politics, could be unduly optimistic. A recent letter to the World Bank president from African churches attacked SAPS for what they called their devastating assault on the physical welfare and basic human dignity of the poor. In the light of these concerns many western countries, the shareholders of the Bank, are demanding that there be some major changes to its policies, and one, Finland, has already cut its contribution to the Bank from US$47 million to US$33 million. Other commentators have noted how the Bank's own previous evaluations had shown that non-adjusting countries in Africa were growing faster than those following the SAPS route: doing what the World Bank insists on is no guarantee of growth. Like all aid agencies the World Bank is helpless in the face of the growing violence and anarchy afflicting the almost leaderless nations of Africa, such as Zaire, Somalia, Rwanda, Liberia and Sierra Leone. The degree of infrastructural disintegration in these countries makes it difficult to envisage any current basis for their reconstruction, while every day that passes brings more misery and death to their wasted peoples. Mikhail Kalashnikov probably had no idea when he designed the most successful assault rifle in the world, that so many African people would suffer from the misplaced arrogance and power it would bestow on those who came to own it.

It is no longer much compensation to recognize that the bloody feuds now tearing apart so many sub-Saharan states in Africa owe their gestation to the curse of the nation state inflicted on them by retreating colonial powers. The highly centralized European way of running states, derived in large part from the English and French revolutions of two centuries ago, made hardly any sense at all to the collections of tribes and peoples who were left with little or nothing in common other than their physical proximity. The colonists could not believe in the stability and political structures that derived their legitimacy from the old tribal kingdoms, and strangely, given their own chequered history with regard to warring neighbours, the Europeans assumed that those who lived relatively close together were likely to get on reasonably well, and so could plausibly be constituted as a nation state. What they did was replicate the status of the European city elite, giving the urban intellectuals complete power over distant rural communities who had little or nothing in common with them. Depending on the accident of numbers and location, only one tribe was likely to be on top at any one time and they were the ones who did the 'running' when it came to running the country, including access to the perks. Decentralizing some of the power of national govern-ments to recapture the civil stability that drew its strength from the common interests of the smaller communities of precolonial times, may be the only way forward for some of these artificial states. Their virulent and unsatisfied tribalism might otherwise continue out of control.

The 26th World Bank Atlas, published in 1994, notes that:

> Despite the vast opportunities created by the technological revolutions of the 20th century, more than 1 billion people, one-fifth of the world's population, live on less than one dollar a day – a standard of living that western Europe and the United States attained 200 years ago.

While explaining that the processes driving economic development are complex and still by no means completely understood, the authors of the Atlas noted that some developing countries, notably those in southeast Asia, had achieved impressive progress over the past 40 years in areas like education and health care, proving that rapid and sustained development is achievable for countries starting from a low economic base. However, it was also true that:

> . . . many countries have done poorly, and in some, living standards have actually fallen during the past 30 years. That is why poverty remains such a formidable problem and why substantial economic progress has yet to touch millions of people.

The Atlas had reported, almost word for word, the same picture in its 25th (anniversary) edition for 1993, and in its 22nd edition for 1989 it revealed that:

> . . . more than 10 percent of the world's population live in countries where the real GNP per capita is not growing; more than half live in countries where the average GNP per capita is still under US$500.

In a long-awaited survey of African economic progress published in March 1994 [29], again comparing the potential adjustments possible in Africa with the adjustments seen in southeast Asian economies like Indonesia, Malaysia, South Korea and Thailand over the last 30 years, the Bank is optimistic that readjustment in Africa is working, while just about every one of its own statistics shows the opposite.

As Brittain [30] has pointed out, the repeated comparisons between the current plight of Africa and the rapid progress made by some countries in southeast Asia makes no sense, and do Africa no service at all:

> East Asia industrialized at a time of heavy investment, with the Vietnam war as a dynamo for growth for the region, and with Japan pushing their development. . . . Their economies grew under the opposite policies to those espoused by the Bank. Far from giving pre-eminence to the market, they went for authoritarian state economic management. And in contradiction to the western donors' demand in Africa for 'good governance', code for multi-partyism and more of a failure than a success in the last year or so, countries like Singapore, South Korea and Taiwan made their way up as authoritarian governments.

The countries of southeast Asia also invested heavily in both primary and secondary education, with their sights clearly set on western levels of adult literacy and the information-based businesses that they perceived would gradually replace other forms of wealth creation, whereas following the strictures necessary to secure World Bank aid caused both health and education spending to decline across most of Africa during the 1980s. Some of the figures seem irretrievable, e.g. Sierra Leone cut its education budget by 82 per cent, Nigeria by 70 per cent and The Gambia by 64 per cent [11]. With mounting debt crises, indifferent or corrupt domestic economic policies and the new conditions being set out by the World Bank, the 1980s look to have been something of a lost decade for much of Africa. Interestingly, while we are all celebrating the success story of the economic 'tigers' of southeast Asia, once some of the World Bank's most prolific borrowers, no-one seems to be in any hurry to invite them back as shareholders, to put something back into the system which once helped them so much. I suggest that such an invitation is now long overdue.

A detailed examination of the information coded by the most recent World Bank Atlases, particularly with regard to literacy levels, shows just how slow progress is. Illiteracy rates as shown by the 1989 Atlas have hardly changed at all in the 1994 edition. Whole swathes of sub-Saharan Africa and India remain coded as 60 per cent or more illiteracy rates, while those segments of the world's population enjoying a more than 95 per cent literacy rate hardly seem to have changed at all.

It is a sorry fact that the giving of aid, with the honourable exception of some of the Scandinavian countries, has always been more a question of making friends and influencing people than targeting poverty. Every year 21 rich countries, all of them in Europe except Japan, Canada, the US, New Zealand and Australia, give or lend US$60 billion in aid, either directly or through multilateral institutions. Most of this is directed by a desire to get something in return, usually allegiance or just straightforward commercial gain. For example, US$21 billion of the total US$60 billion – over one third – is given by the US, who earmark at least 25 per cent of the total for military assistance and 25 per cent for Israel and Egypt. Japan is also quite open in declaring that it generally reserves its development assistance for those countries who are most likely to be its future customers. Given how important a supplier Japan is to most of the world, an optimistic interpretation of this policy could be that in reality it would embrace everyone.

UK government aid to third-world countries currently totals around £1 billion, and just to put into perspective the relative size of the contributions from governments and charities, Oxfam, one of the largest, has a total income of around £60 million per year, i.e. about 6 per cent of the UK government's annual contribution. Charities are important, particularly in helping to fund small low-technology self-development projects, but any large-scale withdrawal of government aid in favour of relying on charities would see human disasters across the world escalate on a catastrophic scale:

> Sometimes the interests of security and commerce have coincided; poor countries with big arms budgets get twice as much aid per person as those that spend modestly on military hardware. [31]

In reality this means that the richest 40 per cent of the developing world gets about twice as much per head as the poorest 40 per cent. El Salvador, a big military spender, gets five times as much aid as Bangladesh, even though Bangladesh has 24 times as many people as El Salvador [32].

Only a relatively small amount of the US$60 billion goes to the poorest countries by way of official development assistance:

> A study of America's aid programme conducted by the Overseas Development Council (ODC), a Washington DC think-tank, found that more than US$250 per person went to relatively high-income countries, but less than US$1 per person to very low income countries. [32]

The ten countries that are home to two-thirds of the world's poorest people receive only one-third of all the available aid. This is a disastrous spiral and one which seems more insoluble the more one learns about the politics of aid-giving. A note in The Economist 'Emerging-Market Indicators' in March 1994 noted how the developing countries' share of world merchandise trade (manufacturing, fuel, food and raw materials) was higher in 1950, at around 40 per cent, than in 1992, when its share was just under 30 per cent. This gloom has recently been compounded by a 1994 report into the running of the African Development Bank by David Knox, a former Vice-President of the World Bank. Knox's report finds the Bank, founded to promote and finance development across Africa, to be spreading itself too thinly over too many activities, riddled with intrigue, burdened by a top-heavy bureaucracy and ritual buck-passing, and dogged by a well entrenched attitude towards procedural avoidance. Knox declared the average African to be worse off today than he was 30 years ago, with poverty, ill health and famine threatening more not fewer people:

> Africa's real per capita income fell by more than 15 per cent in the 1980s and has slumped further since. If Africa is to provide enough food, jobs and rising incomes, its economies need to grow by more than 5 per cent a year. Even then, it would take uninterrupted growth just to recover per-capita income losses of the 1980s. [33]

To put Knox's 5 per cent minimum growth figure into context, African economies grew by just 1.4 per cent in 1992.

It is clear that there has been no serious shift in the fundamental balance of international economic forces since the Second World War. Indeed, the state of some countries, poor in 1945, has worsened as the decolonization disturbances of the 1960s, the debt crises of the 1970s and the trading conditions of the 1980s have left them increasingly dependent on richer countries for basic survival. In a world where aid is linked to trade, and where investment in science and technology provides the key source for future wealth creation and stability, there seems to be little chance of any real transfer south of knowledge surpluses to fuel the kind of economic progress made by some of the southeast Asian economies. Those economies, building on cultural foundations that were perhaps more homogeneous and less tribal, also developed stable domestic environments which generated confidence among foreign investors. A literate, educated society that can lift itself up out of poverty and into the dignity of self-sufficiency still seems far away for so many peoples. Even the aid spent on education and health care nearly always seems to gravitate to the better off, either by building bigger hospitals in the wealthier urban areas or by supporting universities rather than universal primary education. The urban hospitals entice doctors away from the rural clinics, where they attended to the poor, to modern wards where they work with the emerging middle classes. Such imbalances give credence to the 'poor people in rich countries helping rich people in poor countries' type of cynicism that is the understandable expression of frustration among those working in aid agencies.

These new economic conditions suggest that now is the time for rich countries to take stock of their humanitarian positions regarding poorer countries. Four key areas need attention:

1. There should be some redefinition of developed, developing and underdeveloped countries as regards contributions to and receipts from international aid organizations, taking the opportunity to revise the list of potential recipients and to embrace new donor members from the Pacific Rim.

2. No international aid organization should link humanitarian aid, including long-term development aid, to any reduction in public expenditure in the areas of health or education.

3. On the completion of the Final Act of the Uruguay Round of GATT, signed in Morocco in April 1994, which turned the GATT into the World Trade Organization, the world's media suggested that there could only be winners in the release of US$4500 billion of new world trade. However, although the emerging markets of Latin America and southeast Asia see themselves doing well out of GATT, many commentators suspect that the chances of the deal improving the competitive position of many African countries, some of whom could lose out heavily, are not so good. An international commission to monitor the effect of GATT on the world's poorer economies, perhaps under the umbrella of the

newly established World Trade Organization, should be set up with a brief to report freely and fearlessly on its impact.

4. The formation of an international forum that can coordinate the diffusion of licence-free science and technology for humanitarian ends. Such a group would seek to help poorer countries address issues of infrastructure and sustainable development by agreeing to the postponement of licence or copyright fees for an agreed period. Rich countries could help to finance such a programme by allocating a portion of the cash they save from the newly liberated defence funds of the post-cold war era. This kind of cooperation and help could draw on the experience that the EU has accumulated in facilitating the transfer of information, knowledge and technology from its northern to its southern members.

It is no secret that the countries of eastern Europe look poised to benefit most from the GATT agreement. In the same week that the GATT was signed, both General Motors and Matsushita completed big deals in Poland. More big changes in capital movements are expected as multinationals move their plants to Poland or China, where labour costs are low. China's prospects have also been significantly improved by President Clinton's declaration, at the end of May 1994, that the US would continue to grant it 'most favoured nation' status, and that in future US trade with China would cease to be linked with its record on human rights. Without some form of international intervention these nations will attract the cream of available investment and aid, while Africa literally withers on the vine.

There are some signs of hope. Ghana and Zimbabwe seem to be working their way out of the worst of their 1980s doldrums, while with the end of apartheid in South Africa and the reduction of tension in the region, the front-line states who once had to deploy so much of their resources to protect their infrastructure from attack, are now able to concentrate on economic and social development. Hopefully the new South Africa will prove to be a potent political and economic motor for the whole of the region.

Under the conditions that afflict the world's poorest countries concepts such as the multimedia superhighway, digital compression, the widespread networking of personal computers among a computer and information-literate population, widespread television and telephone ownership all look very remote. Portable radios are probably the most widespread modern technology to be found in rural Africa, but even these often lie silent for want of batteries. Some western technologies that require no prior level of literacy, most notably radio telephones and satellite technology, could help transform the communication and informational possibilities of the scattered rural communities in many poor countries. Although now superseded by an increasingly liberalized and commercial television regime, India went through a stage where it used both satellite and terrestrial television to promote educational, health care and agricultural training, as well as to send political messages to the people of its 550 000 scattered villages. As the cost of satellite technology falls, this kind of communication should become available to the much smaller nations of Africa much more cheaply.

Although the implementation of any mass communication system is primarily the responsibility of governments and their agents, it is worth asking what those who have profited most out of the information technology revolution are doing to help poor countries. Surely, if only in self-interest, such people should be at the centre of non-profit-making foundations all over the developing world, enabling and stimulating the modernization of their communication systems?

One approach to measuring the impact of the 'information economy' as it evolves is the rate at which a country gains access to telephone lines. Nowhere has this been recognized as a key indicator of economic prosperity more than in the fast-developing economies of the Pacific Rim. Hong Kong, as so often, leads the way, with just over 59 phones per 100 people, ahead of equally small Singapore's 49 per 100. Taiwan and South Korea follow behind with 35 per 100, while Thailand currently with three lines per 100 people, has set a target to achieve its near neighbour Malaysia's current nine lines per 100 by 1997. Surrounded by such telephone penetration India, with only five telephone lines per 1000 inhabitants, Indonesia with six per 1000, and the Philippines and mainland China each with nine phones per 1000 inhabitants, will all no doubt be making moves to improve this as rapidly as possible. In an attempt to plot the progress of information penetration in different countries, Connors [11] has constructed an intriguing 'Information Access Index'. By collecting figures for each country on literacy, newspaper readership, radio and television ownership and telephones per 1000 population, he highlights the tremendous disparities that still exist, even between developed economies so far as access to information is concerned. As we might expect the less developed economies are way below the constructed index average of 100, e.g. Kenya at 29, India at 23, Senegal at 22, Mozambique at 11, Central Africa at 7. The 'wired' island of Bermuda, host to an unsurpassed density of information-hungry offshore insurance companies, and famous for having the largest concentration of qualified accountants in the world, came out top, with an index rating of 373, with each inhabitant clutching 1.3 radios, just over one phone and just under one television set each.

The idea of the intelligent island seems to be catching on. After all, the islands of Great Britain and Japan enjoyed success in the first two (steam and electronic) industrial revolutions. Perhaps it is something to do with having obvious boundaries that do not merge seamlessly into other states. As well as the obvious examples of Bermuda and Singapore (this latter already calls itself the 'Intelligent Island', and has a written information strategy (Information 2000) in place) other island states are busy with their own particular information SWOT analyses (strengths, weaknesses, opportunities and threats). The Balearics, Crete, Taiwan, the Philippines, Barbados and Indonesia are all busy investing in the mainly fibreoptic cable infrastructure necessary to support heavy text, voice, data and image transmission. Their view that businesses and their employees will be just as happy working in environments that combine the benefits of a warm climate, safety, beautiful scenery and access to a wide range of leisure pursuits, as long as they can communicate with the rest of the world as easily as if they were freezing in New York or traffic-locked in London, is one that they aim to test over the next decade.

China, the only other remaining superpower besides the US, is now emerging as a market that all the suppliers of communication and media technology are watching very carefully. This is particularly true of those that produce the telecommunications technology that a partially economically reformed China is now demanding. In going out to meet the world for this technology the rulers in Beijing will inevitably require partnership deals and licensing arrangements that at least assemble things on Chinese soil. With an average factory wage 96 per cent below that of Hong Kong and only 1.8 per cent of that in the US, China has an unprecedented opportunity to build a new manufacturing base on a transitional mix of low wages and a regional propensity to assimilate new technology without too much difficulty. As well as hosting assembly lines for 'higher abstraction' economies, it will not be long before China raises the question of technology transfer, i.e. 'when do we get some?'

During 1993 British Aerospace, seeking a joint arrangement to manufacture regional aircraft with Taiwan, floundered over just such issues. Given their history of inventiveness, ingenuity and stoicism, the mainland Chinese are unlikely to be any more compliant on this issue than their island brethren.

While recognizing that although it may be premature to talk of an 'information revolution', Connors notes that the necessary infrastructure (which he calls the 'infostructure') to facilitate 'universal access to virtually all information', is beginning to be laid down:

> You don't claim something is a revolution unless it shifts the infrastructure significantly, making radical alterations in the way things are run and done. . . . The propensity and ability of mankind to collect, collate, transmit and analyse information has grown to a point from which there is no

going back, and from which far-reaching change is inevitable in the longer run. Which means revolution . . . the nascent information revolution has added a new dimension to human competition. Individuals, corporations and nation states are today competing with one another for intellectual territory as they never have before. [11]

The idea of 'intellectual territory' is a valuable one. It conjures up an image of intelligence as something that you can have a stock of, as with land from which you expect to mine valuable resources. Mining land is approved by ownership, leases, licences, regulations and planning permissions, while raw materials have a market price which fluctuates with scarcity. Mining intelligence, however, has to be agreed via the temporary rental of a mind, by copyrighting and patenting the products of it and then using these to gain an advantage over others. Given the great disparities between rich and poor countries noted above, it is interesting to consider who the future customers might be. According to the theorists, the higher 'knowledge' economies would supply the manufacturing and food-producing nations with all the information and know-how to ensure that they develop their farming operations to a high level and that they build state-of-the-art factories to produce all the goods the 'thinking' nations want. These higher economies would also supply information and experience, at a price, about running social, educational and medical services.

We should not forget how crucial unhindered and reliable access to food supplies is for all peoples, and how total reliance on a distant country for essential foodstuffs is not an option that many politicians are likely to feel comfortable with. One clear concomitant of this 'knowledge goes south, things come north' scenario is that more and more knowledge domains, and the informational infrastructure that supports the maintenance of tradeable stores of knowledge, would have to be held within secure, excludable, 'commercial and in confidence' boundaries. Knowledge that was once shared freely on a fraternal basis could be jeopardized by such a 'trade only' policy. In reality it would, of course, be difficult to know when or how to switch information transfer from a fraternal to a 'trade only' status. However, the possibility that developed countries could begin restricting the kind of information flows that once were exchanged freely, out of deference to new business imperatives that sought to recatalogue the commercial value of the exchange, is one that could strike a mortal blow to the embryonic research and development programmes of many developing nations.

The strongest protagonists for this point of view would probably envisage a gradual hardening of policy in this direction as traditional manufacturing exports decline, resulting in national budgetary deficits. There is a precedent for this in the severe restrictions used to govern the trading of high-technology parts and components (particularly military technology) between the US and western Europe. Before the fall of the Berlin Wall US insecurities about the potential trickle of information between western European countries and the countries of the former Warsaw Pact lent a slightly hysterical air to US regulation of technological transfer to its allies. In the end, with a kind of fatal irony, it was Saddam Hussein who was to turn US technology against US troops.

This particular nervous twitch has, of course, been reversed as the postwar communist regimes of eastern Europe begin to embrace capitalism. There is nothing quite so welcome as a convert: the unthinkable of just four or five years ago turns into order books, and the people of the 'evil empire' become welcome consumers!

In a world where the pace of technological change is only ever exceeded by the pace of political change, the economics of information and the ethical and moral imperatives that determine its use will remain a source of dispute and debate for years. However, in recognizing its power to change so many things we should also remember how fragile and temporary information supremacy can be. 'Here today, gone tomorrow' is an old saying, but one that might be an appropriate warning to those who misread the durability, distinctiveness and value of their current knowledge surplus.

References

1. Maunders, P., Myers, D., Wall, N., and Miller, R.L. (1991) *Economics Explained*, 2nd edn. London: Collins Educational

2. Doyal, L. and Gough, I. (1991) *A Theory of Human Need*. Basingstoke: Macmillan.

3. Hepworth, M. (1989) *Geography of the Information Economy*. Belhaven Press

4. Feigenbaum, A.E. (1986) *The Library of the Future*. Lecture at the University of Aston, November

5. Malchup, F. (1962) *The Production and Distribution of Knowledge in the United States*. Princeton: Princeton University Press

6. Bell, D. (1973) *The Coming of Post-Industrial Society: A Venture in Social Forecasting*. New York: Basic Books

7. Porat, M.U. (1977) *The Information Economy: Definition and Measurement*. Washington, DC: US Department of Commerce

8. Strassmann, P.A. (1985) *Information Payoff: the Transformation of Work in the Electronic Age*. New York: Collier Macmillan

9. Webster, F. (1993) Informed sources. *The Times Higher Education Supplement*, 8 October

10. Colleges becoming practical. *Asahi Evening News*, Tokyo, 1 December 1992

11. Connors, M. (1993) *The Race to the Intelligent State: Towards the Global Information Economy of 2005*. Oxford: Blackwell

12. Jones, B. (1982) *Sleepers Awake: Technology and the Future of Work*. Brighton: Wheatsheaf Books

13. Europe's Top Thirty: largest international companies with HQs in EU ranked by size of workforce. A chart sourced by IPM. *The Times*, 23 March 1994

14. *The Economist*, January 1993

15. Birmingham City Council (1994) *Birmingham Labour Market Bulletin*. February

16. Waugh, A. (1988) *The Spectator*, July

17. *The Economist*, 30 October 1993

18. Hutton, W. (1994) Flexibility will not get West working. *The Guardian*, 14 March

19. The trouble with success. *The Guardian*, 12 March 1994

20. Handy, C. (1994) *The Empty Raincoat, Making Sense of the Future*. London: Hutchinson

21. IEE, Presidential address

22. Friedman, A. (1994) The spectre haunting Europe. *The Independent On Sunday*, 20 March

23. Krugman, P. R. and Lawrence, R. Z. (1994) Trade, jobs and wages: blaming foreign competition for US economic ills is ineffective. The real problem lies at home. *Scientific American*, April, 22–27

24. *Consumer Habits 1994*. London: Mintel International, May

25. Breeden, R. C. (1992) *The World in 1993*. London: Economist Publications Ltd

26. Goddard, J. (1988) Urban and regional development in an information economy: emerging policy issues. Telecommunications Conference, Newcastle, September 1988

27. Peters, T. (1994) Playing the customer card. *The Independent on Sunday*, 20 February

28. Monbiot, G. (1994) Hero and victims. *The Guardian*, 18 March

29. World Bank (1994) *Adjustment in Africa, Reforms, Results and the Road Ahead*. World Bank Policy Research Report, Oxford University Press

30. Brittain, V. (1994) Hope constantly deferred is Africa's lot under the West's economic reform. *The Guardian*, 14 March

31. Empty promises. *The Economist*, 7 May 1994

32. The kindness of strangers. *The Economist*, 7 May 1994

33. Rafferty, K. (1994) Developing crisis mars bank's 30th birthday. *The Guardian*, 11 May

Chapter 4

Information and cultural context

As the inheritors of a fairly narrow tradition that associates 'culture' with education, refinement, manners, classical art and civilized behaviour, modern Europeans find themselves somewhat bewildered by the contemporary regard now afforded to *all* cultures that offer their members a coherent view of the world. Although there has never been an uninterrupted line between classical antiquity and modern European culture, enough information in support of its superiority has been carried forward for it to secure a tenacious grip on a continent. Its disciples then went on to spread it all over the world offering their conviction of its perfectibility to peoples to whom the very concept of perfectibility would have been a nightmare. Western culture was simply the best way to organize things; it sought and deserved its supremacy because it aimed so high. The inevitable concomitant of this was that other cultures, lacking the same origins, were always regarded as less satisfactory, less perfect and thus less worthy of serious attention; certainly they would not be worthy of emulation.

The information embedded in these other cultures has always seemed dispensable when set against the obvious merit of the Eurocentric model:

> It became apparent to Europeans in the 19th century that there were other societies, with other ways; these societies had laws, myths, music, works of art and institutions which owed nothing to classical Greece. Cultural relativism was born. Isaiah Berlin has described its effect: 'This is perhaps the sharpest blow ever delivered against the classical philosophy of the West, to which the notion of perfection – the possibility, at least in principle, of universal, timeless solutions to problems of value – is essential.' Cultural relativism, at its most basic, suggests that all societies produce culture of equal value; these cultures are 'natural ways of conveying a coherent view of the world seen and interpreted'. [1]

As well as suffering something of a crisis of confidence in the continued superiority of our own culture, modern Europeans also have to wrestle with the difficulties involved in distinguishing between 'culture' and the more transient habits and pursuits that we term 'lifestyle'. As we shall see later, there is no shortage of information in support of lifestyle, but contradictions about culture continue to abound. Hermann Goering's famous remark: 'When I hear the word culture I reach for my gun', was made by the same man who then went on to loot occupied Europe of over £20 million worth of art treasures. Did he want to conceal their decadence? Did he want their embedded wealth? Or did he really seek the kind of credibility that has always been accorded those who are seen to possess the tangible lineaments of European culture?

Whatever our state of confidence about a particular cultural ideal, the socially transmitted learned behaviour and sets of rules that we call culture is the operating system within which human information moments take place. We cannot avoid belonging to a particular culture, for a time at least. At any one point in time the ethnic and/or linguistic glue that we call culture can also be seen as the output of the layering of successive information moments. Thus a culture is both the repository of all past information growth and also the slowly maturing 'compost' wherein the loosely arranged ingredients of new information moments potentially reside. When we say that 'information is culturally dependent' we are simply recognizing that we operate within a particular kind of social structure, and that the information and knowledge transmitted to individuals within it will carry strong reinforcing signals about the values, beliefs and roles that underwrite and sustain one kind of social structure rather than another. If a second-hand car salesman confides to me that the profit margin on a 16-year-old Jensen Interceptor is £14 000 on a sale price of £23 000, my cultural socialization history works on this information thus: first wonderment that there could possibly be any buyers who would not know how to get one for £9000 too; secondly mild outrage that there should be such a high profit margin for simply recycling a vehicle; thirdly an understanding that things that are no longer manufactured (the Jensen factory at Coventry eventually closed in April 1993) will be scarce, and that scarce things always cost more. Wonderment, mild outrage and understanding: at least two of these feelings seem contradictory, yet they all operate on the information at once and, despite the ephemeral nature of this particular example, they all stem from important ideas that I have picked up about the value of things, the reasonableness of profit margins, and quaint British ideas about 'fair play'.

The 'Britishness' of the socialization envelope noted above, based on the shared information moments of a recognizable community and often reinforced by linguistic and geographical boundaries, was, until the great transportation breakthroughs of the 15th and 16th centuries, typical of the sort of distinctiveness that separated different cultures. The improved communications of the 19th century brought increasing interference with the established cultures of groups like the nomadic North American Indian, the native Aboriginals of Australia and New Zealand, and the long-suffering Indian tribes of South America, disrupting distinctive cultural envelopes that still contained powerful reinforcements of the values, beliefs and roles that had sustained and satisfied their ancestors.

Even in a Europe experimenting with the national boundaries that we recognize today, linguistic differences were still quite effective custodians of individual cultures, the members of which were generally passive receivers of the information that sustained and reinforced them. They absorbed it naturally and with little questioning of its value or relevance. Indeed, the tools with which to question, e.g. new information sources or suitable vehicles for communicating non-validated information, were generally not available, and the costs in terms of time, potential opprobrium and family and institutional pressures also diluted the urge to experiment. The scope for dissident or alternative information transmission was therefore limited.

The main custodians of the culture usually controlled access to all but the least effective communication technologies. Galileo's inquisition and imprisonment in 1632 for espousing and publishing works that supported Copernican theories, in opposition to the Catholic Church's preferred Ptolemaic 'view of the world', and Paine's indictment for treason in 1792 for publishing *The Rights of Man* in reply to Burke's more acceptable *Reflections On The Revolution In France* (1790), are just two examples of attempts, within particular cultural envelopes, to suppress access to new sources of information that could influence thought and change behaviour. They have their counterparts in nearly every 'governed' community, at all stages of their historical development. It is from examples of repressive behaviour such as this that 'culture' and all that it embodies has gained something of a reputation for stifling creativity and innovation. Other than after a revolution, when a set of completely new ideas replaces the old order at a stroke, or after a war that saw the complete overthrow of a state, the information build-up within a culture was generally slow. Internal repression was real, but disentangling repression from the norms of a particular culture and blaming it fairly and squarely on someone or something is not easy, even in retrospect. All cultures change over time; new information and ideas eventually filter through, inventions and discoveries do emerge from minds and memories inescapably attached to the culture that bred them. In many early communities these abnormal leaps – mixtures of serendipity, coincidence and tenacity – did instigate and catalyse important changes. In these cases the seeds of cultural absorption also came with them. Their origins from within the culture rather than from outside ensured the carry-over of recognizable 'meme-like' characteristics to help speed up acceptance and assimilation.

Information and cultural destabilization

The colonization of huge parts of the world by the seafaring Europeans in the 15th century must stand as the most dramatic example of uninvited cultural invasion and overthrow. Bearing the information gifts of new languages, new technologies, new desires, new diseases, new animals, and not least a new God, the invaders changed the world forever. In 1520 there were 25 million Aztecs living in the area that we now call Mexico; 80 years later in 1600, 24 million of them had disappeared. Human diversity was declining under the weight of the Cross. Five hundred years later, cultural diversity, even in the remotest parts of the world, is still under attack, this time by signals from distant satellite dishes. Nicholson-Lord [2], on an Earthwatch holiday in the remote Chauda-Bisa valley of northwestern Nepal, observed the irresistible march of the television signal:

> You can see the global village in Jumla, the small and grubby town at the base of the Chauda-Bisa valley, where it takes the form of a television aerial. This receives Star TV by satellite from Hong Kong. In a place where people defecate on open ground, wash their dishes in street drains and walk several miles for firewood, you can watch soft-porn films.

Living for a time among a native people who, in terms of western chronological development, belong to a 2000 BC 'post-Neolithic' culture, he also became a part and parcel of the 'development' dilemma. The questions he poses are those of information colonization that should concern any of us who care about the fragile cultures and environments that still make our world a heterogeneous place. The Khas peoples of the Chauda-Bisa valley, once a supreme force in the Himalayas, now seem forgotten and poor:

> Dysentery, diarrhoea, eye and respiratory infections are common, infant mortality high, survival beyond the age of 60 exceptional. The men never bathe, the women do so only once a month . . . Here in fact is the choice facing the valley: can it retain its social heritage while improving its welfare? If you import western rates of infant mortality, do you have to import high crime rates and junk culture too? . . . Will the Chauda-Bisa valley and the Khas people succumb to coca-colonization, following so

many aboriginal cultures into extinction? According to human diversity theory, each culture lost is a subtraction from the world's stock of wisdom: some day, like the Madagascan rosy periwinkle – saved from the devastation of the rain forest and now providing drugs to treat leukemia and Hodgkin's disease – it might have proved valuable. [2]

Earthwatch, via its promotion of 'integrated rural development', hopes to help such peoples find a middle road to better health and education without destroying their local cultures.

There was no such thought in the minds of the colonists of old. From our perspective the pain inflicted on the peoples they found in 'new worlds' seems unduly violent and harsh, yet given the fierceness with which Catholicism was being reaffirmed in Europe at that time, it was also inevitable. As usual, the speed and pain of the inevitability was largely determined by various kinds of greed: greed for new sources of gold and silver, for slaves, for coastal settlements for trade and for safe harbours. The strength of these desires led unerringly to wholesale cultural destruction: the invaders never had the time or the inclination to master the art of serious cultural connecting.

Not surprisingly, given the seafaring nature of most colonization, the languages of the colonizers, English, Spanish and Portuguese, still feature in the world top ten of both mother-tongue speakers (MT) and official-language populations (OL):

English, number 2 MT and number 1 OL

Spanish, number 3 MT and number 4 OL

Portuguese, number 8 for both MT and OL. [3]

It is interesting to reflect on how the world might look today if other nations had developed and sustained the military and maritime technology that carried these languages around the world. A largely Greek-speaking South America? An African continent speaking mainly Swedish or Italian? Norwegian as the common language across most of North America, with small pockets of Danish here and there? Given that language is a key element in the repeatability of information, the force and ubiquity of a particular language must have been a powerful motor in the later development of these colonized peoples. Their often fragile records, their largely oral collective memories, their stores of ideas about themselves and the icons that helped reinforce their beliefs, were changed out of all recognition. The more permanent technologies and memory stores of the invaders reduced them to dimly remembered mysteries that only archaeologists have been able to recover. It is chastening to note that the Incas of Peru, so well developed in the technologies of irrigation, intensive farming, tax collection, military organization and communications over inhospitable terrain, had little or no science of writing. They had no collective memory of any permanence other than the remains of stone buildings, monuments and the intriguing 'information knots' of the quipu noted earlier. Paradoxically, the invasion of the modern tourist, in search of the original people, customs, places and information about the original 'experience' has given a commercial boost to rediscovering information about precolonial cultures.

Arabic also features in the top ten of both mother-tongue speakers (number 5) and official-language populations (number 7). Europeans use Arabic numerals, the highly successful Portuguese navigators used Arabic-inspired designs for their long-distance ships, and Arabic science, particularly in the areas of mathematics and medicine, has a long and distinguished history. Yet within a few decades of Napoleon's arrival in Egypt in 1798, the entire Arab world had fallen victim to domination by one western power or another. During this time Arabs grew fascination and repugnance for western technology and culture in the same garden. This schizophrenia continues to feed the conditions of Arab-Islamic suspicion towards all modern carriers of western sources of information. The more conservative guardians of the old Muslim traditions yearn for a return to the slow pace of pre-colonial information growth. Such a pace allowed communities time to develop a system of beliefs which gave them confidence and security. It enabled them to set up systems of government, to create records of procedures and rules; it provided the foundation for artistic representations of their world and it fuelled discovery and technological change at a rate which caused minimal discontinuity. They were able to add to their history in a way which did not involve a wholesale rejection of the past or make significant chunks of it irrelevant. Unlike the seemingly absurd rates of change that modern industrial societies encourage, and the wholesale disorientation of individuals it often brings with it, the bearings and priorities of non-industrial societies could still display uninterrupted time-lines directly related to the values and beliefs held by their predecessors. Such vestiges of the measured pace of change can sometimes be seen in rural village communities of industrial economies. They touch something within us, something to do with size and population, something to do with a community which knows all there is to know about itself and is not too bothered about knowing any more, but modern communication technologies and modern definitions of convenience have probably rendered even these rare outposts more of a facade than a reality. Laurie Lee [4], growing up in a Cotswold village during the first two decades of this century, probably experienced the last remnants of this way of life:

> . . . They occurred at a time when the village was the world and its happenings all I knew. The village in fact was like a deep running cave still linked to its antic past, a cave whose shadows were cluttered by spirits and by laws vaguely ancestral. This cave that we inhabited looked backwards through chambers that led to our ghostly beginnings; and had not, as yet, been tidied up, or scrubbed clean by electric light, or suburbanized by a Victorian church, or papered by cinema screens.

Under the umbrella of these trickling rates of change, where the imperative was as often as not to 'look backwards' for inspiration, new information, particularly if it contradicted key assumptions within a culture, often remained within the minds of its sponsors. Its time would eventually come, slowly if left to its own internal rhythms, faster when prompted by outside intervention.

Although concerned with Anglican missionary zeal at work in Australia during the early part of the 20th century, Diener's [5] cautionary tale of information and cultural dissolution shows just how misplaced 'fast-forward' information civilization can be:

> The three basic elements of human society are people and their interactions, artefacts and knowledge. The people and their interactions constitute the life of a society. The artefacts constitute the physical tools and environment through which the society exists. The knowledge constitutes the information base of a society, including its culture, world view, or social reality as well as the knowledge necessary for everyday life.

He tells the story of the establishment of a mission station near to the Yir Yoront group of Aborigines in Queensland. Within this group only adult males owned the polished stone axes which provided the core of their paleolithic technology. Children, uninitiated young men and women could use an axe owned by an adult male relative but, as part of a strong obligation and bonding structure within the society, they could not own one. Although the axe was used primarily by women to carry out many day-to-day tasks, the knowledge of how to acquire the materials and construct them was strictly reserved for initiated adult males. Unaware of this, the missionaries distributed short-handled steel axes to anyone they thought would be able to make good use of them. The cultural information once embodied in the fabrication, acquisition and ownership patterns of stone axes was thus quickly rendered redundant, and a key element in the information glue of the Yir Yoront was destroyed.

Given the natural urge of humans to enquire, to explore, to interact and to communicate, it is understandable that if an advanced group comes into close contact with a less technologically advanced one, then changes are bound to occur. With greater care and understanding on the part of the more advanced group, the rate of intrusiveness can be controlled so as to avoid wholesale cultural disintegration and conflict. The information that the modern business explorer brings, embedded in factories, engines, huge earth-moving vehicles and a plethora of portable devices and artefacts, can still disrupt the rhythms of a simple culture 500 years after Columbus. The old colonial imperative of the 'quick buck' is still alive and well, and short-term profitably expedient solutions continue to drown out the cries of those who see the danger of moving too far, too fast. I recommend Diener's [5] lucid commentary on the issues involved in assessing the strength or fragility of the 'informational fabric of a society' to anyone interested in exploring further the idea of new information as a serious disrupter of a particular way of life. His four key issues, openness, informational complexity, structural complexity and dynamics, are well worth the contemplation of anyone involved in devising aid policies or educational programmes for developing countries. It has always been a characteristic of slow-moving information communities that the dissemination of new political and economic ideas would be seen as a serious threat to the current custodians. There is still nothing quite as subversive as persuasively presented information on how people might organize to govern themselves differently, or ensure a more equitable distribution of the rewards of their endeavours. Even when the information has lost the ability to persuade, as with the Marxist theories that until recently provided the rationale for so many postwar communist states, just continuing to exist may be enough to prompt serious opposition:

> In March 1960, the Eisenhower administration formally adopted a plan to overthrow Castro in favour of a regime 'more devoted to the true interests of the Cuban people and more acceptable to the US – the two conditions being equivalent – emphasizing again that this must be done 'in such a manner as to avoid the appearance of US intervention'. [6]

Every American president since then has tried, one way or another, to effect this policy, and the plan is still in place 35 years later. The great crime of 1959, i.e. Cuban independence from US control, will never be forgiven until Cuba rejoins that happy band of US-approved countries in Latin America which enjoy the obvious and tangible benefits of democracy and US hegemony. After several attempts to invade or destabilize the Castro regime, the US has now settled on a fierce economic blockade in tandem with information bombardment via satellite. Pop music and soap operas are dropped on the island for hours at a time, just to remind the Cuban people of what they are missing. Such a conscious invasion of a country by television may be the precursor to the 'visual information wars' of the future.

The Clinton administration, to its credit, has recently indicated that it intends to stop funding the 'TV Marti' satellite invasion but the unilateral economic embargo is to continue. As Cuba no longer poses a threat to the security of the US, we must assume that it is just the continued existence of the 36-year-old communist regime that still makes politicians in the US feel nervous. The courage to change 30 years of ignoble foreign policy towards Cuba has so far proved to be lacking. President Clinton has an opportunity to show just how magnanimous the last superpower can be.

Information acceptance and rejection: open and closed

The dissemination of new or different political ideas and their repression or acceptance within and between cultures is well documented, but new information offering different explanations about the world via scientific experiment and discovery may still come too fast. Such ideas will eventually become accepted of course, but not necessarily when the discoverers would prefer: cultural clocks run to the rhythm of groups not individuals. There are still serious differences of view over the time that should be allowed to elapse between the discovery, announcement and eventual cultural absorption of certain discoveries. The wider public acceptance or rejection of a new technology, as opposed to acceptance by the scientific community, varies quite surprisingly. Although this probably has more to do with how the message is broadcast than with a deep understanding of the issues, the opposition is often concerted and effective.

Some messages, such as those associated with nuclear power, start off well (cheap, safe and pollution-free electricity for all) and finish badly (expensive, dangerous and creating harmful radiation wastes that may never die). Some, like the development of computer technology, seem to carry the 'symbol of progress, torch of ingenuity, vital part of our civilization' label almost from day one. Although there have been some dissident voices, usually concerned with the legal, social and political applications of computers, there has been a near-total absence of organized public concern about these issues. Computer technology has gained the status of an unquestionably 'good thing'. The development of biotechnology, on the other hand, is now the focus of quite persistent public agitation, particularly in the US.

The concern about the future role of biotechnology and its potential disruption of the links between biological reproduction and our traditional ideas of kinship is a very topical example of how late 20th century science may be racing well ahead of our cultural ability to cope with the outcomes. It has always been a powerful component of most cultures that we are all related 'by blood' to someone else, and one of the great bonding satisfactions within a culture is that we also know who these 'relations' are. To help confirm these important blood-line links societies have constructed information maps of them: mother, brothers, uncles, cousins etc., and we are each given a precise longitude and latitude on a kinship chart which is unique to us. Bioengineering threatens to disrupt this social cartography by screening out the social identities of some of the 'blood' involved, introducing ambiguity where most cultures require certainty.

At the point of technological conception none of this seems relevant – after all, science is just making possible what a genetic flaw has made impossible. But the new technology that makes anonymous conception possible cannot displace the overwhelming tenacity of kinship, nor can it deny the urge of children thus produced to seek out their own specific place on the map. Strathern [7] sets out some of these contradictions:

> New reproductive technologies enable conception to take place outside the usual social arrangements by which people organize family life, and enable families to create themselves irrespective of people's capacity to conceive. Kinship is the enterprise that organizes this demand: fertility becomes an issue because people wish to have offspring. At the same time the (harsh, cold, brute) reality of the situation is that, in having the child, the parent is creating relations, not just with the child but through it with the child's other parent(s), and with its grandparents, siblings, cousins and so forth. It is no surprise that these implications should be on people's minds when they think about the difference it makes to the fact of relatedness how conception itself is contrived.

Some 3000 children are born every year in Britain as a result of artificial insemination. In a recent book Snowden and Snowden [8] chronicle both the psychological and the social trauma that often results from the separation of practical from genetic parenting. The UK Human Fertilization and Embryology Act of 1990 sets out the legal status of children born as a result of donor insemination. It states that the identity of the donor, the child's genetic father, must never be revealed and that only limited information, to avoid intermarriage with relatives of the original donor, can be made after the child reaches the age of 18. As such children become adults in a culture that still regards genetic links as a key ingredient of kinship, and as it is known that the authorities hold precise information about donors, it looks as if a number of litigious 'time bombs' have been set to go off in the not too distant future. The early months of 1994 in the UK witnessed public repugnance and alarm over the publicity given to proposals involving the possible use of ovaries retrieved from aborted fetuses and ovarian tissue from corpses in order to overcome the relative scarcity of 'live' donors and satisfy the increasing demands for eggs by infertile women. The British Human Fertilization and Embryology Authority issued a 10-page explanatory document. This was intended for wide public discussion over a five-month consultation period, and covered the key scientific, social and moral issues involved. Not least of these is the potential for one biological parent to be traced back to an aborted fetus. This highlights some of the dilemmas governing information sharing, and the age-old issue of the ethical appropriateness of disseminating certain kinds of information and the control or lack of it that should accompany its availability, for example:

1. The dilemma facing scientists about how and when to reveal the new opportunities arising out of potentially sensitive areas of the science/culture interface.

2. The dissemination of information about nuclear technology which could be used to construct and deliver nuclear weapons.

3. Our growing inability to ignore new information until we can handle it. Because it is there, and because there always seems to be an urgent reason to apply it, it is recommended and used, many years before the cultural consequences can be felt or understood.

4. Many scientific and technological outcomes are now so complex in their interaction with society that they probably could not be predicted or tested in any meaningful way apart from full-blown injection into a culture.

5. The information that should be made available to a child whose genetic map is not the cultural norm and the concomitant social responsibility of all those involved, i.e. the donor, the practical parents and the authorities who hold the key information.

Governing access to certain sorts of information will always be a provocative issue. Who should do the governing? How will they be selected? This brings us back to the issue of control which, as we shall see below, is becoming much more difficult.

The face of a seemingly confident and very modern nation may be a mask behind which a legacy of strict controls, isolation and separateness still conditions behaviour. The draconian seclusion laws invoked by the Tokugawa (Edo) Bakufu Shoguns of Japan to restrict the flow of personnel and information from the west for nearly 200 years, between 1639 and 1853, is one such legacy. Put in place principally to prevent the spread of Christianity, these laws were clearly intended as cultural protection, not just from new sets of ideas, but from the idea of ideas [9]. The Tokugawa did not want the closed cultural envelope of Japan diluted or polluted with information that might threaten Japanese institutions of social control or Japanese cultural and political stability. A small Dutch trading post restricted to the island of Deshima in Nagasaki remained the only official western presence throughout this time. Trade with western nations was thus severely curtailed and the import of books and materials that might carry western information, knowledge and ideas was banned. Although this ban was relaxed somewhat in 1720, the 'exclusion' was almost total until the arrival off Tokyo in July 1853 of a four-ship naval squadron under Commodore Matthew Perry.

Perry was carrying orders from the US government to initiate relations with Japan in order to facilitate the provisioning of US ships in the Pacific, and to arrange for the proper treatment of shipwrecked sailors. He returned in the spring of 1854, this time with nine ships, to conclude a US–Japan Treaty of Friendship (the Kanagawa Treaty). The same year saw similar treaties signed with Britain and Russia and the opening up of two ports for foreign ships to acquire supplies. Needless to say, superior western military technology ensured Japanese compliance in these unequal treaties. These changes eventually led to the dissolution of the Tokugawa shogunate and its replacement by the Meiji dynasty of emperors in 1868. Accepting that it was industrial power that gave the western nations unassailable military strength, the Meiji embarked on a speedy programme of industrialization for Japan. They also accepted that information on best western practices and processes would be necessary to help bring this about. Thus the important Charter Oath proclaimed in April 1868 included a declaration that knowledge would now be sought throughout the world, and that the evil customs of the past were to be abolished.

For 200 years the Japanese had missed out on the exchange of information and ideas that occurs as a natural byproduct of trade. At a time when key intellectual, economic, political and technological forms were being developed in Europe, Japan's progress in all these spheres was limited to what could be achieved by growing and building on internal knowledge. The Meiji were keen to fill in the gaps. Hunter [10] notes the residual tensions that, 140 years after Perry's second mission, still lurk in Japan's cultural background:

> Herein lie the origins of a fundamental dichotomy that has dominated Japan's recent history; the simultaneous existence of both 'indigenous' and western modes of thought and behaviour has resulted in acute cultural conflict. Japanese attempts to change Japan in the last 150 years have been both imitative and derivative, but have been accompanied by conscious and unconscious retention of indigenous characteristics and the 'simulation' of traditional Japanese attributes, plus a fair measure of

originality. Although accommodation between the two cultural traditions is often achieved, the conflicts provoked have also been intense. Reconciliation sometimes proves impossible, and continuing strains within Japanese society are the result.

Many westerners would be surprised to hear about Japan's 200 years of self-imposed isolation. Add to this our knowledge of current Japanese economic power and we might be forgiven for regarding this as somewhat ironic. In the decade following the Second World War Japanese industry gained a reputation for copying everything that was not nailed down. They sent out businessmen and observers to Europe and the US with a clear brief to bring back information on just about every aspect of western management and production techniques, good, bad and indifferent, and we have had ample confirmation over the last three decades that they did not fail. Despite the insecurities and strains noted above, western technology, assimilated and applied within a Japanese cultural context, has so far proved an almost unbeatable mix.

After the Second World War the communist governments of eastern Europe and the USSR, in contrast to Japan, opted for the old isolationist approach, but their problem, as for the Shoguns, was that information carrying new ideas is difficult to keep out of even the most closed cultural envelope; all it takes is time. And time is definitely not on the side of constraining or regulating forces. The inexorable progress and facilitation of modern communication technologies, all increasingly available to large numbers of the population in developed economies, makes it virtually impossible now to interfere effectively with transborder flows of information. Popular commentators often refer to this as the globalization of information, which can be something of a misnomer if accepted uncritically. Most of the world's population is still excluded from access to the new tools and instruments, and therefore have no access to the information they hold or provide a gateway to. Also, most of the information that is disseminated on a global scale is information to secure profit. It is the information that helps some form of business, not information for education and enlightenment. Much of the information that we all access daily is of this profit-making kind, and we seem happy to pay for it one way or another. The apparent invisibility of the payment mechanism, often embedded within the costing of a product or service, can have the inadvertent effect of persuading us that it is cheap or even free.

The greatest impact of the 'global village' must surely be that although new information is received by people who still live and operate in recognizable cultural envelopes, they are now much more likely to have absorbed alternative cultural values that fundamentally change the way they process it. Japanese or Finnish pedestrians may still wait patiently at a red traffic light while gazing at the empty road junction in front of them, dismissing as dangerous or subversive an Australian or Italian culture that might take a more relaxed view of automated instructions. But at home, in front of screens or behind the pages of glossy magazines, Finns, Australians, Italians and Japanese have become multicultural receivers, switching seamlessly across the boundaries of their own socialization, to accept quite different values and behaviours. Just how comfortable this process is depends on a number of important local factors, e.g. age, education, family traditions, social and economic status, familiarity with the transmitting media and the social depth of surviving cultural traditions. There are always local tensions that by turns accept and then reject externally generated information, or defiantly stand out against even a limited acceptance of any of it. The role of women in Asian or Islamic countries, compared to the predominantly western role-models portrayed in the media, is an obvious issue. The impact of gratuitous violence on children and the unrestrained dissemination of western fashions, consumer lifestyles and sexual values are others. Most of this information will be absorbed from the predominantly visual images of television. The recent impact of Italian television on the material hopes and restlessness of the people of the once severely 'closed' Albania, and the general impact of western television images on all the former regimes of eastern Europe and the former USSR, bear witness to the power of this medium. In addition, popular magazines, popular music, film and theatre productions, long-distance telephone contact and cheaper air travel continue to accelerate the breakdown in the dominance of home-grown information. The reception of information is clearly becoming less and less culturally dependent. The codes and signals put out by Gucci, Nestlé, U2, McDonalds, Steven Spielberg and western 'soap operas' are anticipated and processed in much the same way by Russians as by Brazilians. Faced with such universality the protective Shoguns may be in for a tough time, but they will not be giving up. Devising new forms of cultural protection from unwanted information flows will just get more frantic as the technology makes it more difficult to stop.

Suppression and misuse: still going strong

Given the state of communication technologies in the late 15th century it was an easy matter, in 1499, for the two founders of modern (Catholic) Spain, Isabella of Castile and Ferdinand of Aragon, to order the burning of all Islamic books. Four hundred and thirty years later it was comparatively easy for Hitler to order, and in part achieve, the burning of all Jewish and other 'subversive' books inside Germany and its conquered territories. Sixty years after Hitler, Muslims in England took to the streets to burn Salman Rushdie's book *The Satanic Verses* and to condemn the author to death. In October 1994, Salman Rushdie still lived under the threat of death, there was still a US$2 million price on his head, and he still had to live and travel in secret. Throughout these years Rushdie secured only grudging support from the British Foreign Office, although the Prime Minister did meet with him in May 1993 and issued a statement to the effect that he underlined the government's full support for Rushdie's fundamental rights as a British citizen, and expressed concern that the Iranian authorities had failed to repudiate the incitement to his murder. Coincident as it was with the 1993 Teheran Book Fair, at which a number of British publishers were exhibiting, this must have given the lonely author some modest comfort. However, without a more interventionist stance by the British and other governments in support of free speech and free expression, it is difficult to see how Salman Rushdie will ever be free to live a normal life again.

Although alone in one sense, Rushdie may not be alone in another. The anti-expression ripples that have confined him look set to embrace anyone who has or may have some involvement with him or his work. In July 1991 Ettore Capriolo, the Italian translator of the *Verses*, was stabbed and wounded in Milan by a hit squad demanding the author's address. Eight days later the Japanese translator, Hitoshi Igarashi, was stabbed to death in Tokyo by unknown assassins. In early July 1993 Muslims besieged and set fire to a hotel in the Turkish Anatolian town of Sivas, killing 45 people and injuring 145 others. They were protesting against the presence of Aziz Nesin (who had previously translated parts of *The Satanic Verses* into Turkish), at a gathering of intellectuals and writers, and in October 1993 Rushdie's Norwegian publisher William Nygaard was shot and badly wounded outside his home in Oslo. Both Nygaard and the Norwegian government have consistently adopted a high profile in continuing to champion Rushdie's right to freedom of expression.

The suppression of alternative information sources by fundamentalist followers of Islam may turn out to be the big censorship issue of the 1990s. Strident and uncompromising, their messages convey confrontation rather than ecumenicism, a message of insistence rather than fraternity, the closing up and turning inward of a rich culture rather than an opening out of it as part of a community of learning and exploration. The continuing civil war between the military regime in Algeria and the militant Islamic party which was on course to win the cancelled Algerian election of 1992, the continuous fuelling of fundamentalist ideology by Iran and the Egyptian government's increasing crackdown on anyone suspected of sympathies towards the Islamic movement all suggest that some terrible conflicts within and around Islam are likely in the near future. The betrayal, desperation and dislocation felt by many European Muslims about the west's perceived failure to protect the Muslim populations of Bosnia will add a further dimension to what has until now been seen as a predominantly Middle-Eastern issue.

The savagery and physical terror of war will inevitably be foreshadowed by the brutalizing of information and ideas. After participating in a widely publicized debate at the Cairo International Book Fair early in 1992, the controversial Arab writer Farag Fouda was assassinated in the following June. The same book fair witnessed an unprecedented confrontation between President Mubarak of Egypt and al-Azhar, the leading Sunni Islam organization based in Cairo. Al-Azhar officials wanted to remove books by Judge Said Ashmawi, the head of the Egyptian state security court and a scholar active in opposing attempts by Islamic fundamentalists to use Islam as a political tool, and the Egyptian President resisted. However, notwithstanding this high-level intervention, several books by Arab writers were removed from the 1993 Cairo Book Fair at the insistence of al-Azhar, and their powers of intervention seem to be growing. Salman Rushdie may be an Iranian prisoner on British soil, his books may be burnt and some government authorities and publishers may take fright at the threats of a fanatical minority, but his ideas will still be repeated many times, via television and radio, and in newspapers and magazines. Replicated in so many forms, it is becoming difficult to burn the idea now!

An interesting example of the consequences of stimulating economic reform, and hence a desire for all things western, within a censorious political system, is the current dilemma facing the Marxist government of mainland China. In October 1993 the Beijing government issued new rules banning individuals and 'work units' from setting up or using satellite television dishes, in an attempt to reinforce restrictions first introduced in 1991. Faced with an explosion in back-street dish fabrication, sales and installation, the old men at the helm of the People's Republic fear the social and political consequences that might arise out of the liberated access to information that a dish on every roof might bring. They may stem the tide for a while, but they are just sticking a finger in an electronic dyke that will eventually burst over them. It is now almost impossible to block the flow of information travelling electronically, or to prevent the installation of ingenious devices for receiving it. This is the much heralded liberation of access to information by technology.

This same 'liberating' technology can of course be turned, in even the most benevolent political system, against the individual. At various times the British government has used sophisticated electronic surveillance equipment to eavesdrop on the Pope, a Falklands war hero, a Scottish trade union leader and a 93-year-old woman peace campaigner [11]. In July 1993 the National Westminster Bank, one of the UK's largest clearing banks, confirmed, with hardly a twinge of regret, that it kept details of the political and religious affiliations of some of its 6.5 million customers. Spokespersons for the bank, obviously astonished to have this practice queried at all, simply noted that these were just two of 50 approved categories that the bank had registered under the Data Protection Act, along with others such as physical descriptions and personality traits. As many banks in the UK have been accused of selling information about their customers to third parties, continuing fears that computerized information might turn up in surprising places seem to be well founded. It is intriguing to reflect on what kind of 'personality traits' the bank feels are worth recording!

The incredulity shown by the bank over the media attention given to this particular case is increasingly typical of corporate responses to criticism arising out of the computerized diffusion of personal information. I mentioned earlier the almost total lack of public concern about the potential for intrusiveness, control and misuse that can arise as computer technology spreads into every sphere of our lives. Nelkin [12] has compared this complacency with the vigorous opposition that has characterized the dissemination of other technologies:

> Both information technology and biotechnology promise enormous benefits to society, and both present certain risks. Comparing the public response to these technologies and laying out the issues that have generated opposition, suggests the hierarchy of values that more broadly shape public attitudes towards science and technology. It also exposes certain contradictions between rhetoric and reality. We give lip service to the importance of the right to privacy, the freedom from social control, and the preservation of democratic values. But the issues most likely to generate resistance to a given technology have more to do with its potential risk to health, its impact on organized interests, and especially its effect on moral and religious agendas.

This seems a very apt summary. The commitment that individuals, corporations and governments have to privacy has proved to be ephemeral. There is no broad consensus on the seriousness of the risks because they are largely invisible. A single incident can arouse concern, but it is soon swept away by the day-to-day need to collude with a technology that most of us believe we cannot now live without. Also, intrusions into personal privacy often happen at sensitive points in our engagement with institutions: maybe when we seek credit, request a licence of some sort, open a bank account or attempt to adopt a child – times when we least want to complain or draw more attention to ourselves.

In many countries ordinary citizens are now powerless to control the information that government and other agencies hold on them, usually in multiple electronic databases that interface with each other via national bridges. This personal information may be benign, it may be mildly inaccurate or it may be inaccurate and defamatory; whatever its status, redress, despite the Data Protection Act, is usually hard to obtain, and is often secured only after serious damage has been done to the individual or organization concerned. A BBC 1 'Panorama' programme entitled 'Secrets for Sale' in October 1993 revealed just how easy it was for private investigators in the UK to acquire confidential information on just about anyone. The programme demonstrated how, for a price of between £50 and £200, they could collect information on the private bank and credit card accounts, health and criminal records, national insurance, tax details and ex-directory telephone numbers of four well known individuals (with their permission, of course). Those willing to pay – mainly companies seeking information about their competitors and customers, as well as information about their current and potential employees – seem to be impervious to the fact that this information can only be accessed illegally. Bank staff are routinely bribed, as are senior police officers with access to the Police National Computer. The security of this latter facility is no doubt hindered by its online link to over 1500 local police stations throughout the country. One seasoned investigator noted how many of the contacts that he had built up over his 15 years in the business had now moved up into more senior positions. Having helped once with a 'favour' it was difficult for them now to withdraw from his service. It is ironic that so much information that people feel is their due as citizens and voters they often cannot get, while personal information about themselves that should not be available can be traded so cheaply. We have to accept that the new technologies will facilitate all kinds of information-seeking misbehaviour on a much grander scale than hitherto, and that we will tolerate this because we want the convenience of the underlying technology. The alleged misuse of computer information by British Airways for competitive advantage over Virgin Airlines during their recent 'dirty tricks' campaign, and the transparent attempts by the French Intelligence Services to gain commercial information from the US participants at the 1993 Paris Air Show, are just two recent examples of hostile information collection fuelled by the coincidence of smart microelectronics and the pressures of global competition. It is also getting much harder to find out what governments and corporations are really up to, to get at the truth behind the rhetoric on almost any issue. This is certainly not an area where a 'free' press has much freedom, not in the UK at any rate. In Britain the notorious 'catch-all' and ambiguous Section 2 of the 1911 Official Secrets Act was, for nearly 80 years, the envy of despotic powers everywhere. Its 'reform' in the new Official Secrets Act of 1989 at least now focuses on the nature of the information disclosed and the harm arising from its disclosure, rather than on the act of disclosure itself, as was the case before. However, it is clear from the debates that accompanied the passing of the 1989 Act that the British government intends to tighten up the terms of employment of civil servants, seeking a scrupulous code of lifelong confidentiality for all members of the security services. This code insists that civil servants and the media will no longer be able to argue that information relating to matters such as government misconduct, fraud, threats to public health, or malpractice by members of the security services was or should be disclosed because it was in the public interest to do so. This means that the 'public interest' verdict of the Clive Ponting jury in January 1985 (against the wishes of the presiding judge), concerning his disclosures to a Member of Parliament about the circumstances leading up to the sinking of the Argentine warship the General Belgrano, would no longer be an acceptable defence in a British court, whatever the jury thought. Ponting admitted leaking the information but he maintained, and the jury accepted, that his actions had been motivated by a higher principle of public service than that which normally guides the Ministry of Defence. The latter had clearly misled parliament and the British people over the Belgrano affair, and the chances are that they will do so again now that they feel confident of protection by the courts. The 1989 legislation still puts certain government misconduct and malpractice outside the law and makes the publication of information about such misconduct unlawful. Under it a judge would have no option other than to direct jurors to ignore a public interest defence.

The typically British 'everything is secret until proved otherwise' approach to all information collected by government, irrespective of its sensitivity, has been integrated into the laws and procedures of many former British colonies. The sight of the Singapore government taking the *Business Times* and its informants to court under the country's Official Secrets Act over its early reporting of some quarterly GDP statistics during 1992, demonstrates just how deep and all-embracing the phrase 'official secrets' can be, as well as how long the habits of a colonial power can linger on in the system. Based on the 'old' UK Official Secrets legislation, the Singapore Act is very widely drawn and identifies as secret any information that has been 'classified' by the government, irrespective of its nature or content. The fact that the Attorney General himself attended to the prosecution of this case, and that all five defendants were found guilty and fined, indicates the degree of importance that the Singapore government still attaches to such disclosures, as well as reinforcing Singapore's reputation as an information-repressive regime:

> The case is really about whether prosperous, educated Singapore wants or needs a more open, plural society, or should stick with the authoritarian system developed by Mr Lee. The fact that *Business Times* is fighting the case indicates that the establishment is divided on the issue. [13]

Interestingly, this case revolved around a document left on the desk of the chief economist at Singapore's Central Bank. Two stockbrokers spotted the document, extracted the information and sent it, unannounced and unrequested, by electronic mail to the editor of the *Business Times*. Thus one man had no intention of passing on the figures (indeed, the prosecution eventually changed the charge against him to 'endangering the secrecy of official information', or as one local wag put it, of 'not keeping his desk tidy'), and another was found guilty despite having received the information involuntarily. As one of the defence lawyers argued, if receiving information unintentionally constituted an offence, then all the readers of that particular issue of the *Business Times* had also broken the law. Such nonsense will proliferate as the technology of information distribution races ahead of laws and regulations compiled to cope with the media of another age.

Politicians in the UK also get confused about where they stand on information access issues. Kenneth Baker, then Secretary of State for Education, addressed a group of 400 students at Moscow State University in 1988, when the USSR was still the 'evil empire', along the following lines:

> What's the point in having computers and information technology if you are not allowed access to anything more than the contents of a modest library? . . . The information technology revolution cannot bear fruit without the free flow of information within society and between societies. [14]

Such fierce info-liberalism was scarcely seen or heard of in Britain at this time, where 'market forces' and 'the reduction of hidden costs' tended to condition the political approach to all public goods and services, including access to information.

Another challenge that UK ministers discovered around this time was the enriching effect that added value can have. This was something that was definitely right for British industry and commerce, but somewhat less acceptable when associated with other forms of intelligent information gathering. The collecting together of information into something that looked new and which might have an impact much greater than the sum of its individual parts, as well as offering up some surprises, was also perceived as being subversive. A month after Baker's speech in Moscow, the then Home Secretary, Douglas Hurd, unencumbered by the shackles of overseas packaging, addressed the Royal Television Society Conference:

> The disclosure of certain information was always harmful whether or not it had been published before. [15]

In July 1993 the British government, perhaps becoming more sensitive to the charge that it is still one of the most secretive governments operating in a democracy, published a brochure explaining the role of MI5, accompanied by 'authorized' photographs of its head, Stella Rimington. In October 1993 they went on to issue a 28-page booklet, *Central Intelligence Machinery*, explaining in very general terms the work of the Joint Intelligence Committee (JIC) which assesses the value of all raw intelligence gathered by MI5, MI6 and GCHQ concerning the 'national security and economic wellbeing' of the UK. They followed up these public relations exercises in November 1993 by announcing that MI6, which gathers intelligence abroad, and GCHQ, which intercepts communications from all around the world, were to be placed on a statutory basis for the first time. These moves represented little more than a publication of what most journalists and commentators already knew. The government still has no intention of making the work of the JIC accountable in law, or the budgets of the intelligence services available to parliamentary, or even ministerial, scrutiny. The tradition that the JIC still has of marking some of its reports 'not for ministers' eyes' [16] seems unlikely to change as a result of these largely cosmetic exercises. It is salutary to note that, despite their lack of accountability, the price of which, they might argue, is their supreme effectiveness at information assessment and prediction, the JIC still failed to foresee the two most important foreign crises of the last 11 years, the Argentine invasion of the Falklands and the Iraqi invasion of Kuwait. They were also taken completely by surprise, as were most other intelligence services around the world, when the Berlin Wall came down. When the UK intelligence services do manage to get it more-or-less right, as with the information they secured on ministerial connivance in the recent 'arms for Iraq' scandal, on those British companies involved in sanctions-breaking in Rhodesia during the 1960s and 1970s, and on the illegal activities of the Bank of Credit and Commerce International, their reports are either ignored, heavily sanitized to protect something or other, or just quietly suppressed.

There are always ironies with regard to calls for legislation affecting access to information about individuals. Such calls are often aimed at people who perform duties on behalf of the state, or who operate in a domain where their private behaviour could have serious repercussions on their public responsibilities. These ironies are particularly true with regard to the balance between reporting information that satisfies a legitimate public interest and the reporting of information that really only satisfies the more salacious appetites of readers or viewers. Following the two Calcutt reports on the press, the British government signalled its intention to introduce a 'privacy law' to protect individuals from the worst excesses of media intrusion. The first Calcutt report on privacy, produced in 1990, supported a 'give the press a chance to prove themselves' stance by advocating voluntary self-regulation under the code of practice operated by the newly formed Press Complaints Commission. This was accompanied by an open threat that if such a system of self-regulation was seen to be ineffectual or breaking down, it would have to be replaced by a publicly funded statutory tribunal with far greater powers of enforcement.

The second Calcutt report, really a review of how the press had been behaving over the last two years or so, was published in January 1993. This found that the 'voluntary' system had failed to curtail the worst excesses of press intrusion and called for sweeping statutory constraints on newspapers. It called on the government to introduce a new tort of infringement of privacy; three new criminal offences of trespass; and a statutory tribunal chaired by a judge with powers to restrain publication, to require apologies and, where necessary, to impose heavy fines. Towards the end of 1993 the Lord Chancellor issued a Green Paper, *Infringement of Privacy*, as a discussion document on the changes in the criminal law that might now be taken up by the government, and although at the time of writing the outcome is still uncertain, it looks like something of a legislative minefield is about to be laid down around access to information of all kinds. As is so often the case, just one high-profile act of perceived invasion of privacy can accelerate a process, the seeds of which were sown some time before. Such an act may have been the publication by the *Daily Mirror* of photographs of the Princess of Wales working out in a private gymnasium in London during November 1993, taken with a cunningly concealed camera. The outrage that this series of photographs provoked among politicians, and (not surprisingly) among rival newspapers, all complaining that the *Daily Mirror* had broken that part of the voluntary code that specified 'that the use of photographs taken without consent on private property was forbidden', was just the kind of catalyst that those clamouring for legislation on privacy needed to help secure their case. Ironically, while some sections of the press have done their best to prompt legislation, the British government has made it clear that it really does not want to get embroiled in the politics of a comprehensive privacy law. The accelerating practice among newspaper managements of writing the 'voluntary code' into the employment contracts of all journalists and editors may help. This development, together with the appointment by the Press Complaints Commission, in early 1994, of a Privacy Commissioner who will be free to adjudicate speedily on matters of individual privacy, might just be enough to stem the legislative tide. The Privacy Commissioner will not be able to impose fines but will be able to summon editors to explain their conduct and, if warranted, recommend that publishers take disciplinary action against them. Newspaper and television editors rightly fear that investigative programmes dealing with issues such as police corruption, or public figures who have clearly been acting against the public interest, will become tangled up in any legislation primarily designed to protect the great and the 'good' from having photographs of their holidays and reports of their infidelities strewn around the press. The 'prior restraint' that individuals would be able to use under such new legislation would inevitably result in editors having to queue up to see a judge in chambers before running a story, to prove in advance that it was clearly in the public interest to do so. Many believe that a privacy law would simply be a handy charter for the rich and the powerful to prejudice serious investigative journalism which, in the UK, is already beset by excessive legal restrictions. Whatever the politicians may say or mean, redress via such legislation would almost certainly be too expensive for the majority of ordinary citizens.

Governments, as the collectors and custodians of so much information, almost without trying, acquire the power to prevent access to it, or to manipulate it in such a way as to render it as reliable or unreliable as they see fit. Paradoxically, the very cult of secrecy that pervades the security and intelligence services can also serve to protect all citizens from invasions of their privacy. The current UK government's policy of seeking to privatize public agencies that currently carry out discrete civil functions is giving rise to a new set of fears, i.e. the future security of privatized information. Highly sensitive records, often crucial to the discharge of a particular public function such as tax collection and social security provision, will inevitably have to be handed over to the private operators. Whatever its failings, the British Civil Service has a culture that requires a clear respect for the confidentiality of information that it holds on individuals. It is difficult to see how such information could be protected once it is in the hands of a private concern.

One example of the kind of information at risk is that held by the UK Employment Service (ES), currently a separate agency operating within the Employment Department Group and widely tipped to be a candidate for future privatization. The ES is currently engaged in updating and rationalizing its information networks and hopes, by the mid 1990s, to have linked all UK Job Centres together, so that all ES information can be accessed from one terminal. The NUBS2 system which the ES will be using to implement its IT strategy belongs to the Department of Social Security, and it is intended that it will provide a dynamic Job Centre interface with the DSS to help job applicants and administrators alike. Such an information system, with its transparent bridges to other big information-holding agencies, would hold a tremendous amount of detail on individual citizens which, in the hands of an unscrupulous or disgruntled private operator, or even the occasional malicious employee, could be a serious threat to individual freedoms. The potential risk of leaks is all the more alarming when one considers that privatization is inevitably an exercise in cost-cutting. The maintenance of secure systems and interfaces is probably not cheap: the staff need careful training, they require a reasonable reward for their work, and they want reasonable security of employment. A private firm pledged to do the job for a fixed price will have to cut the cost of information security somehow, and there will be a limit to this beyond which the security of the information becomes vulnerable and the likelihood of serious breaches of confidentiality becomes greater.

Government plans to place the confidential details of millions of UK personal and company tax affairs into private hands are also well underway. During May 1994 Electronic Data Systems (EDS), the US computing services company currently owned by General Motors, was successful in gaining a contract from the Inland Revenue to handle their tax records. In a lovely bit of irony, representatives of a nation that resisted being taxed by a UK parliament in the 1770s end up charged with storing and safeguarding its taxation records in the 1990s. As everyone is obliged by law to disclose the most confidential information about their affairs in their tax returns, any part of this rich mixture, if leaked or made public knowledge, could result in serious invasions of privacy. The competitive position of major companies could also be put at risk. For example, some of the information in company tax returns, if made public, could affect share prices, destabilize them or leave the company vulnerable to hostile takeovers. The Deputy Chairman of the Inland Revenue, Steve Matheson, noted in a letter to staff [17] that:

> Revenue staff had never sold or exchanged any details contained in tax returns, and that the department had never been penetrated by industrial or commercial spies or computer hacks.

The Group 4 loss of prisoners on the way to a court hearing in the UK during 1993 may be one antisocial result of lax supervision by private operators; losing the personal records of half a million people or leaking market-sensitive information from the tax records of British Aerospace, BP or Lucas could prove catastrophic.

There has recently been a growing concern in the UK about the veracity of information given out by the government and its agencies concerning accidents and incidents involving nuclear materials. Information about the scale and seriousness of the nuclear accident that occurred at Windscale (now Sellafield) in Cumbria in 1957 which only recently emerged from papers released under the government's 30-year rule, is just one of a number of belated 'information moments' that is now causing concern. BBC 1's 'Panorama' investigation in June 1993 into the conspiracy of silence surrounding safety conditions at the Atomic Weapons Establishment at Aldermaston in December 1992 is another. During this latter incident four men checking canisters of highly toxic plutonium were showered with invisible particles of the substance after oxidation had caused one of the containers to split. Official silence and the remarkable compliance of the Health and Safety Executive, theoretically the only source of independent information on work-based risks to health, make it almost impossible to identify the extent of the damage. Reports of numerous barrels of radioactive material being stored within old buildings whose porous brick allows the escape of radioactivity, are difficult to confirm or deny as the Aldermaston managers retreat behind the Official Secrets Act.

The official information given out on unemployment in the UK has long been regarded by many as one of the longest-running information illusions in the western world. John Wells of Cambridge University has provided compelling evidence that 1993 ended with something like 4.01 million people out of work in the UK, rather than the 2.81 million estimated by the DOE. Whether this discrepancy is accurate or not is not really the point; the issue is that the official information is no longer trusted, and as the method of presenting the official statistics has been changed no fewer than 24 times, it is now almost impossible for researchers to compare current and past trends in unemployment [18, 19]. On the other hand, the retail price index, the basic collection of statistics compiled by the Central Statistical Office that informs the British public about the official rate of inflation, is conscientiously reshuffled every year in order to maintain some semblance of reality. This provides a statistical snapshot of what 7000 'average' households buy (the annual expenditure survey) over a given two weeks in a particular year. Although just another official list, the annual expenditure survey is one that offers particularly important information to those, now ubiquitous, researchers of consumer behaviour, who seek to identify trends among out various wants that astute marketing might be able to translate into future needs.

Consumer information: coca-colonization

Consumption is what those of us who are employed in the industrialized world do a lot of. After all, industrialization developed so that more of us could consume the artefacts of production. Industrialization has democratized consumption and unchained it from the small-scale craft production techniques and outputs that could serve only the wealthiest 5 per cent. Now, with leaner manufacturing and production techniques, there is much more to consume at increasingly competitive prices. In order to consume we have to know what is available, and the rapid spread of information about consumer products and the instruments used to deliver it can tell us a lot about cultural receptivity.

This is information packaged to perfection, designed to grab your attention, to thrill you with its message and to suggest all kinds of things about your life, your loves and your place in the scheme of things, and it is without exception driven by the most powerful motors that current artistry and technology can provide. We might think that as modern, sophisticated information processors we are immune to its ubiquity, but not so! This information is designed to stick. It forms a potent part of the global information business and is funded on a scale that the providers of more life-critical information systems, such as the World Health Organization, Oxfam and the providers of domestic opportunity information, like law centres, Citizens Advice Bureaux and public libraries, can only dream of.

A tremendous amount of current artistic and technological resource is bound up in the dissemination of consumer information through music. The much-celebrated advertising campaigns funded by Coca-Cola and Pepsi-Cola are only made possible by the universality of popular music and its potential connectability with their products. The makers of Pepsi-Cola have been particularly aggressive in securing, at various times, the expensive talents of Michael Jackson, David Bowie, Madonna and Tina Turner, all powerful icons in a global youth culture. Not to be outdone, Coca-Cola responded in early 1992 with a video of Elton John extolling the virtues of Diet Coke to the long-gone Humphrey Bogart and James Cagney. A campaign perhaps designed to appeal to the slightly older cola drinker? Whatever its target, Elton John was fronting Coca-Cola's first global advertisement, to be shown in nearly all the 90 countries where the drink is sold. Interestingly, the Pepsi and Coke songs are always in English, a tribute to its acceptability as a currency of communication, to the powerful cultural values that it communicates, and to the grip that the US and the UK have on the worldwide popular music business. The Elton John video was also recorded in French, German and

Spanish, with reserve 'sign-off' tags in Italian and Japanese, just in case there is still a corner of a foreign field where pop songs sung in English need translation [20]!

Although often a powerful endorsement, the risks in so clearly associating any kind of product with celebrities, pop stars and sports personalities can also be high. Some of these people are notorious for their unpredictable lifestyles and behaviour, and damaging information about an individual, once they are linked with a product, can soon turn into poor customer reception. The images and music put together with such skill for modern promotional campaigns are intended to form lasting memories. Whether or not it results in directly related consumption, the television advertisement has become a key 'information moment', with recall levels that are often much higher than those for other informational transactions. To paraphrase Lady Macbeth, 'What is done cannot be easily undone': damage these memories and you are well on your way to damaging profits. In 1989 Pepsi dropped an expensive television advertisement featuring Madonna when consumers were found to confuse the promotion with her then controversial 'Like a Prayer' music video. Pepsi also dropped heavyweight boxing champion Mike Tyson after reports that he had punched his wife. It also brought its long-term sponsorship deal with Michael Jackson to an end in 1993, when bad publicity about alleged child molesting, an addiction to painkillers and the eventual cancellation of a world tour looked like spoiling a lot of Pepsi memories. But the singer had worked considerable magic by that time: over the previous ten years Pepsi had sponsored three Jackson concert tours and paid him some US$20 million. During the same period Pepsi had notched up two market share points over their arch rival Coca-Cola, at an estimated increase in income of US$500 million in annual sales per point. Not a bad investment.

The information content of popular music is probably the most powerful contemporary agent of indigenous cultural breakdown. Buddy Holly only recorded his music for 18 months, and yet his tunes are still played all over the world 40 years later. The songs of Joan Baez, Bob Dylan and John Lennon still enthuse the young in countries where a record player would have been a scarce commodity when the recordings were first made. Lyrics made popular by Elvis Presley, Rod Stewart and the Rolling Stones live on in day-to-day social interaction and conversation longer than anyone would have dared think possible. In more recent times we have seen the power of popular music harnessed to put across information about more serious issues. The Band Aid, Live Aid, Nelson Mandela and the Freddie Mercury AIDS concerts were staged to carry messages of charity, caring and concern. Television marathons and phone-in campaigns linked to events like

Comic Relief's Red Nose Day in the UK have also mobilized the power of popular entertainment to raise significant sums of money for charity.

But these are small blips on the screen of information power. Much more typical of modern information packaging for global receptivity was the 1992/1993 advertising campaign launched by the Italian family business of Benetton. Specializing in colourful, fashionable clothing, Benetton had, for a time at least, given up on language for their advertising campaigns. Amid international controversy Benetton had worked closely with a photographer, Oliviero Toscani, to produce images that challenge and disturb. Pretending little or no association with the products they are supposed to be promoting, the photographs (a blood-spattered newborn baby, a nun kissing a priest, and a picture of the bloodstained jacket of a Bosnian war victim, among others) were used worldwide in conjunction with the name 'Benetton' to draw undivided attention to the brand name. Even members of the family joined the parade. One full-page advertisement in a 1993 newspaper presented the reader with a naked Luciano Benetton covered only by the words 'I WANT MY CLOTHES BACK'.

The company's explanation for this interesting approach to marketing was that, given the difficulty of promoting clothing products worldwide, the reception of which is climatically dependent and seasonal, standard methods of brand specificity were inappropriate. Far better to get the brand name across in association with striking and memorable images than having to work out several different advertising campaigns to cater effectively for a global market. Spokespersons for Benetton also added that the images touched on some of the big contemporary issues which intelligent people would welcome being aired in this way. Luciano Benetton, via a public face of hurt and amazement at some of the published responses to his campaign, has confirmed that these were indeed the intentions:

> What we are trying to do is use our advertising budgets to do something a little more useful . . . to teach the world about itself and have a spirit of sensitivity and care for others. [21]

Another theory might be that these messages were the work of an astute entrepreneur seeking to test the limits of public acceptability, and engineer controversy. The outcry about the campaign itself would provide a second layer of publicity which would keep the campaign going a little longer and help to increase market share. Whatever the reasons, what is much more interesting in terms of human information acquisition and processing is that this kind of global advertising campaign could exist at all, that it could assume that such stark and shocking images would have the same (or very similar) effect in so many different places, that the codes and taboos implicit and explicit in the photographs could be as eye-catching in Reykjavik as in Paris, in Bogota as in Bombay. The popular magazine Elle in the UK refused to carry a picture portraying a dying AIDS victim, as did most media in the US. It assaulted their view of the context in which such a picture should or should not be shown; they understood the information embedded within it and they knew that their readers would understand it, but they wanted to control the context. They also wanted to send a signal to Benetton about the unacceptablity of these kinds of shock tactics. Magazines need advertising to survive, advertisers need magazines to carry their messages; their respective and mutually compatible interests rarely involve this kind of judgemental angst, and this kind of editorial censorship of advertising is unusual: editors are much more likely to turn away news and feature material that would not appeal to advertisers. The readership profile of a popular magazine is very much the profile that is likely to consume the products it advertises, and theoretically the stories and articles readers want should naturally coincide with what advertisers want. There should be no conflict, no need for risk: it's a fully integrated package!

Regional and local newspapers have taken these economic strictures to heart with a vengeance. As recently as the late 1970s local newspapers in the UK were still interesting. They were vehicles for significant local news that also carried appropriate advertising. Now they tend to be vehicles for significant advertising that also carry some local news. It seems to be an unstoppable truth that each generation should get less and less news from its newspapers. Given the range and diversity of competing forms of media in the modern world some might say that we are lucky to have any news in newspapers at all!

Cartoons and Gabriella, coffee and Cheers

Children may have viewed the Benetton images with the incomprehension of innocence or the comprehension of minds open to everything and anything. Whatever their views on shocking static images, most Saturday mornings will find large numbers of them glued to television screens filled with animated cartoon characters whose bizarre world they know very well indeed. These characters zoom through space, blow up and reconstitute themselves, assume fantastic shapes in the wink of an eye, all to ensure that their enemies end up as piles of brightly coloured dust. On a regular weekly basis good will overcome evil within wildly futuristic landscapes, palaeolithic caves and dark caverns which, to their young consumers, seem as real as the cat next door. Walt Disney could not have guessed when in 1927 he gave birth to a cheerful, energetic and somewhat scrawny-looking black and white mouse that he would grow up to be the most recognized personality in the world. Disney had identified and capitalized on the public taste for animals with the speech, skills, personality traits and failings of human beings. 'Steamboat Willie' issued in 1928, starred Mickey Mouse for the first time. Although complete with the novelty of a voice and music soundtrack, viewed today it shows no sign of being the precursor of the hi-tech and surreal cartoon worlds that have become one of the most potent forms of communicating with children in the 1990s. Disney would no doubt have been surprised to learn that Donald Duck's nephews Huey, Dewey and Louie would be used by the Italian magazine *Topolino* (the Italian name for Mickey Mouse) to help explain to its 8–12-year-old readers the meaning of European integration and the role of the Maastricht Treaty in trying to achieve it [22].

With a popularity akin to children's cartoons, television 'soap operas' also travel around the world carrying information about AIDS, divorce, abortion, violence, unemployment, family disruption, homosexuality, affluence and poverty to every television set capable of receiving the signals. Their particular brand of heightened reality – real life with the boring bits left out – has proved a potent mix. It enables them to secure their viewers identity with some very individual destinies while at the same time suggesting that they are somehow typical. There can be no doubt that the modern soap opera has become a vehicle for enabling agendas and stimulating everyday discussion about issues that other media have much more difficulty addressing. Their serial format enables 'soaps' to explore such controversial issues as lesbianism and senile dementia, within the context of seemingly 'normal' social relationships, over a much longer period than other forms of programming. The escape-promise of weekly drama has thus become a major source of hard information for many people who would not regard themselves as particularly well informed. Information-intensive soap operas might of course lose viewers, disenchanted with the exploration of too many serious issues too close to home. Towards the end of 1975, programme controllers at Granada, who produce the UK's longest-running drama series 'Coronation Street', sought out Bill Podmore, a successful producer of comedy programmes, to lighten the content of their flagging serial:

> 'Coronation Street' appeared to be limping along on a diet of heavy social comment or flighty romance, and everyone seemed to agree with my initial diagnosis that the show was suffering from a lack of laughter and fun. [23]

Notwithstanding this particular mid 1970s concern, the 1980s and 1990s have seen both an explosion in twice-weekly television drama series and a continuance of their role as backdrops for serious social comment. Such drama series are now rivalled only by popular music and television advertising in their global impact. Individuals and families now interact with the characters in soap operas as they would with relatives and friends. They attend their weddings and their funerals, they endure anger and suffer disappointment with them, they cry and laugh with them. They also retain the information embedded in these dramas in a far more tenacious way than they would with a book or more formal presentations.

In Brazil the steamy 'Body and Soul' series was screened by TV Globo during 1992 and 1993 six days a week just after the main evening news at 8 o'clock. This 'novela' attracted a dedicated audience of 50 million viewers, who accepted its improbable plots and bizarre situations as if they were the faithful yardsticks of normality. In December 1992 one of its leading actresses was murdered, allegedly by her male co-star. After the discovery of her body on a piece of waste ground close to the studio, everyone – police, audience, cast, the accused actor and his pregnant wife – became embroiled in a drama that for many of the viewers became just an extension of the nightly fiction, and subsequent episodes included a number of thinly veiled calls for justice.

Obsessed as we are with the output of the mainly North American and western European media networks, it is chastening to remember that there are major media developments, addressing large audiences and using the most modern technologies, going on all over the world. This is particularly true in India, Asia, South America and the newly free eastern European countries, where unlearning censorship and control is just one of the many challenges facing programme makers and information providers. The producers of 'Body and Soul', TV Globo, with 30 years of broadcasting behind them and with 50–55 million viewers every day, is typical of a non-western operation which is a major media player by any standards, ranking as the fourth largest commercial television network in the world. Operating in the absence of any strong tradition of public service broadcasting, with politicians using broadcasting licences as a sort of high-denomination currency and with little or no regulation of advertising standards, TV Globo has grown to produce 80 per cent of all Brazil's programming. It now employs over 15 000 people and has made its owner, Roberto Marinho, one of the most powerful men in Brazil. Not averse to doctoring news and avoiding the reportage of dissent, TV Globo has quietly sought out comfortable arrangements with every Brazilian government of whatever complexion. It survived the military dictatorships of the 1960s and 1970s by always seeking an accommodation and never using its power to threaten them, and from 1964 onwards the military regimes in Brazil spent over US$14 billion extending and integrating modern telecommunications across the country.

Whatever the original reasons for this investment, it completely changed the nature of life in Brazil. It offered a conduit for developing a national identity where previously, due to the size and nature of the terrain, there had been only regional and parochial perspectives. These communications links also opened up new opportunities for the dissemination of commercial entertainment to a massive population of 100 million viewers. TV Globo, quick to see the possibilities, soon established itself on a fast track of programme and broadcast development. Since 1966, when it was the only television station to cover the extensive flooding in Brazil live, TV Globo has gone from strength to strength, achieving a near monopoly of Brazilian air time. Its major contribution to Brazilian life and culture is via its thrice-nightly six-days-a-week 'novelas', one subdued and dull at 6 p.m., one slightly more lively at 7 p.m. and the most elaborate offerings, 'Stone Jungle', 'Gabriella', 'Dancing Days', 'Belly for Rent' and 'Body and Soul', at 8 p.m. [24]. 'Gabriella' is said to have achieved the almost impossible statistic of having 100 per cent of Brazil's television sets tuned to it during one particular episode. Only the erotic 'Pantanal', put out by its much smaller competitor TV Manchete, has ever challenged Globo's predominance for novela viewing figures. Globo's highly successful formula is to make 12 episodes of each novela before transmitting the first one and then to take viewers' reactions on board in the construction of the episodes due to follow. The novelas are always steamy romances and intrigues, usually set within affluent consumer lifestyles. They are so successful that Brazilian politicians strive to be included, in the briefest of cameo roles, US pop songs provide the sound tracks and consumer products are shamelessly plugged by all of the characters. Many Brazilian commentators complain that TV Globo is engaged in a grotesque manipulation of the population, that the novela seriously distorts the reality of poverty, sedates the viewers against political and social realities and reinforces stereotypical images of Latin men. There can be no doubt, in a country where the gap between rich and poor is one of the biggest in the world, that much of this is true. But, as elsewhere, people yearn for escape, even for just a few hours, into a world where their daily realities do not exist. While at other times and in other moods they might seek out something more serious or more politically aware, there are clearly times when the novela serves them as much as they serve it.

As if to remind us that we still control the knobs that turn the media on and off, Heilman [25] wound up his introduction to a 15-page *Economist* survey on how interactive television might change the world by remembering an incident from a 1993 episode of the popular US weekly TV show 'Cheers':

. . . a beer-bellied character named Norm was awestruck by a bank of big-screen satellite-linked televisions on the wall of a Boston bar. 'Well, Normie,' said his friend Cliff, 'this is the information age. We can get up-to-the-minute stock prices, medical breakthroughs, political upheavals from all around the world. Of course we'd have to turn off the cartoons first.'

Less excitable than the Brazilians, but no less drawn by the seduction of visual stories, the British during 1992 also enthusiastically embraced a new kind of media construction. Among the regular debates and discussions about prices, the infidelities of politicians and royals, Europe, privatization and the plight of the Bosnian Muslims, there emerged the intriguing story of two lovers. Alexandra and Matthew had spent no more than 40 seconds on the television screen at any one time, and those interspersed between what the television companies thought was the main event. In 11 40-second television commercials to promote Nestlé's 'Gold Blend' coffee, just 7.3 minutes in total, they had built up a following of millions, all desperate to see how their tentative early contact would develop. In order to put some flesh on the bones of these brief but tantalizing glimpses of love over the coffee cups, Corgi books distributed 150 000 copies of *Love Over Gold* by Susannah James to British bookshops during one week in February 1993 [26], while a concurrent campaign of excerpts from the key moments of the original advertisements was run during prime-time TV. Total sales of *Love Over Gold* reached 178 196 at the end of 1993, placing it 49th in *The Guardian*'s 100 'fastsellers' list. We are all familiar with the film of the book, or the play of the book, or even the book of the film. The book of the television advertisement is obviously going to be the new literary genre of the 1990s. The information transfer in the coffee story was skilfully arranged to be brief, i.e. undemanding, incorporating strong human emotions (love) and, in true Dickensian style, it always left the audience wondering what would happen next. The cliffhanger ending has always been a key component of the television soap opera, but recently, in a gesture that confirms the power of such endings in a violent and complex world, the BBC made an announcement about the outcome of a child-kidnapping incident, set in its popular 'Eastenders' series, prior to the transmission of the episode where the child's fate would be disclosed. The kidnap episode had been transmitted during the week in which the funeral of a murdered two-year-old boy, kidnapped from a shopping centre in Liverpool, was to take place and the BBC wanted to confirm that, unlike the real kidnap, the fictional incident ended happily.

Undemanding, emotional, unfinished, these are obviously important ingredients in getting messages about lifestyles and behaviour across to mass audiences in the 1990s. The undemanding element

confirms that, despite 100 years or so of mandatory secondary education in the UK, to successfully get the attention of a large number of
people the content still has to be brief, easy to assimilate and easy to
digest. Slogans and short stories look likely to dominate the successful
information and entertainment currencies of the future. To these
ingredients we should, of course, add humour.

During the time that I was working on this chapter the long-running
weekly US television serial 'Cheers', referred to above, was transmitted
for the last time in the US. This last episode attracted 70 million
viewers, the kind of figure normally reserved for moon-landings and
the Superbowl in the US. Despite almost being closed down by NBC
in 1982, due to poor initial audience response, 'Cheers' went on to
occupy 274 episodes of prime-time TV for over ten years. In these days
of even speedier assessment of audience response it would more than
likely have been closed down after as few as five or six episodes if it did
not achieve what advertisers regarded as a sufficient audience rating
within that time. 'Cheers' had good writers, good plots, lots of humour
and fine actors. The characters convince because they seem to have no
idea that what they are saying and doing is amusing: 'They were just
making obtuse, panic stricken, bewildered attempts to come to terms
with the world and their miserable lot within it' [27]. Their humour
also grew out of the absurdities of human behaviour, particularly seeking or avoiding relationships. It also exploited the fun to be had from
familiarity, the knowing that is the key ingredient of comradeship and
the unusual levels of tolerance that comradeship often gives birth to.
These brief extracts of lives leaked out over a fictional bar in Boston
reinforced what many US males would regard as the 'American way',
and the 'Cheers' bar, as if to confirm its place as a national icon, has
now been erected as a permanent display at the Smithsonian Institute
in Washington DC.

Situation comedy might not be high on our list of vehicles for hard
information, but the social solidarity and bonding that humour
encourages can, and often does, package within it hard information
that might be less acceptable in any other form. Current examples of
issues covered in situation comedy programmes in the UK include
unemployment, moonlighting, racism, issues affecting single-parent
families, tax avoidance, medical problems, coping in old age, public
service cutbacks and class rivalry.

The medium may be different but there are many precedents for the
conscious application of 'infotainment'. Dickens and others used the
popularity of penny magazines and serialized stories, often peppered
with some very dry humour, to draw attention to the plight of those
oppressed by Victorian poverty and injustice. A later master propa-
gandist, Dr Goebbels, sought to convey his messages of the 'new

order' in Germany via films made primarily for entertainment. Goebbels rarely ever sought to change the German view about anything, his aim was to reinforce existing views and beliefs in an entertaining way.

Media habits, lifestyles and culture

For many people, however, the written word still represents the single most important facilitator of cultural continuance. Indeed, some would argue that this is the most important key to the preservation of western culture. Our classical Eurocentric heritage is increasingly seen as needing protection from the waves of mediocrity posing as enlightened multiculturalism. These threats are nearly always perceived in association with changes in the way that information is put together and made available for consumption. For those of us in 'electro-cultures', the range of information media available and under development, covering everything from geometry to democracy, is almost a matter of daily astonishment. Printed information is now just one of many options competing for our attention, among which television is currently the most powerful and popular. During July 1993 the UK-based Henley Centre for Forecasting published *Media Futures*, a report suggesting that many people in the UK were turning away from television. Based primarily on interviews with 1500 people, *Media Futures* claimed that people are watching less TV and getting less satisfaction from what they see. It went on to note that television is becoming the refuge of an underclass made up predominantly of the poor and the old, and that the more intelligent, younger and better-off UK citizens were as likely to get their information and entertainment from newspapers, magazines and radio as television. This trend has been known since the late 1960s, when accurate statistics on viewing figures became available. However, the continuing fall in newspaper circulation and readership, particularly among the young, a decline that can also be traced back to the late 1960s, and a 25 per cent increase in television advertising over the same period, makes these suggested trends difficult to reconcile [28]. Noting down what viewers and advertisers say they do rather than monitoring what they actually do is a notoriously unsatisfactory way of gaining reliable information about behaviour, and reports of the imminent death of television should be regarded as greatly exaggerated. Television has always suffered from a deep social schizophrenia in the UK, assigned enormous power and influence on the one hand and dismissed as a lower form of life on the other. Those who see themselves as discerning and discriminating viewers often have difficulty in believing that any one else can share the same characteristics, particularly the young, the old and the poor. This is not new. Dunkley [29], in responding to the Henley Centre report, remembered the habit of the television-owning intelligentsia of the 1950s and 1960s, of pretending never to watch television, as the 'au pair syndrome': 'We only have a set to help the au pair with her English'. It ought to be surprising that this kind of sham and snobbery should still continue. It says a great deal about the lack of underlying social change in Britain that it does, and that we are still not surprised by it:

> . . . doctors and businessmen often have jobs which keep them out late, and compared with nurses or centre lathe turners they are better able to afford seats at the opera or dinner in a restaurant. The fact remains that though they may watch less they still watch a lot – and experience suggests that they are ashamed of this. When like so many they switch on to watch the 6 o'clock news and then stay for 'Top of the Pops', they blame television for its triviality rather than themselves for lack of will power or discrimination. [29]

Moore [30], in a robust 'what is good about television is special to it' piece in *The Guardian*, also chipped away at this peculiarly British mix of patronage and self-denial:

> Like David Bowie in the film 'The Man Who Fell To Earth', these poor things sit mesmerized in front of a bank of screens, zapping mindlessly from one channel to another, lost in the great undertow of television time. The model here is one of addiction: they will want more and more.
>
> The Henley Centre's research proves that model incorrect, although it points to a widening gap between those rich enough to choose from a variety of leisure pursuits and those who watch television mainly because they cannot afford to do anything else. You can bet any money you like that those who talk about TV's declining standards are those who do not watch very much. Indeed their cultural capital comes from an innate distaste for what is actually one of the most democratic media available.

A tremendous amount of information is now conveyed in ways that seem alien to the paper-based worlds of academe and the professions. As custodians of a higher culture they continue to regard the old quality control of 'refereeing' to be a fundamental prerequisite of approval and validation. That 13 million people can hear an accurate account of the effect of contracting HIV via a popular television programme without the prior approval of a medical panel, while fewer than 5000 may read about it in a serious monograph, is typical of the shift in information penetration that has taken place during the latter part of the 20th century.

The issue of the quality of information is growing ever more complex, and to talk of quality in simple media-dependency terms is to ignore both the depth and the pervasiveness of information quality in media of every kind. Paradoxically, the media campaign to prevent the imposition of VAT on newspapers, magazines and books in the UK during the run-up to the Chancellor's budget in November 1993 seemed to re-emphasize the great media divide. Articulated as a 'tax on knowledge, learning and education', it was really a campaign against the taxation of paper as a medium for storing and collecting knowledge. An advertisement in the *Amateur Photographer* magazine during November 1993, sponsored by the Periodical Publishers Association, read:

> A tax on newspapers would after all, represent a tax on information and the right to know. And a tax on books, magazines and periodicals would mean a tax on education. . . . It can only have a detrimental effect on our and our children's education.

An encyclopaedia sold on CD-ROM is subject to VAT but the paper version is not. The book component of a language learning pack is exempt from VAT, while the audio tape or video cassette that comes with it is rated at the standard 17.5 per cent. Charles Dickens' *Little Dorrit* is exempt as long as it is restricted to paper, but the video of Christine Edzard's glorious film of it is taxed at the standard rate. Such anomalies and contradictions seem doomed to continue as long as 'knowledge and learning' are seen to be derived from the medium of delivery rather than the nature and content of the information itself.

Unlike their more pious supporters, the publishers of print media have never been embarrassed by their growing role as part of the entertainment business. Romance novels made up 46 per cent of all mass market paperbacks sold in the US in 1991, accounting for some $750 million in retail sales [31], while pulp fiction has always been a mainstay of the UK publishing industry. Margolis [32], in a timely piece in the Sunday Times at the end of 1993, began to pull the beards of some of Britain's ostensibly quality publishers. Quoting some interesting examples of recent works from 'reputable' publishing houses such as Bloomsbury, Macmillan, Century and Sidgwick and Jackson, he notes:

> . . . unfortunately, wacky or contentious books are nowadays no longer the province of small or fringe publishers. Indeed, look at bookshop non-fiction shelves with a good, sceptical eye, and you may well conclude that the standards required by even the most reputable publishers today are approaching that of the tabloid press. Many of these books are probably true as far as the authors are concerned; the difficulty comes with accepting that the publishers believe in them, and are not just exploiting their companies' highbrow image for profit.

With the doyen of literary publishers, Faber, linking hands with a television gameshow via the 'Win a Lifetime of Travel' promotion, and cheerfully joining with ITV to publish *The Hypnotic World of Paul McKenna*, from a televsion series, the sight of publishers living off their past reputations for the credibility and validation of their current material, looks likely to be a common one.

Despite the obvious mix of information quality in all media, the confusion between 'format' and 'value' still continues. Van Peer [33] wrestled with some of these issues in 1988:

> One may add to the previous considerations the matter of quality. Most, if not all, European cultures distinguish between 'high' and 'low' products of culture, and use similar criteria to this end. Thus a contrast is created between, on the one hand, cultural products which are valued as 'high', 'artistic', 'original', 'classic' or 'canonical', whereas other products are labelled 'low', 'trivial', 'stereotypical', 'pulp' or 'popular'. It also tends to be assumed in this cultural practice that 'low' forms emerge more or less spontaneously and hardly need the support of other bodies in society. Simultaneously, the 'high' forms are usually viewed as dependent on, or in need of, extra incentives from local or national authorities or from some kind of patronage.

The degree to which we serendipitously acquire information from 'popular' entertainment moments is an issue which needs more research. I am personally confident that entertainment is a seriously underestimated source of information acquisition. So many valuable information moments have accrued to me and others I know, all from time that we would describe as primarily spent in entertainment, that I cannot believe it to be exceptional. What is undeniable is that television now carries much of this information. Though perhaps not central to their schedules, most commercial television companies have always given over a portion of their air time to news, documentaries and in-depth reports on contemporary or historical events. Indeed, some governments would only give them licences to transmit after they had pledged a certain minimum percentage of this kind of programming. The rise in the output of consumer-choice offerings such as travel, fashion, automobile and health and diet programmes has added a further information dimension by feeding on a consumer culture that commercial television cannot help being a part of. There may be less hard information on television than appears annually in print, but what there is is often as well researched, as accurate and, not least, more likely to be retained by much larger audiences.

It is difficult to correlate the impact of two forms of media, one of which measures its output in hours and its audience in millions, the other by the total packages sold numbered in hundreds or thousands. Most commercial television providers would not, however, claim to be big on information provision, although some, like the CNN news channel, offer what can only be described as a purely information service. The content, timing and balance of television ebb and flow faster than print media, and the advance publication of television schedules often represents more the kind of programming that was available rather than the result of careful planning. In a debate on independent television programming in September 1993, Marcus Plantin, Director of the Independent Television Network Centre in the UK, noted:

> . . . that he would be vastly increasing the amount of peak-time factual programming in the coming months. This was partly in response to popular demand and partly because ITV had been unable to find sufficient high-quality comedy programmes. [34]

Despite their involvement in some serious information and 'cultural' programming, commercial television companies would claim that government-funded or public-service television is the natural vehicle for such output. However, given the general move towards the deregulation of television services, fears are growing that such public-service missions may be jettisoned in order to save money and gain the audience ratings that some governments now demand before agreeing to continue funding. New market-driven political ideologies now require public-service television to demonstrate a market share which is at least as good as their commercial competitors' while holding the line with regard to peak-time news and current affairs programmes. The British government's repeated warnings that the BBC's royal charter may not be renewed when it comes up for scrutiny in 1996, unless it can cut its costs and show itself to be more responsive to audience concerns, is just one example of this. Indeed, the BBC's current task to achieve 'tabloid' ratings via 'broadsheet' programming looks increasingly like a modern-day labour of Hercules, designed to undermine and eventually humiliate one of the world's most respected providers of information.

In places where electricity is accessible or commonplace, major structural changes have taken place in the dissemination and acquisition of information, and the most significant issue arising out of this is the way people use their time. Many commentators fear that in future people might never get around to learning, or refining their ability to access printed forms of information, not because they lack the facility to become literate but because it no longer seems as necessary to acquire these skills as it once was.

The use of time, particularly by children and young people, is a key issue in contemporary debates about information quality. Still often focusing on modes of information presentation, current fears about the poor literacy rates among the young of western countries (see Chapter 2) are clearly founded on the way they now split their (unsupervized) time between written and non-written forms of information. All the signals suggest that less time is now being spent developing the skills to use printed information, despite their continuing centrality in education, business and commerce. Away from the classroom reading has clearly declined since the 1950s. However, recent evidence shows that reading for pleasure is by no means dead, but it is widely differentiated between boys and girls. More than half the girls and 37 per cent of the boys interviewed during 1991 and 1992 by the Exeter University Schools Health Education Unit [35] said that they read books for pleasure after school, generally ranking this as their fourth most popular out-of-class pursuit, after watching television or videos and playing computer games. The preponderance of solitary recreational pursuits among the 8–10-year-olds interviewed in this survey suggests that children are losing out on socializing and family conversation, and thus run the risk of missing important contributions from the traditional testing grounds of social skills development. With keyboard and screen-based entertainment occupying more and more of children's time away from school, many teachers fear that the coherence that written language has always given to information acquisition may become fractured, and this could harbour serious consequences for the continuation of culture as we know it:

> The transmission of cultural, scientific and technological knowledge is virtually dependent on sophisticated literacy skills. Although it may be presumed that the role of the new AV media in educational settings may also grow, it is inconceivable that they will take over the basic functions of PRINT in the near future. This is even less likely in another area where PRINT fulfils a major cultural function, i.e. that of theory and analysis, of rational argumentation and of criticism. The (written) discursive practices which have developed in European cultures since early modern times, not only in education, but similarly in the legal and religious, economic and scientific, medical and political institutions, are at the very heart of European culture, and as such form a basic precondition for participation in democratic structures and organizations. [33]

Information is now trickling out from various local education authorities and the National Foundation for Educational Research in the UK concerning the decline in literacy levels in British schools over the last decade. These trends are serious and should be taken seriously, but I do not believe that European culture or democracy is threatened by the tendency to enjoy using a variety of media. Brunelleschi, Michelangelo, Sir Christopher Wren and Ansel Adams all left us many rich gifts which could not have been written down. If time spent with keyboard and screens can lead to a loss of social skills, we should also remember that excessive absorption in the written word has always been a solitary affair, often prompting adult concern for the potential social alienation that might afflict young 'bookworms' who had little interest in play or conversation.

The huge archives of audiovisual material now available to us offers no shortage of the 'rational argumentation and criticism' that Van Peer attributes so exclusively to print. Sir Kenneth Clarke's 1969 television series 'Civilization' for the BBC probably represents one of the most formidable marriages of a popular medium with cultural issues and ideas more often reserved for a smaller audience. In his foreword to the ensuing book, Clarke was moved to note just how limiting print can be in presenting certain kinds of information:

> Going through these scripts and comparing them in mind with the actual programmes, I am miserably aware of how much has been lost. In almost every one of them the strongest impact depended on factors that could not be conveyed in words. To take examples from one programme only, 'The Fallacies of Hope': the sound of the Marseillaise and the prisoners' chorus from 'Fidelio', and the marvellous photography of Rodin's Burghers of Calais: all these said what I wanted to say about the whole subject with a force and vividness which could never have been achieved by the printed page. I cannot distinguish between thought and feeling, and I am convinced that a combination of words and music, colour and movement can extend human experience in a way that words alone cannot do. For this reason I believe in television as a medium, and was prepared to give up two years' writing to see what could be done with it. Thanks to skilful and imaginative directors and an expert camera crew, I believe that certain moments in the film were genuinely moving and enlightening. They are lost in a book. [36]

The critical and popular welcome given to the repeat showing of this series by the BBC during the autumn and winter of 1993, 24 years after its original release and ten years after the death of its creator and presenter, stands as a testament to how audiovisual information can become both 'classical' and 'canonical'.

What is clear is that the contemporary imperative for adults to acquire information is restless and unforgiving. In developed economies we are constantly reminded that to understand something or to get the best results from some potential action or other, we will almost certainly need to arm ourselves with further and better particulars before proceeding. Simultaneous with these expectations our opportunity to digest and reflect on the information that we acquire suffers as our time is constrained by a real or imagined urgency to assimilate it. This attracts us to media that will give us quick digests, abstracts and extracts, the gist but rarely the context. Under these pressures we nearly always leave the information table unsatisfied, hungry for more but lacking the time or the energy to fill in the gaps. In looking at the media options available we should look carefully at the roles they play and the expectations they satisfy. We should not expect the qualities of a learned monograph from television, and to invest it with expectations that it is not very good at satisfying will always disappoint. Every medium eventually gives up its novel cultural dominance to become just one choice among many, and we can expect the options to multiply, the devices to get smaller and more portable, and information access points, for those that can afford them, to get even more diverse.

However, it is my guess that television, in one form or another, will retain a strong cultural dominance in the foreseeable future. A number of 'interactive' television experiments are underway in the US and the UK which will eventually confirm whether or not such services are what viewers really want, and whether a 'one-box' solution for information and entertainment offers the kind of services and facilities that people are happy to pay for. The 20th century has seen the development of the home as a place where we expect to experience music, news, entertainment, information and discussion, all accessed via a growing range of electronic devices. We no longer expect to have to go out to find these things. Most of us still go 'out' to work and come 'in' to play, our recreations now shared with smaller and smaller families, secure behind locked doors. At the end of the 19th century entertainment and relaxation were generally sought out of doors, or at least in another place:

> During the 20th century the conception of entertainment has changed from a number of activities interposed at the edges of the working day to a cluster of industries which attempts to provide for all the leisure time available. Entertainment was, for the great majority, a communal experience, something available for the most part outside the home. But at the end of the 20th century we can see how entertainment has gradually taken over the home and transformed its organization. [37]

There are signs that home-wired entertainment can sometimes get a bit claustrophobic. The emulation of situational reality that has been the hallmark of most postwar drama for instance, can make it look too familiar, too reminiscent of the confined spaces and pressures that its audiences occupy. In seeking diversion from the routines and the tensions of domestic life people may again feel the need to escape to another place:

> In these long recession years the home has also become the location of frustrated economic expectations . . . One might predict, therefore, that in coming decades a new generation will find a place for entertainment that assists escape from home into places less fraught with social and financial stress. [37]

The development of plush multiscreen cinema complexes in recent years has attracted more of us out of our homes to enjoy the spectacle of big-screen, special-effect productions. Cheaper air travel has carried us to destinations that we first discovered on small screens, and a veritable explosion of open-air 'live' museum developments has tempted us off the sofa for a hands-on trip down memory lane. The financial uncertainties still affecting the Disneyland complex in Paris, however, suggest that catering for a mass audience away from home (without sunshine at least) can still be a precarious business. Despite attracting over 17 million visitors over its first 18 months of operation, Disneyland, Paris lost £610 million in the year up to September 1993. The less gregarious attractions of the wired home still look good, safe and relatively cheap to investors, equipment manufacturers and software providers alike. Predictions of even more spectacular and diverse offerings in the pipeline, some of which are outlined in the next chapter, look set to keep us addicted to 'the box' for some time to come.

The advantages of more convenient forms of communication via the convergence of telecommunications and computer power – 'telematics' – may also begin to reverse the 'going out to work' habit. Teleworking, although confined to very small numbers at the moment, is growing in popularity with certain types of information-intensive businesses, notably software houses, and it clearly has the potential for expansion in a large number of other information-handling activities. This work currently seems to operate either at the higher, sophisticated added-value end of the market, e.g. computer programming, features writing, systems designing, translating and management consulting, or at the more repetitive clerical end, such as data input, but by the end of the century teleworking could begin to embrace many more people who had never imagined that they would work from home. Personal and domestic convenience, work access for the disabled, overcoming the disadvantage of distance and scatter in rural communities, reducing pollution in cities, retaining scarce skills, reducing congestion and travel times in crowded cities and towns, and not least reducing costs while increasing output, all of these factors could begin to reform our views on when and where we work. The impact of such developments on the current role of towns and cities, not least on the social and economic investments in their fabric, could be enormous: empty office buildings could mean empty pension funds! The problems of exploitation, emptiness, boredom, lack of social contact and confusion over where work ends and home life begins are also not insignificant. This is particularly true of exploitation, which has always been interpreted as 'opportunity' by the suppliers of even the most grotesque working arrangements. It is a generally accepted truism that all outworkers, be they working at looms in India or in front of screens in Indiana, have always been exploited, finding it impossible to represent themselves effectively via collective bargaining and enjoying little or no contractual protection.

As with all the economic opportunities embedded in the new computer-driven networks, teleworking has the potential to bring both liberation and bondage. Interestingly, the numerically most important of the potential beneficiaries of these remote work opportunities, the unemployed, are not in any position to engineer change, be it in teleworking or in any of the other potential effects of technology on work and work availability.

The long-term relationship between television and telephony is difficult to assess at this point in the convergence of their technologies via the microchip. Suffice it to say that the current role of the viewer as a largely passive receiver, switching between a limited number of channels on a dumb terminal is likely to change dramatically. When a similar receiver can interact fully with bandwidths that are plentiful and whose options can be numbered in thousands, the old limitations of channel choice will disappear and give way to new modes of decentralized audience empowerment.

It is envisaged that such personal formatting of reception will embrace an almost unlimited choice of educational, information and entertainment programmes drawn from libraries unrestricted by geographic or cultural boundaries. The restrictive power of central stations and transmitters will thus be surrendered to networks, whose intelligence can be controlled by the user. It is a vision of what the technology can do, rather than any certainty about how people will actually behave. There is always a high premium to pay for increased choice and yet it is a startling contemporary paradox that those who are able to afford such a rich variety of information and entertainment, piped directly to their homes via infinitely hospitable broadband cables or satellite links, seem to be seriously disinterested in signing up for it. While those who find the idea of being awash with 'infotainment' attractive are those least likely to be able to afford it. The men and women building the great media empires noted in the next chapter will no doubt be seeking to turn this paradox around.

Receptivity to information between cultures is increasing at an exciting or alarming rate, depending on your point of view. The upside of this is that different races can now understand more about each other as language barriers break down in favour of English; the downside is that, as language is the main conduit of cultural heritage and the key to distinctiveness, there will be less to fascinate and excite us because the richness of difference will be replaced by the poverty of sameness. A bland global conformity, created by marketing departments and advertising agencies, will be draped over a worldwide communications network beneath which cultural colours will all turn black and white. We will both surrender and suffocate.

Whether or not the worst fears of the cultural guardians are realized with regard to the impact of new media on future literacy levels, it is clear that children are increasingly becoming the main targets of the cultural cleansing of information that is the prerequisite for global appeal. They cannot help but be hypnotized by a fast-moving, highly visual street culture which often simulates only a narrow band of reality and leaves them full without room for further curiosity. In this world, attention span is at a premium. Retention and recall of anything earlier than a few minutes old is at best boring, and at worst unlooked-for hard work. Much commercial television aimed at younger viewers is skilfully organized to give brief spates of satisfaction, and is invariably linked with suggestions that create strong desires for consumer products. Merchandizing and tie-ins create a reiteration of fast lifestyle information that has become the sought-for reality of many children. The guardians of print as the home of literate information acquisition see the book being displaced by the cartoon and the soap opera, with inquisitiveness and curiosity being replaced by the mirage of complete satisfaction.

The anarchic 'Beavis and Butthead', two 14-year-old cartoon characters with foul mouths and equally foul minds, currently proving very popular with teenagers on both sides of the Atlantic, represent probably the lowest ebb in popular youth culture. Mimicked as trendy icons, Beavis and Butthead shoot down jumbo jets, drive down singing hippies, set their friends' hair alight, get involved in arson, petty theft, shoplifting, car theft, fraud and all kinds of cruelty to animals in a non-stop journey of menace and mockery. This house and hair-burning duo currently operate in the UK via MTV and Channel 4. Both networks have already been criticized for the mindless violence which provides the main platform for the programmes. No doubt some room will be found for them as phenomena worthy of sociological study, echoing the sentiments of *Time* magazine:

> They are not just any losers. They are specifically our losers, totems of an age of decline and non-achievement. [38]

Some commentators are sure to credit them with being the 'voice of a generation'. Parents and teachers motivated to offer antidotes to this slick and cruel culture face a tough time: the ubiquity of audiovisual sources of information, relentless peer pressure to join in, and the need to commit to lines of discourse which can only be comprehended or informed by regular access to certain sounds and images, are all too strong for them.

Consumption is now the dominant theme in the culture of all developed economies and multi-interest corporations now mix information with product promotion and consumption messages in ways which are getting harder and harder to disentangle. So 'correct' has the consumption habit become that governments and political parties, once famed for preaching thrift and good housekeeping, have begun to urge active consumption, including, if necessary, the taking up of credit to facilitate it. All the UK media regularly report information about the extent of domestic borrowing and monthly retail spending figures as a frontline news item. The consumption culture has also spawned great families of information sources specifically designed to help us differentiate between the multiplicity of products and services on offer. There is now so much to consume and we are so 'spoilt for choice' that this has become a major information industry in itself.

The discriminating consumer was not born in the 1980s, but the sophisticated information sources available to help consumers select or dismiss what is on offer definitely were. Fashion clothes, by their very nature doomed to a short life, now also carry strong informational messages embedded within brief, vivid symbols. The direct marketing of clothes is currently supported by lifestyle information networks among young people, embracing unstructured signals associated with pop music, video images, club lifestyles, fashion magazines and actual sporting events, to build up a global demand for a disposable product. Building on personality endorsement techniques modern sportsmen and women have become household names in the most unexpected places: a survey of schoolchildren in China recently discovered that, as far as they were concerned, the two greatest men in history were Zhou En Lai and the basketball star Michael Jordan [38]. Sports shoes (trainers or sneakers) seem to be a particularly potent form of fashion information, indeed potent enough, sadly, for some young people on the west coast of the US to kill for. The outer design of some of these shoes may be changed three or four times a year, the colours and motifs ranging over various environmental and futuristic themes. A pretty paradox will thus find teenagers in Bangkok and Mexico City, two of the world's most polluted cities, walking around in sports shoes carrying ecological and environmental symbols derived from the popularity of 'green' information in countries on the other side of the world.

The key point here is that the absorption of information about what the fashionable teenager is wearing is multifaceted and fast, using all the conduits that modern technology has at its disposal. Its success depends on the breakdown of culturally dependent information handling and processing among an age group hungry for novel impressions and from which the decision makers of the future will be drawn. Given the perceived need to continually expand markets for consumer goods, this kind of popular information pollenation will continue to support the marketing of globally standardized products carrying all sorts of powerful information. Pockets of cultural resistance will no doubt remain, but image makers all around the world will be doing their best to break them down.

Minamata and the rain forests

Since the 1950s the relentless urge for economic growth has required more and more access to information, to support research and development, to learn about potential markets, to understand (or avoid) regulatory conditions in different parts of the world and to ensure efficient and competitive production. Sometimes this invades the space of less developed cultures, often without a thought for the consequences. The destruction of the primeval rain forests of Malaysia and the Amazon Basin has been well documented, as has the deadly pollution emanating from factories in India, Japan, Taiwan, South Korea and many of the countries of eastern Europe. Information on the dangers of unbridled industrialization and the pollution that often accompanies it is abundantly available, but still it goes on. People still suffer great harm and their legal redress, if any, may take years to come: the 100 000 people who were poisoned during the 1950s, after eating fish affected by the mercury pumped into the sea at Minamata off Southern Japan by the Chisso Chemical firm, had to wait 40 years before a Tokyo court ruled that the Japanese government should be absolved from all responsibility in the affair.

It is ancient knowledge that mercury is poisonous if ingested, and that it is a particularly difficult poison to shift once it is established in the ecosystem. Indeed, we now know that it can linger in soil and water for over 100 years, and yet the gold-miners of the Amazon Basin, as well as contributing to deforestation by ruthlessly clearing away thousands of hectares of rain forest, also do their bit to help keep mercury poisoning up there as one of the world's most deadly killers. First they clear the forests in order to be able to force-pump the earth with water to break it up. They then separate out the gold from the resulting sludge using mercury, which binds with it to form an easily collectable amalgam. In order to retrieve the gold the miners, at considerable risk to themselves, burn off the mercury in the open air, where it becomes a deadly gas. Around the much-polluted Tapajos river small dredgers suck up alluvium from the river bed, which is then treated with mercury in the same way. Once in the water the mercury becomes methyl mercury, a concentrated poison that becomes even more concentrated as it moves up the food chain. It has been estimated that for every ton of gold extracted in this way two tons of mercury are discharged into the environment [39]. The information is known, the damage being done is known, but the gold equals GNP now and the damage it does comes later.

Sometimes, although we are aware of the physical damage, both to the environment and to the people in it, simultaneous losses from the store of human knowledge are often invisible. Despite its clearly 'belonging' to a particular community, the disappearance of a natural environment often takes away with it valuable information and knowledge that is a loss to the much wider world. The peasant farmers of South America, driven into open-field cash-crop mono-farming in the wake of deforestation, were once the masters of considerable ecological knowledge. Using age-old techniques of slashing and burning that allowed the forest to reseed and re-establish itself during long fallow periods, they exploited the natural cover and protection of a dense and seemingly inhospitable tropical environment. By a subtle mixture of carefully paced intervention and the nurture of natural growth, they developed a diverse multicrop harvest that sustained all their needs and produced surpluses for sale. By 'farming' the forest they cultivated a much wider range of shrubs, trees and plant life than can ever be grown in the poor soil of the open fields they now have to work in. The loss of the genetic resources themselves and the good 'eco-sense' that facilitated both human exploitation and forest succession is a clear example of the intimate relationship between information and environments and vice versa. We can of course store all the information about 'forest farming' in our electronic memories, so that when priorities change we will be able to avail ourselves of some clear descriptions of how it was once all done. But finding a man who knows how to farm a forest, whose eyes have seen the ripeness of its fruit and whose hands have handled the bushes, herbs and vines that have grown in it, that will be much more difficult.

In a related but slightly different context, the government of Malaysia seized the passport of Cecil Rajendra in July 1993. A British-trained barrister, Rajendra writes poems that focus on the environment and social issues, and is known particularly for his poetic condemnation of what he sees as indiscriminate logging in Malaysia. His passport was seized because the government felt that his persistent anti-logging message could damage the country's image overseas. Extensive logging in Sarawak (eastern Malaysia) continues to deplete one of the world's oldest tropical forests, and while neighbouring Thailand, the Philippines and Sabah, all once covered by vast forests, have now stopped exporting timber, Sarawak has yet to weigh the price of GNP now against ecological disaster later. The existence of accurate information about the terminal and fatal outcomes that stem from certain consequences has never prevented governments and corporations carrying on as if it did not exist, or of silencing those who might find too big an audience for it.

Despite the current proliferation of information systems and models, now often capable of giving 'expert' advice, the time-worn but profitable imperatives of convenience, ownership and gain still override the antisocial or fatal outcomes that they might predict.

As important as it is, information has never been power. If it was, we would not have to keep asking why so many powerful people retain their power while being so poorly informed, and why so many well informed people remain powerless. In these days of global influence and reach, poorly informed power will always be a match for brilliantly informed powerlessness. Being casual in elevating information to any status that is divorced from the realpolitik required to mobilize it effectively, serves only to undermine its influence when it is so allied.

The data on the sabre-toothed tiger (see Chapter 2) have come a long way. Many information moments are just as critical in the mid 1990s as they would have been during the middle Pleistocene period; the big difference is that there are now so many more of them. So many, in fact, that we are rarely aware of them as discrete events any more, and for most of us they become a frantic weave of mental accumulation that we would have difficulty recalling and retelling after just a few hours. Our retention periods fill up too quickly with too much. A primitive tribesman's acquisition and processing journey has not been any less complex than ours. Often operating in a harsh and unforgiving environment, he will have to assimilate and interpret the critical information to fuel basic survival. While not trivialized by information overload, derived from endless messages about consumption, it will often be derived from environmental phenomena over which he will have little control. The tribesman will also make something of telling the story of his day, as part of a bonding process between family and friends, summing up and sharing the kind of information and experiences that make a day worth having and the next day worth preparing for. Whatever this kind of bonding end-of-the-day exchange is really worth, those of us rushing home in crowded towns and cities most probably lost the joys and benefits of it a long time ago.

In the developed world we are currently faced with shifts in the distributive forms of the mass media, and hence the information that we gain access to, that call into question the exclusive role of the intellectual in the creation of cultural products. While welcoming the wider range of cultural choices now available, we do not have to belong to an elitist club of cultural guardianship to declare ourselves sensitive to some of the dangers. In so far as independent thinkers ever had the power to promote wisdoms at variance to those held by the current orthodoxies, it was through the institutions of an understandable nation state. The global nature of multimedia corporate operations is beginning to blur the landscape where intellectuals once operated, marginalizing their forums and privatizing some of the information that was their lifeblood. The critical discourse that once illuminated issues, exposed humbug and highlighted new imbalances in the exercise of power, is trickling away as nations respond to global imperatives which seek peace and stability at all costs. Citizens, once involved as actors in a vibrant and public national polity, have also been seduced. Lodged more and more in private rather than public worlds, they face becoming units of consumption rather than the lifeblood of a democracy. Within such changes hard-won community priorities can come to seem less important and may be easily surrendered in favour of more immediate, if trivial, private conveniences. In such private worlds we may also lose that sense of community wherein the information which fuels liberty and oils the limbs of dissent also lies. By envisaging a world of home-wired information, we may be feeding new depths of isolation where families have little connection with each other, other than by the common use of similar services. The political association and social kinship that has always been the prerequisite for articulating the common demands required to satisfy common needs, will find little to nurture it in this new privatized social life. Such conditions may lull people into a somnambulance where they will discover too late their loss of authoritative citizenship. Their participation will increasingly be limited to that expected from the members of a market, a place where the rights of consumers always have more protection than the rights of citizens.

The new technologies of information processing and communication can offer us both optimistic and pessimistic scenarios. They can increase the scope for entertainment and diversion, individual choice and rational decision making, but a lot of the information is not freely available, nor is it designed to help us to influence events. Indeed we face the prospect of an increasing privatization of many different forms of information. Paradoxically the commercial organizations that now produce most of the information that we consume also have a primary interest in keeping a lot of it secret to protect their commercial advantage. Their secondary interest is to build on their exclusive information holdings to produce commodities for sale. Some of the information that was once available to the public as of right, may in future only be available at a price, while information for which there is no perceived market will not be produced. The ongoing digitization of information that was once available only in books will also begin to restrict access, with only those who can afford it enjoying access to it. The cost of all the electronic components will of course decrease over time and, as we will see in the next chapter, one aim of the multi-national media combine of the future will be to own as many of the different information packages as possible, so that they can feed them into one another.

The challenge for us has to be to ensure the survival of cultural and ideological diversity. Technology is not destiny, it is not awesome, it is not God. The quality and quantity of the information that it carries are still determined by humans in engagement with their peers. If we use our energies to turn it in on ourselves, if we are satisfied to use our technological ingenuity for paltry pleasures, if we avoid struggle and choose to manufacture the consent that nurtures Noam Chomsky's 'necessary illusions', it will be because we are whispering when we should be shouting, indolent when we should be energetic and resigned when we should be angry.

If information is to be the lifeblood of a new order and facilitate a new mosaic of wealth and cultural fulfilment, it will be because it has been forged by humans harnessing machines, not the other way around. Our mission must be to seek engagement in this process at every level, so that we can confidently chart, without addiction to exclusive forms of media and without limiting ourselves to narrow definitions of excellence, the differences between information solely designed to support consumption, lifestyle and fashion and that which truly facilitates our search for richer domains of human existence. One critical part of this engagement must be an active reaffirmation of our hospitality to the positive role that robust investigation and debate play in the development of all cultures, and that, whatever information may be put out to the contrary, no community claiming to embrace a whole way of life can be without its dimensions of struggle and confrontation between opposing ways of life.

References

1. Cartwright, J. (1993) Culture. *The Independent Magazine*, 3 July

2. Nicholson-Lord, D. (1993) Into post-Neolithic Nepal. *The Independent on Sunday*, 1 August

3. Crystal, D. (1987) *The Cambridge Encyclopedia of Language*. Cambridge: Cambridge University Press, p. 287

4. Lee, L. (1959) *Cider With Rosie*. London: Hogarth Press

5. Diener, R. A. V. (1991) Cultural dissolution, a societal information disaster: the case of the Yir Yoront in Australia. In *Great Information Disasters*, ed. F. W. Horton and D. Lewis. London: Aslib

6. Chomsky, N. (1993) *Year 501: The Conquest Continues*. London: Verso

7. Strathern, M. (1993) Society in drag. *The Times Higher Education Supplement*, 2 April

8. Snowden, R. and Snowden, E. (1993) *The Gift of a Child*. Exeter: University of Exeter Press

9. Cortazzi, H. (1990) *The Japanese Achievement*. London: Sidgwick and Jackson

10. Hunter, J. E. (1989) *The Emergence of Modern Japan: An Introductory History Since 1853*. London: Longman

11. Katz, I. (1992) Elton and assembled ghosts put boot into Pepsi. *The Guardian*, 7 February

12. Nelkin, D. (1993) Against the tide of technology. *The Times Higher Education Supplement*, 23 July

13. Bowring, P. (1993) Singapore takes stand over secrets. *The Guardian*, 25 October

14. *The Guardian*, 4 October 1988

15. *The Guardian*, 3 November 1988

16. Norton-Taylor, R. (1993) Spymasters come under the spotlight. *The Guardian*, 2 October

17. Harper, K. (1993) Tax secrets 'open to abuse after sell-off'. *The Guardian*, 6 September

18. Elliot, L. and Kelly, R. (1994) Unemployment and figures of speech. *The Guardian*, 10 January

19. Line, M. (1990) Knowledge is power, and power is dangerous: reflections on the availability of knowledge and information in Britain today. Presidential Address, *Library Association Record*, **92**(11)

20. *The Guardian*, 7 February 1992

21. Profile: Luciano Benetton, salesman extraordinary. *The Independent*, 4 April 1992

22. Marshall, A. (1993) Mousetricht explains the European idea to baffled Bambini. *The Independent*, 27 March

23. Podmore, B. and Reece, P. (1990) *Coronation Street: The Inside Story*. London: Macdonald and Co

24. Channel 4, 'Brazil: Beyond Citizen Kane, TV Globo', Monday 10 May 1993

25. Heilmann, J. *The Economist*, 12 February 1994

26. Perrick, P. (1993) Book review *Instant Satisfaction*. *Sunday Times*, 14 February

27. Hornby, N. (1993) Three tears for 'Cheers'. *The Guardian*, 7 June

28. Lind, H. (1993) Long view and short sight. *The Guardian*, 9 August

29. Dunkley, C. (1993) Of course we never watch it . . . *Financial Times*, 28 July

30. Moore, S. (1993) TV or not TV. *The Guardian*, 30 July

31.   *The Bookseller*, 21 May 1993

32.   Margolis, J. (1993) Truth or dare. *Sunday Times*, 19 December

33.   van Peer, W. (1988) Reading, culture and modern mass media. *Journal of Information Science*, **14**, 305–309

34.   Frean, A. (1993) BBC to run repeats throughout year but only by demand. *The Times*, 18 September

35.   *Very Young People in 1991/92*, a report by the Schools Health Education Unit, Exeter University, 22 November 1993

36.   Clark, K. (1969) *Civilization: A Personal View*. London: BBC and John Murray

37.   Smith, A. (1993) The electronic circuits: the homely roots of escapism. *The Economist*, 11 September

38.   Tran, M. (1993) Sony stands by Jackson as singer is sighted in France. *The Guardian*, 18 November

39.   Pettifer, J. The price of gold. BBC 2, 'Assignment', Tuesday 19 October 1993

40.   Not yet out of the woods. *The Economist*, 16 October 1993

Chapter 5

Information concentration: more or less?

If the information associated with consumption is crowding out the disposable time available to access other kinds of information, the challenge of the new media moguls is to ensure that they claim as much as they can of whatever is left. In complex economies the media are now part of a relentlessly unfolding paradox, that is, that people now need more information to help them understand their world and multiple forms of entertainment to help them escape it. However, if they are employed they have less and less time to stop and discover it, and if they are unemployed they have all the time in the world but no money. The inexorable drive of big media combines to get bigger is all part of claiming access to the disposable time of the employed. They exercize this claim by promising diversity, which requires that they collect together as many ingredients of the information and entertainment chain as they can under one umbrella. The sheer size of the investment now necessary to offer even the limited diversity that we have become accustomed to, would seem to rule out any kind of cottage-industry approach. Driven by the ambitions of individuals like Silvio Berlusconi, Rupert Murdoch, Ted Turner, Conrad Black and Sumner Redstone (Viacom), and the less personality-conscious corporations such as Time Warner, Sony, Pearson, Bertelsmann, Matsushita and Reed Elsevier, the drive to integrate every form of informational package within one family has continued apace. 1993 was a particularly busy year on this front. It may be that the stage was being set for the even greater changes to come, but nonetheless I would suggest that 1993 will come to be seen as a year that saw the beginnings of a new world order in media integration. It was certainly a year that saw telephone companies flexing their cash-rich muscles to gain a slice of programming capacity wherever and whenever they could find it.

In January 1993, Reed announced its merger with the Dutch-based Elsevier. In August a US Federal court ruled that Bell Atlantic, one of several US regional phone companies, could offer video services in Alexandria, Virginia. This signalled the crumbling of a traditional barrier to supplying video services which will have a profound impact on the future of US cable and telephone operations, as well as sending out powerful signals to other media regulators all over the world. In September Rupert Murdoch made a key statement outlining News Corporation's new global strategy during a major speech in London. In October Bell Atlantic announced its proposed merger with the cable operator TCI. Although this deal eventually collapsed in early 1994, the powerful forces behind the original idea are still at work. Southwest Bell paid US$650 million for two cable systems in Washington DC, and US$1.6 billion for 40 per cent of Cox Enterprises' cable operations. In November the British government announced some relaxing of the conditions governing mergers between the 14 regional ITV companies, prompting an instant spate of courtship dances.

During the last four months of the year the battle between Viacom and QVC for the ownership of Paramount Communications raged on until it was finally settled in February 1994. These, and many other moves like them, began to take the now well-established process of 'vertical integration' to new heights. Like the great dash to forge mergers and alliances that deregulation is prompting among the world's airlines, the key players in the media business want marriage, particularly that part of the marriage vow that emphasizes 'to the exclusion of all others'. Telephone companies, publishers, movie studios, cable operators, computer manufacturers and television companies are all now jostling to see who fits, who is available and, just as importantly, who might be denied to another suitor. They are seeking to secure control of all the components of creating, owning, distributing and recycling information; they want ownership of every genre and every medium. They want them exclusively and they are willing to pay way over the market price to get them. Below are some typical examples of this phenomenon. Although this is a snapshot rather than a complete review, it is intended to give a flavour of what is happening now and what is likely to happen in the future.

Reed Elsevier

The statistics of the Reed Elsevier group give some idea of what it means to be even a modest player in this business. Reed and Elsevier merged in January 1993. By mid 1993 the market capital of the new group stood at around £6.8 billion (Reed £3.7bn and Elsevier

£3.1bn). Pretax profits for the same year, the first year of trading as a group, were 19 per cent up on 1992 at £518 million, making it the most profitable publisher in the world. Why should two successful companies want to join together when the lesson to be learnt from the big media mergers of the 1980s was that size was no substitute for strategy? Reed, with interests in business and professional publishing, travel information and consumer magazines (including Britain's *TV Times*), papermaking, printing and packaging, secures around 40 per cent of its sales income from advertising. Tough times in recession-hit north American and British markets have seen Reed's advertising revenues decline. The Dutch-based Elsevier, on the other hand, the world's largest publisher of scientific journals, secures most of its income in the form of high-margin journal subscriptions (including those it bought when it acquired Robert Maxwell's Pergamon Press in 1991), giving them an annual profit margin of around 20 per cent. These almost recession-proof profits (constant price-hikes, mainly institutional buyers and hardly any author costs) would help insulate Reed during cyclical ups and downs and also give it the kind of footprint in continental Europe that it had always wanted. In return Elsevier would be able to plug itself into a wider world of publishing, especially the world 'at the top of the information pyramid'. It also gets to share Reed's experience in CD-ROM and other new publishing technologies [1].

As with any merger the combined group also expects to make 'rationalization' savings of around £20 million a year when its restructuring is completed. It is interesting to note that during 1993 Reed Elsevier's sales, excluding currency factors, grew by only 2 per cent. Most of the company's profit growth came from within, via improved systems, increased use of new technology and strenuous and ongoing efforts to contain costs:

> It is scarcely a secret, however, that the powerhouse of future growth will come from takeovers: the merged group has enormous fire-power and its business palette is broad enough for almost the entire media world to be its oyster. [2]

The gathering in of 'the entire media world' could look understandably foreboding to those already worried about the current levels of media concentration, but the company spent more than £400 million on acquisitions during 1993. Its largest purchase was the *Official Airline Guides* for some £277 million, followed by the acquisition of a 40 per cent stake in the leading Italian legal publisher Giuffre and its sister company Mori in late 1993. Giuffre has a backlist of over 5000 book titles, and is strong in subjects like economics and political science as well as law. It publishes some 60 journals and, like some parts of its new partner, it is developing a strong presence in CD-ROM products.

The publisher of this book, Bowker-Saur, is just one of over 20 publishing imprints, most of them once independent publishers in their own right, that are now owned by Reed Elsevier. This kind of concentration within traditional publishing has been accelerating since the mid 1980s and is no longer regarded as a new phenomenon. Publishers also need bigger worlds to bustle in. Their home markets now represent much more of a base camp from which they sally forth to the bigger profits that lie in wait around the globe.

Other examples of imprint collecting include Random House, which now provides a home to over 20 imprints; Penguin and Longman, themselves part of the Pearson Group, own 13 and 10 imprints respectively, and HarperCollins, itself owned by Rupert Murdoch's News Corporation, has over 17 imprints.

Pearson

Among other things Pearson owns the *Financial Times* and Thames Television. It also owns Penguin and Longman, who in turn own Ladybird, Pitman and a number of other publishing imprints. Like Reed Elsevier, Pearson is also seeking a bigger share of the cake. Pearson have quite openly declared that their objective is to become a more tightly focused media and entertainment group concentrating on the creation and exploitation of intellectual property rights in a variety of packages [3]. In the search for a truly global presence such an objective requires a serious policy of acquisition for fulfilment, and Pearson have not done so well in this area, gaining something of a reputation as a company that starts well but finishes badly when it comes to completing deals. Having failed to tie the knot with Elsevier, not proceeding with its interest in Mirror Group Newspapers, getting pipped at the post by Rupert Murdoch for a major stake in Li Ka-shing's pan-Asia Star TV satellite group, and losing out to Paramount in the bidding for Macmillan in the US, caution rather than excitement seems to have been the Pearson watchword. Despite offering more money than Murdoch for a 70 per cent stake in Star TV, Pearson's insistence that the Li family retain a major shareholding in the group until 1998, thereby keeping Li Ka-shing's valuable political influence in mainland China within the company during the all-important 1997 handover of Hong Kong, eventually resulted in the deal going to News Corporation. Ironically, Pearson still has a 17.5 per cent stake in News Corporation's flagship TV operation BSkyB, in addition to a 14 per cent stake in Yorkshire–Tyne Tees Television,

15 per cent in UK Gold, 15 per cent in UK Living and 10 per cent in Astra. Pearson's formation of a new television division to help expand its media interests in both Europe and Asia towards the end of 1993 was intended as a clear signal of its continuing commitment to forging further partnerships in television programming and distribution. As if to show that it really was in earnest, in May 1994 Pearson and the BBC announced a 'global strategic alliance', designed to ally the BBC 'brand' with Pearson cash to mount satellite programmes in Europe, Asia and the Americas. Obviously aimed at News Corporation, this was diplomatically heralded as the first-ever joint venture between a publicly funded national broadcaster and a private-sector company. The 'alliance's' first project will be to launch two new BBC satellite channels towards the end of 1994, one, funded by advertising, carrying news and information, the other, funded by subscription, offering general entertainment. Following, what now seems to be a fairly predictable formula for such marriages, Pearson will provide around £30 million in cash, some programming and, most importantly, some commercial nous, while the BBC will provide one of the best media brand names on earth, top-quality news provision, programming, infrastructure and access to massive libraries. As well as taking the BBC's World Service television news around the world, the new partners hope to look at the possibility of launching channels devoted to educational, documentary and children's programmes.

Longman book publishers, responsible for 50 per cent of Pearson's total operating profit in 1992, and for some time a believer in locating subsidiaries in its main overseas markets, has had more success than its parent in turning its far eastern aspirations into significant business. With Longman Group Far East restructured and renamed Longman Asia, and with companies in Hong Kong, Singapore, Malaysia, Taiwan and Japan, Longman expects to become a market leader in the fast-growing economies of the Asia–Pacific region in areas like business, professional, educational and medical publishing. They also intend to become the clear market leader in the growing business of teaching English as a foreign language [4]. The phrase 'seeking to be the market leader' occurs with monotonous regularity in the world of media concentration. Although it can mean 'we intend to offer the very best', it can also be read as 'determined to use whatever muscle we have to crowd out the competition'.

Time Warner

After staving off a US$12 billion bid by Paramount Communications in 1990, Time Inc. acquired Warner Communications Inc. in the same year for US$14 billion to form Time Warner, then the world's largest media empire, with interests in book and magazine publishing, music, films, theme parks and cable television. Since the merger Time Warner has proved to be a magnet for cash-rich corporations like Power Corporation and US West. This latter, an American telecommunications company with industrial interests in Japan, invested US$2.5 billion in Time Warner during 1993. The giant Canadian-based drinks company Seagram also took a US$2 billion (5.8 per cent) stake in Time Warner in 1993 at around the same time as Power, with whom it shares some directors. During 1994 Seagram admitted to raising this stake to 11.7 per cent via stock buying in the open market, thereby prompting some nervousness among other shareholders that the company could be the target of an unfriendly takeover bid by Seagram. Seagram had always made it clear that it was looking to increase its stake in the company to a minimum of 15 per cent. Time Warner's 1994 defensive tactic, of a 'shareholders rights plan' designed to limit the ownership of shares by any person or group to 15 per cent of common shares, seems designed to ensure that 15 per cent is all that Seagram will get.

Rich in film libraries of its own, Time Warner also has access to a stock of hard news information via its 19 per cent stake in Turner Broadcasting, best known for its round-the-clock news channel CNN. The most serious challenge facing Time Warner after its merger was the US$14 billion debt that the new company was saddled with in 1990. Although blunting its aspirations somewhat with regard to making further big acquisitions, this debt has not prevented it from exploring some facets of the multimedia future. In early 1993, building on the success of its more modest experiment in the borough of Queens in New York, where it had been delivering 150 channels of interactive television to cable customers, Time Warner announced that it was to begin building the world's first 'full-service network' (FSN) 'interactive television' (I-TV) service for 4000 households in suburban Orlando in Florida. Despite some initial problems with the underlying system software and the configuration of the set-top terminal, these homes are expected to be at the cutting edge of modern communications and digital compression technology by the beginning of 1995. They will be served by high-capacity advanced digital storage devices capable of holding up to 1000 gigabytes of digital information (equivalent to 500 two-hour movies). The network itself will take the form of a hybrid. Built of fibreoptic coaxial (copper) cable, capable of almost infinite data capacity and delivering interactive services, video games, home shopping, movies on demand, normal telephone services and any interactive information services that future providers might consider worthwhile to put on the system. The high-speed digital switching facilities serving the network will transparently accommodate the normal routing of telephone calls as well as all the anticipated bursts of video and data traffic. Building on the convergence of personal computing and television made possible by advanced digital technology, this experiment is an example of the much anticipated electronic superhighway linked to an equally super household appliance handling all the functions now performed by separate boxes.

The digitization of TV broadcasts, utilizing intelligent video dial-tone systems, will eventually allow viewers to programme their hitherto passive TV set by remote control. They will be able to capture and download pay-per-view movies selected from big film-banks for both instant and future viewing. Such a network would provide almost unlimited opportunities for marketeers. For the first time they would be able to target individual households via a range of highly differentiated approaches, including traditional timed advertising, more detailed 'infomercials' and even a quick spot-on-demand facility which could be used to take advantage of a particularly opportune selling moment. Consumers, in their turn, would be able to tap into individual product or service messages at their own convenience. It is interesting to see that many of the most rapidly assimilated of the new technologies have proved to be those that extend the convenience of an old technology, or which convert screen-based information back into paper. Mobile phones are an example of the former and facsimile machines are clear examples of the latter.

Given the tenacity with which we hang on to familiar and comfortable technologies, especially those that still produce something on paper, it should come as no surprise to hear that Time Warner have done a deal with Hewlett-Packard (HP) to provide each of the 4000 targeted subscribers with a specially modified HP colour printer, offering them the option of a home media printing service. Developed from their 'Vidjet Pro' printers which were produced to meet the needs of video production professionals, these printers will store and reproduce individual frames, or sequences of frames, on plain paper at a fraction of the cost of current technology. Linked up to the TV cable, the printer will enable users to make paper copies of screen images, frames of a home video, even selective news and information taken from menus off the screen, and all in colour. Given that most subscribers will switch away from advertising during their interactive viewing, the printer waiting quietly in the living room could prove a boon to advertisers, who could send it special discount vouchers or coupons for printing out on the spot. They could send details of new lines or new models, unannounced or promptly on demand. This experiment will allow Time Warner to gauge just how much time and money middle America is prepared to spend on accessing various mixtures of information and entertainment. As a company seeking to continue its global presence in the face of fast-growing competition, it will also be looking for new strategic alliances, perhaps building on its existing relationship with US West.

Sony and Matsushita

Sony acquired Columbia studios in 1989 (it had already acquired CBS Records, the world's leading record company in 1988) for a top-of-the-market price of US$5.4 billion, while Matsushita, the home of Panasonic, purchased MCA/Universal in late 1990 for US$6.59 billion. To many observers this was to be a collision of two clearly incompatible cultures. On the one side the cautious, consensus-obsessed Japanese, whose loyalty to the company or the group usually transcends personal ambition and self-serving; on the other the out-rageous flamboyance and cult of the volatile individual which is almost a prerequisite for success in tinseltown.

Recognizing that the culture of making movies is nothing like the corporate culture of Japan, both Sony and Matsushita have, for the time being at least, sensibly left the management of their Hollywood acquisitions in American hands. Characteristically they both have very long-term objectives. They are not looking for success this year or next year: their aim is the total integration of entertainment hardware and software and, as all western observers should know by now, one resource the Japanese never seem to run out of is patience. Future movies and TV series would not only be made by Sony and Matsushita, they would also be packaged on their video tapes, laser discs and cassettes, to be played on their own make of video, tape and laser-disc hardware. The soundtrack would of course be recorded on their own brand of compact disc, recorded by an artist under sole contract to them.

Just six companies now dominate the worldwide US$29 billion music industry: Sony, Thorn EMI (who bought Virgin records in 1992 for £560 million), Warner, BMG, Polygram (owned by electronics giant Phillips) and MCA. Like the old Hollywood exclusive studio-contract system that died in the 1950s these six record companies like to keep their artists tied to long-term 10- and 12-year contracts. They also keep the rights to a singer's back catalogue, which in recent years, with the growing popularity of compilations, TV spin-offs and revivals, has proved a lucrative source of income, now often accounting for 70 per cent of total profits. Despite occasional blips, e.g. Sony's defeat in the 1980s in its attempt to dominate the VCR market with its better-quality but poorly marketed Betamax video system, the Japanese corporations can afford to watch and wait. All Japanese electronics companies invest heavily in research and development and there can be no doubt that they will achieve many of their objectives with regard to long-term product and service integration. Matsushita is continuing to explore thinner and wider screen television technology, and the ever-innovative Sharp is seeking to build up particular knowledge and expertise in the all important thin/flat screen areas of liquid crystal displays and in the development of flash memories.

One area of technological development which looked like confusing consumers for the next decade was the development of high-definition television (HDTV). In many ways the more trivial of the developments taking place in the electronic laboratories of the world, this was nonetheless poised to deliver two competing standards. The decision, after 30 years of intensive investment, by Japan's Posts and Telecommunications Ministry in early 1994, to pull out of its 'Hi-Vision', analogue HDTV programme, opened the way for a worldwide digital standard based on the more flexible and technically superior US HDTV system. Being completely digital rather than analogue, it can coexist with analogue TV broadcast standards and is well suited to cope with the needs of interactive television, in which the US also leads the world.

One dead, one out, one still in the ring

In November 1988 Robert Maxwell's highly publicized £1.6 billion bid for the US publisher Macmillan Inc. was unashamedly declared to be part of a strategy to make the Maxwell Communication Corporation a £3 billion a year publishing group by the turn of the decade [5]. Although Maxwell's particular brand of personal acquisition and control was terminated by his death at sea in 1991, this kind of personal ambition shows no signs of going the same way. As the owner of Mirror Group Newspapers, Maxwell was notorious for his interference in editorial matters, in which he parallelled the behaviour of another would-be media mogul, 'Tiny' Rowland. Condemned in 1973 as the unacceptable face of capitalism by the then Prime Minister Edward Heath, an unperturbed Rowland later orchestrated the purchase of *The Observer*, a quality Sunday newspaper, for Lonrho, a company largely founded on African mining interests. One of many stories of editorial interference by Rowland goes that during the British general election campaign of 1983 the then deputy editor of *The Observer*, Anthony Howard, after discussions with his colleagues, wrote an editorial in support of the Liberal Democrats called 'Stopping a Tory landslide'. He then left the office for a time.

When he came back the editorial had been changed to reflect an entirely different point of view [6]. In another instance of gross partisanship in March 1987, Rowland insisted on bringing out a special edition of *The Observer* to publicize and comment upon a government report which made some criticisms of the financial affairs of the Fayed brothers, with whom he had been engaged in a fierce boardroom battle for the control of the House of Fraser [7]. The independence of this once great British Sunday paper had clearly been eroded by its new role as a mouthpiece for Rowland's world of political and commercial influence. Perhaps as a result its circulation declined, and its losses eventually became too much for even Lonhro to bear. It was eventually sold to Guardian Newspapers in April 1993, bringing to an end a glaring example of UK media ownership for the clear promotion of personal interest. It is nice to know that, sometimes at least, 'you can't fool all of the people all of the time'.

Unlike Maxwell and Rowland, the Canadian newspaper entrepreneur Conrad Black is still very much in the acquisition business. Head of the UK Telegraph Newspaper group, which he acquired in 1985 and which publishes the *Daily Telegraph* and the *Sunday Telegraph*, and with significant newspaper holdings in Canada and Australia, Black is every inch a newspaper mogul in the old style. The leader of a syndicate that won a bidding competition for the Australian-based and debt-ridden John Fairfax press group from the receiver in 1991, he is no stranger to controversy. Indeed, his 19.9 per cent stake in the now reconstituted and publicly listed John Fairfax Holdings has been legally challenged by one of the rival bidders. The claim against Black's successful Tourang syndicate was that it gained an unfair advantage from the banker advising on the sale, that they struck an exclusive agreement with the American junk bond holders (the main holders of the Fairfax debt) which tied them in to the Tourang deal, preventing them from talking to rival bidders, and that Tourang was allowed to submit an improved offer for the group two weeks after the tender date had elapsed. Despite the family feuding and financial mismanagement that eventually led to its collapse, Fairfax was worth a battle. It is the second biggest newspaper group in Australia, after Rupert Murdoch's News Corporation, controlling three of the world's most profitable daily papers, the *Sydney Morning Herald*, Melbourne's *The Age*, and the national *Australian Financial Review*, as well as a healthy group of regional titles. The Sydney and Melbourne papers dominate the classified advertising market in Australia's two largest cities. Bucking the recession, they have both consistently returned substantial advertising earnings back to the group while continuing to maintain their roles as key opinion formers among the country's leading policy and decision makers.

The Fairfax family had run the newspapers for 149 years, and had cultivated a strong tradition of editorial independence. The opposition to the Tourang bid within Australia, although basically aimed at the growing concentration of newspaper ownership in the country, also contrasted this tradition of independence with the interventionist reputation of both Black and Kerry Packer, who was an original partner in the Tourang syndicate but was forced by political pressure early on in the bidding process, to make a hasty withdrawal. Australia's richest person, Packer already owns the leading commercial television network Channel Nine and most of the country's magazine titles. Not a man to take disruption of his plans quietly, he has already picked up 14 per cent of the shares in Fairfax since its reflotation in 1992. Like Packer, Black's role in the media business of his home country, Canada, is rarely out of the news. Through his Hollinger group Black owns around 19 per cent of Southam, Canada's biggest newspaper group, publishing 17 titles every day. Like Australia and the US, the Canadian newspaper market consists of large-circulation daily papers produced in each of the country's main cities. Only two Toronto newspapers, *The Globe* and *The Mail*, owned respectively by Thomson and the *Financial Post* (Pearson owns a 19.9 per cent stake in the latter), have anything approximating a national circulation. Power Corporation, Hollinger and UniMedia, another Conrad Black company, now control the quality newspapers of six of the eight largest cities outside Toronto, as well as the leading quality newspaper in each of Canada's French-speaking cities. While Canada is relatively active in monitoring competition among the broadcast media, other than for limiting the foreign ownership of newspapers to a 25 per cent stake it has no regulatory panel that examines the impact of mergers in the newspaper market. Early in 1994 through its subsidiary American Publishing, which already publishes 280 small-town newspapers across the US, the Hollinger group made its first excursion into the urban US market. For US$180 million it bought the tabloid *Chicago Sun-Times*, the country's ninth biggest daily newspaper, whose assets also include around 60 community papers in the Chicago area. The Sun-Times will undoubtedly be the beneficiary of Hollinger's now well rehearsed formula of tight cost control linked with the latest in labour-saving technology. Conrad Black comes from eastern Canada, a region that has often exported embryonic media magnates to Britain. Max Aitkin (later Lord Beaverbrook) came from this area to take over the then puny *Daily Express*, the *Sunday Express* and the *Evening Standard*. He eventually created a formidable press empire that he used unashamedly to propound his strong pro-Empire views. It was Beaverbrook and Lord Rothermere (*Daily Mirror*) who prompted the then British Prime Minister Stanley Baldwin to castigate the press barons for seeking 'power without responsibility, the prerogative of the harlot throughout the ages'.

Roy Thomson (later Lord Thomson) also came to Britain from Ontario. Building on his experience at buying and selling Canadian newspapers and radio stations, he eventually took control of Scottish Television, *The Scotsman* newspaper, the *Sunday Times* in 1950 and later *The Times* itself in 1967.

Power Corporation

Another quiet but determined player in the information and communication business is Power Corporation of Canada. This cash-rich financial services and media group recently paid $99 million for a 1 per cent stake in Time Warner and a 19 per cent stake in Southam, Canada's biggest newspaper publisher. Power will have joint control of Southam with Hollinger, the holding company controlled by Conrad Black. Power Broadcasting, a 100 per cent wholly owned subsidiary of Power, owns several radio and TV stations and has recently formed a partnership with the Canadian Broadcasting Corporation to provide two channels to DirecTV, the planned US direct broadcasting satellite service nicknamed 'Death Star' [8]. Through its interest in Pargesa Holdings, a Geneva-based holding company, Power also owns part of Radio-Television Luxembourg, which itself owns ten radio stations and six TV channels broadcasting into France, Germany and the Benelux countries.

News Corporation

In 1952, the Australian newspaper proprietor Keith Murdoch laid the foundations for his son Rupert's career as a media baron by leaving him a daily and a Sunday newspaper business in Adelaide. The 22-year-old heir promptly entered into a bruising circulation war with the competition. Today Rupert Murdoch's News Corporation's (NC) widespread newspaper interests – three dailies and two Sunday titles in the UK, representing 35 per cent of all UK national newspaper circulation, and around 60 per cent of Australia's metropolitan and national newspaper titles – form only a part of a modern media empire that has no continental boundaries. With its ownership of Fox film studios and its invasion of the UK satellite television business, first via Sky and then the enlarged BSkyB, NC is now probably the most controversial example of contemporary media acquisition and control.

The epitome of the modern media-baron, Rupert Murdoch, at 63, must now be very close to his dream of a truly global multimedia network. Like the great US railway barons of the 1880s, he is always on the lookout for new ways of extending his reach, of controlling the strategic passes of the modern communications network. Anyone with electronic, satellite or print-on-paper 'rails' to sell will always be of interest.

On 1 September 1993, relishing his role as both futurologist and executive chairman of News Corporation, Murdoch gave a speech at the Banqueting Hall in London, ostensibly to celebrate the initiation of Sky Multi-Channel's new 14-channel network. He used the occasion to announce an array of new initiatives and partnerships for NC that would secure its place at the centre of just about every form of information and entertainment production and distribution. During his speech Murdoch emphasized the liberation that technology was now bringing to all peoples in terms of their access to new information and ideas. Clearly a follower of technological determinism, he also noted how:

> . . . it has also liberated people from the once powerful media barons. The days when a few newspaper publishers could agree to keep an entire nation ignorant of an important event are long gone. Technology is racing ahead so rapidly, news and entertainment sources are proliferating at such a rate, that the media mogul has been replaced by a bevy of harassed and sometimes confused media executives, trying to guess at what the public wants. The consumer is in the saddle, driving the telecommunications industry. The technology is galloping over the old regulatory machinery. . . . Five of the world's biggest industries – computing, communications, consumer electronics, publishing and entertainment – are converging into one dynamic whole. [9]

He went on to outline the particular draughtsmanship that would ensure NC's future economic expansion, concentrating on eight key strategies. These aspirations are worth noting in detail as, irrespective of whether they all succeed, they help illuminate the many different facets and technologies that any media operation with global pretensions needs to embrace:

1. Probably his most important announcement concerned a possible deal with British Telecom and Cellnet in the UK to explore the creation of an information superhighway. This would link NC's expertise in satellite technology with BT's ownership and knowledge of the telephone network, initially via a 500-home experiment combining access to telecommunications, television shows, films and specialist information. This new relationship would build on the rapport NC already has with BT concerning the sale

of NC's satellite receivers and dishes through BT's 90 high-street retail outlets. BT is banned from broadcasting live programmes over its telephone network until 2001 and, although OFTEL is still insisting that no easing of restrictions will happen until then, most commentators expect this restriction to be reviewed in 1998, if not before. BT believes that its proposed ventures with NC constitute 'narrow' rather than 'broad' casting, and thus do not constitute a breach of the current regulations. No doubt one serious objective of the relationship will be for BT and NC to join together in testing the nerve of the UK regulatory authorities.

2. He confirmed the acquisition by NC of Delphi Internet Service, a small electronic online data service in the US, with the potential to move into the electronic newspaper/magazine area.

3. He also confirmed a new joint venture between NC's Fox Broadcasting and Televisa of Mexico to produce 500 hours of multilingual drama. This package will include a series of soap operas that will first be produced in Spanish and then redone on the same set with the same script using American actors.

4. He announced a joint venture with Pro 7, the German broadcaster associated with the Kirch Corporation, to develop pay television in Germany covering as many as six channels. The idea is to eventually target up to 100 million German-speaking viewers throughout Europe.

5. He noted the launch of several new programming initiatives in Asia, including an 'open university' and educational channel using the Star satellite system, in which NC recently bought a controlling interest.

6. He outlined his plans to expand Sky News, already seen in 33 countries, to South Africa from October 1993, plus further plans to extend the service to all other continents through ventures with local partners.

7. He announced the launch of a second Sky sports channel in 1994. Sky hopes to gain exclusive rights to Wimbledon in 1995, showing matches from different courts simultaneously on four or five channels. It is also preparing a bid to secure an exclusive contract for domestic Test cricket by 1995 or 1996. Sky already has a monopoly of the live play from the UK's premier league football, an exclusive contract to cover England's overseas cricket tours and an exclusive right to Ryder Cup golf in 1994.

8. Last but not least, he unveiled a new agreement between News Datacom, NC's media access and encryption company, NTL, the UK research and telecommunications group, and Comstream, an

American high-tech company, to develop a common digital satellite system throughout Europe, Asia and the Americas.

Although sounding the most technical and least glamorous of all the new strategies, this last is probably one of the most important planks in NC's future domination of pay TV. NC currently has a UK monopoly of the encryption or scrambling technology necessary to prevent non-subscribers gaining access to satellite programmes. Whether or not a reliance on income direct from viewers' pockets proves more predictable than raising it from advertising remains to be seen. The current view among satellite TV providers is that, despite its potential pitfalls, funding via subscription is a less volatile source of income than that dependent on advertising alone. If this new funding wisdom turns out to be correct it will be a major boost for NC, since whereas it only has a 50 per cent stake in BSkyB it is the sole owner of News Datacom and its sophisticated 'Videocrypt' subscription technology, the system used by all British-based subscription channels. Armed with new partners, NC will no doubt be capitalizing on its patent of this particular piece of intellectual property to dominate the world market for encryption devices. Its expertise in handling subscription accounts is also a unique (as far as the UK is concerned) knowledge base which is very marketable. BSkyB has been through the learning curve associated with selling, coding and collecting subscriptions within a culture more used to licence fees and advertising. Around 3 million homes in the UK now have satellite dishes accessing around 30 channels, and all the pioneering work involved has been done by BSkyB. Of all the initiatives announced by Murdoch, this agreement between News Datacom, NTL and Comstream could prove to be the most significant in terms of NC's future monopoly of regional satellite power.

News Corporation, Hong Kong and the battle for China

Although he already held a 50 per cent stake in Hong Kong's immensely profitable *South China Morning Post* and *Wa Kiu Yat Pao* newspapers, it was no surprise to hear, in mid 1993, that Murdoch was on the look-out for a television partner in the far east. His first move was to seek a one-third share in TVB, the main domestic TV station in Hong Kong. With a huge library of Mandarin language programming, TVB is sitting on something of a gold mine for anyone aiming to develop future services in mainland China, but in the end the TVB deal was thwarted by political and regulatory opposition to the ownership of media companies by non-Hong Kong residents.

However, in the language that often characterizes temporary setbacks in this business, 'doors have been left open'. Murdoch's next move was to explore the possibility of an association with the other Hong Kong satellite operator, Star TV. Since 1991 Star TV has operated five 24-hour channels free to anyone with a dish that can receive the signals. Currently this amounts to some 45 million people in 38 countries, a 'footprint' that extends from Turkey to Japan and from Mongolia to Indonesia. Murdoch paid £352.34 million for a 63.6 per cent stake in HutchVision, Star's parent company. The deal was concluded just one day after the Pearson negotiators had retired from their discussions with Richard Li in London, convinced that their offer for 70 per cent of the company had been accepted. So important was this purchase to Murdoch, the most significant financial transaction for NC since its serious debt problems in 1990, that for the first time ever in an acquisition he gave the vendor a large number of NC shares as part of the agreed price.

Li Ka-shing will be the third largest shareholder in NC after the Murdoch family and the US bank Citicorp. The obstacles that hindered the TVB deal had been overcome. NC's 48 per cent stake in the Hong Kong segment of HutchVision neatly falls below the 49 per cent non-resident maximum holding set by the Hong Kong government for operating the satellite service, and the Li family retain the remaining 52 per cent. Everyone gets something. Star TV needed programmes to satisfy its increasing audience share, and NC needed to establish a base close to the world's largest potential television market:

> In programming terms Mr Murdoch can offer Star TV the library of 20th Century Fox and Fox broadcasting. In addition Star TV is keen to plug into BSkyB's resources on sports programming – there being a large appetite for European sporting events, including football, athletics and cycling – and arm Star TV's news services with feeds from BSkyB's expensive news operation in west London. [10]

'The boss' is certainly optimistic: 'We will build a business out of Asia as big as two BSkyB's' [10].

The big prizes that await those who are poised to reach the embryonic satellite audiences of India and mainland China have an attraction and excitement akin to that which drew Marco Polo to the terrestrial wonders of Cathay and the palaces of the Kublai Khan in the late 13th century. With NC's help Star TV will be able to improve its programme offerings on its five existing 'free air' channels, helping it to compete more strongly in those Asian countries where domestic television production is established. From October 1993 Star began to operate its first pay channels, using the technology and expertise gained from NC's BSkyB experience. As Star TV is still short of Mandarin language programming there may still be room within the new arrangements for NC to do a deal with TVB, whose own involvement in a wider consortium that includes Home Box Office Asia, Turner International, Australia's AUSTV and the ESPN sports network is more of a declaration of cooperation rather than a formal agreement.

In September 1993 Murdoch announced that, in order to concentrate on his interests in Star TV, he intended to divest himself of his holding in the *South China Morning Post*. Many commentators saw this as a clear signal to the Beijing government of Murdoch's intention to tread carefully with regard to his ownership of news and information media in southwest Asia. The eventual buyer of the 110 000 circulation daily was the Kerry Group, owned by Robert Kuok, a Malaysian–Chinese businessman with major investments in mainland China. He is also known to be close to the government in Beijing, who have appointed him as one of their advisers on Hong Kong. Among other things Kuok owns the Shangri la hotel chain; he also owns a 32 per cent interest in TVB. Although on the face of it this was just a normal sale and purchase agreement between two independent and powerful businessmen, the coincidence might suggest that some connection with TVB and Star TV may still be on the cards, perhaps when the regulatory pressure subsides. In the true spirit of 'doors have still been left open' the Mandarin programming of TVB probably took a small step closer towards Star TV, via a deal that apparently had nothing whatsoever to do with television. The Beijing government will welcome a friendly hand on the editorial tiller of the *South China Morning Post*. A highly respected English-language newspaper, whose reporting of world and regional events has generally known no fear or favour, its ownership and control by a friend of China will reinforce the view prevalent in Hong Kong that self, rather than imposed, censorship is likely to be the order of the day after 1997.

Given the creeping influence of the Beijing government over every aspect of information provision in Hong Kong, the move by the pro-democracy Oriental Press, the most profitable Chinese-language publisher in the colony, to launch a new English-language newspaper, the *Eastern Express* (the first such launch in over a decade), as a direct competitor to the *South China Morning Post*, has to be seen as the work of great optimists. Welcomed by many the *Eastern Express* promises editorial integrity, freedom of debate and resistance to the creeping self-censorship noted above. However, Chinese businessmen, like their counterparts in the west, do not embark on new projects lightly. Having been summoned to Beijing in 1993 for a lecture on how to become more compliant in readiness for the Chinese takeover, the top men of the Oriental Press group suddenly (some might say bravely) saw how a Hong Kong newspaper clearly perceived as free from Chinese influence could be a winner. If it works, the *Eastern Express* could prove an interesting and unusual example of how a threat became an opportunity, and perhaps more importantly how 'freedom' might be made profitable.

Similarly, the heavy start-up costs incurred by the new Cantonese Wharf cable channel in Hong Kong during November 1993 looks like a remarkable act of faith, given the regulatory cloud that could burst in 1997. But like Robert Kuok, Wharf's chief Stephen Ng is close to the Beijing bureaucrats, already owning a 20 per cent stake in one of China's first cable joint ventures, in Sichuan province. Wharf's expertise could hold more future appeal to a mainland government currently finding satellite TV a little too hard to control. Although expensive to lay, cable does at least have a physical presence: it can be seen, it can be cut, it can be switched off. But it also takes a long time to go live, and back in television-hungry Hong Kong, where 99 per cent of homes own television sets, and 82 per cent own VCRs, the natives are getting restless. In response, Wharf has decided to begin by delivering its programmes by microwave signals that can be received by the current roof-top aerials which just require an easily installed decoder to unscramble. After three or four years all of Wharf's services will arrive via a state-of-the-art fibre network that could carry 40 TV channels and, regulators permitting, telephone and data services. Wharf has begun with seven Cantonese channels and four English-speaking channels, i.e. CNN, the BBC World Service, Prime Sports and MTV Asia, the last three of these supposedly being bought in from Star TV. This latter partnership no longer seems certain, as both Star and Wharf wrestle to establish the dimensions of their own aspirations in the region. Four other channels are also expected to be available for an additional fee. The current government of Hong Kong seems keen to help Wharf take on the costly task of underground cabling, and has granted Wharf a 12-year licence and a three-year monopoly in providing programming in Cantonese. It is also allowing Wharf to use the city's subway tunnels to install the fibreoptic backbone of the network, and is offering the conveniently grouped government housing schemes for first wiring. Many mainland Chinese also live in large government housing schemes and, like their 6 million Hong Kong cousins, they too are compulsive television watchers.

When asked in the 1950s to comment on what effect the French Revolution of the 1780s had had on the modern world, Mao Tse-Tung is reputed to have replied that 'it was too early to say'. Faced with two of the oldest challenges, lack of money (India) and governmental insecurity (China) those media moguls currently investing in the east might be saying something similar for a few years yet. Their small stocks of patience look like being tested to the limit by negotiators who have come to know the worth of the huge audiences that they can offer. Sometimes the discussions will be inexorably complicated by the ghosts of past histories and alignments that will not lie down.

When Murdoch bought Star TV in 1993 a number of voices were raised against what they regarded as a continuation of western imperialism by other means. One of these, Malaysia, was later to accuse his *Sunday Times* of retaliating against their opposition by exposing the links between British aid for the Pergau dam project and a later contract for £1.3 billion of British arms sales.

Despite his insistence that satellite technology is 'an unambiguous threat to totalitarian regimes everywhere', enabling the information-hungry residents of such regimes to bypass censorious state controls, Murdoch has come to learn that even satellite beams can be searched at the border. The People's Republic of China has shown itself to require sweetening by some pretty robust self-censorship if it is to return favours later. Murdoch's agreement to stop transmitting the BBC World Service television news to Hong Kong, Taiwan, Korea, Mongolia and northeast China, replacing it with a Mandarin-language film channel, is a direct result of the Chinese government's sensitivity to western sources of news. China had expressed anger with the BBC over a number of documentary and news programmes broadcast in 1993 and 1994, and had made its displeasure known at the highest levels. Although Murdoch could not be expected to hold any kind of brief to protect the BBC, an interesting twist of info-geopolitics has seen the free market, buccaneer of the airwaves, joining with a totalitarian regime to suppress certain forms of information in order to secure future licence agreements.

Given the weight of the local circumstances, the BBC, which had been broadcasting across Asia on Star since 1991, accepted the loss of its northern beam eight months before its contract was due to run out at the end of 1994. The final deal bought the BBC a two-year reprieve for its service to viewers in India, Pakistan and Bangladesh, which it transmits on the satellite's southern beam. NC had earlier objected to plans by the BBC to launch an Arabic news and information channel, complaining that its proposed transmission area overlapped Star TV's satellite footprint. These objections now seem to have been withdrawn and BBC World Service television news is set to go ahead with this service, as well as plans to expand its satellite news services in both Japan and the US. Torn from the arms of Murdoch, the BBC moved to embrace the somewhat more compatible corporate values of Pearson. The satellite wars in the east seem to be warming up!

Turning BSkyB around in the UK and lifting the Fox network out of the doldrums in the US may be nothing to the cultural, political and geographical contortions that Rupert Murdoch may have to perform to bring Star, currently losing about US$50 million a year, into some kind of profit. Meanwhile the nations of Asia are learning how to turn offers away. Also many other media groups are coming to realize that the number of local programmes available in local languages may in the end determine future winners. With a dozen or so satellites due to be launched in the region over the next two years, Star TV's current scarcity premium will begin to evaporate, and MTV's embryonic policy of language localization could become the norm.

Paramount, Viacom and QVC

The multimedia era's first takeover battle, between Viacom and QVC for Paramount Communications, the last independent film studio outside Disney, began in September 1993 and raged for over five months, eventually ending in a US$10 billion 'victory' for Viacom in February 1994. It is a story replete with all the optimism and the awkwardness that characterizes such acquisitions. Initially Paramount struck up a US$7.5 billion takeover deal with Viacom, the successful cable TV company run by the 70-year-old Sumner Redstone.

Paramount investors feared that without a broader base the company would have difficulty thriving in an environment increasingly dominated by diversified giants such as Time Warner, Sony and News Corporation. Their preferred partner, Viacom, owned MTV, an all-music channel that is arguably one of the world's most successful cable networks. With MTV advertising income continuing to grow at around 25 per cent a year, despite deep cuts in advertising revenue everywhere else, Viacom certainly looked like a robust partner to have on board. Viacom also owned Nickelodeon, a 'wacky' children's channel, and Showtime, a popular film channel. This valuable programming synergy was declared by both sides to be the rationale for the friendly nature of the proposed takeover. However, within days of the Viacom offer Barry Diller, head of QVC, a highly successful 24-hour home shopping cable network in the US, came out with a higher but unfriendly US$9.5 billion counterbid, which the Paramount board was, by law, obliged to consider. A key element in the QVC approach was that, initially, it contained a higher, and therefore more attractive, cash component than the Viacom bid. In order to fund this attractiveness QVC sought backing from other partners, including John Malone's TCI (a cable operator), his Liberty Media (a cable programmer), Brian Roberts of Comcast and Bell South telephone company. Paramount's attraction rested on a number of features, including a rich dowry of legend – Hollywood studios still exude an air of magic and mystique – programme and production assets that would be almost impossible to duplicate, and a television production division. It also owned six television stations, Madison Square Garden in New York, the New York Knicks basketball team and the New York Rangers hockey team. Paramount also offered valuable opportunities in print-based communication, owning the publishing interests of Simon and Schuster and Pocket Books. In an interesting move, and while still under offer itself, Paramount confirmed the importance of the print media component of its portfolio by successfully bidding US$552.75 million for the prestigious Macmillan Publishing Inc., the largest US business in the empire of the late Robert Maxwell. Martin Davis, the chairman and chief executive of Paramount, had no doubts about the soundness of such a move. It was:

> . . . a significant step in furthering our strategic objective of creating proprietary intellectual properties that can be distributed through a wide variety of media, from printed pages to computer and video screens . . . [11]

Macmillan's publishing interests extend over general fiction, reference and children's books, and an extensive backlist of authors that includes Ernest Hemingway and William Faulkner. As with the Reed Elsevier merger, considerable savings are expected once Macmillan is fully integrated into Paramount Publishing.

In order to help fund its bid, Viacom, like QVC, sought help from a variety of other partners. Early on in the bidding process Nynex, one of America's Baby Bell telephone companies, invested US$1.2 billion in Viacom to help things along. In early 1994, Viacom announced a surprise US$8.4 billion merger agreement with Blockbuster Entertainment, a large video retailer and rental chain, who also injected US$1.25 billion in cash. In order to protect their deal from hostile predators, Viacom and Paramount had originally incorporated a codicil to their agreement stipulating that if Viacom's bid was frustrated by a successful, unfriendly intervention, the successful bidder would have to honour a US$600 million payback to Viacom. If all this seems a bit over the top, so are the perceived stakes, especially as Paramount is the last sizeable media group likely to be on offer in the immediate future, and scarcity always fuels demand. After many weeks of securing partners and putting new stock and cash packages together, QVC eventually got a Chancery Court Judge in Delaware to declare the codicil illegal and trumped Viacom's bid by offering over US$9.9 billion for Paramount.

A $2 billion increase in the bid value of a company requires a lot of funding, and many commentators saw this frenzied bidding as being more about ego enrichment than sensible business. Viacom eventually paid US$2 billion more than it wanted to pay for Paramount. Only time will tell if the resulting 'synergy' was worth it. Estimates of the combined debt of the new Viacom–Blockbuster–Paramount conglomerate on day one of the combined merger run at around US$10 billion, and under current trading conditions only Blockbuster has the kind of cash flow that could service it.

While the battle between Viacom and QVC for Paramount was the main event, one of a number of interesting sideshows going on alongside, and one that illustrates the tentacle-like nature of the media business, was the simultaneous link being forged between Blockbuster in the US and Virgin Communications in the UK. During October 1993 Blockbuster, with its 3200 video rental stores worldwide, bought an equity stake in Richard Branson's Virgin Communications, which currently operates a £200 million interactive games business. This link gave Branson's investment in intellectual property access to the retail outlets of one of the world's largest media conglomerates. Blockbuster in turn gained some welcome diversification into the kind of technology-based entertainment that is expected to feed part of the home-entertainment revolution of the future. After all, video rental and sell-through sales are destined to be the big casualties if and when the technology to deliver video on demand gains a mass audience. Video games, on the other hand, are likely to be just the kind of service that prospers from being rented rather than bought.

Bell Atlantic and Telecommunications Inc (TCI)

While the Viacom/QVC/Paramount battle rolled on, what American commentators often describe as 'a defining moment' took place at the Macklowe Hotel in New York on 13 October 1993. On that day John Malone, head of the world's largest cable television company TCI, shook hands with Ray Smith, the head of Bell Atlantic, a telephone company with 18 million subscribers in several mid-Atlantic states. They agreed to a US$32 billion merger that would have created, at an eventual valuation of US$61 billion, the sixth largest company in America. To put this figure in some sort of perspective, the GDP of Malaysia was US$46 billion in 1991.

In February 1994, and this time in a moment clearly defined by the economics of the present rather than those of a largely unknown future, both parties agreed to discontinue the merger arrangements. Ray Smith blamed 'the unsettled regulatory climate [which] made it too difficult for the parties to value the future today'. Both parties also blamed the Federal Communications Commission (FCC) who, early in 1994, had ordered that all cable TV companies would have to cut their rates by 7 per cent during the year. This price cut would reduce

TCI's anticipated cash flow by US$144 million a year, and coming on top of the 10 per cent cut which the FCC had already enforced in 1993, it probably represented the last straw for a deal that had always been keenly balanced with regard to price. Given that the deal was entirely based on an exchange of shares, and that Bell Atlantic had seen its share price fall from US$66 to US$53 since the merger announcement, this factor would also have required some serious adjustments to the original exchanges of 'paper'. Bell Atlantic was already paying roughly one and a half times TCI's pre-deal market value and 20 times its cash flow for 1992, as the price of its stake. Future cooperation and 'synergy' could perhaps be bought at a cheaper price. Also, the things that Bell/TCI would have been good at putting together – a cable-based telephone service, videophones and video on demand – are the very things that all deregulated telephone and cable companies will soon be offering. Competition will thus become very intense, prices will have to come down and margins will get slimmer.

Notwithstanding the seriousness of these potential competitive issues, it is worth looking at why the proposed merger of these two companies, still considered by many as the ultimate marriage of communications technology with content, stirred up so much excitement. TCI owns the largest cable network in America, with 1200 separate cable systems linking up more than 10 million subscribers in 49 states. This, together with its own programming company, Liberty Media, which also has stakes in numerous other cable channels, including QVC, puts TCI in pole position to benefit from any eventual relaxation in the regulations restricting cable companies to television. TCI also owns 23 per cent of Turner Broadcasting Systems, giving it access to retrospective stocks of hard news material and other very information-rich programming. Turner also owns a 3000-film library that it acquired from MGM/UA Communications, and for which Bell Atlantic's 18 million telephone customers could one day be hungry subscribers. Bell Atlantic is also a determined player in the development of interactive technologies. In an experiment similar to that planned by Time Warner in Florida, Bell Atlantic is currently testing an interactive television network among 70 of its employees at Alexandria, Virginia. More importantly, it has developed its own digital compression technology for carrying video images over standard copper telephone wires, something that was once thought only possible via fibreoptic technology. The big breakthrough that would have been heralded by Bell and TCI is that they were willing to join together to scupper the conventional wisdom that holds that each type of service needs a discrete wire into the home, that the consumer would have a choice about what services to buy, thus ensuring competition, low prices and a continuous improvement in services. The 'two-wire' wisdom is of course costly, and neither partner could afford to create the information superhighway alone. It looked like a marriage made in heaven; that it ground to a halt in the face of economics is really just a blip.

Via joint ventures and contacts of a less formal kind TCI and Bell Atlantic will continue to stay in touch, while alliances like the one that they proposed will continue to take place. Indeed, in November 1993 Cable and Wireless (C&W), the home of Hong Kong Telecom and Mercury Communications in the UK, announced that it too was looking for partners to develop a set of multimedia services. Entrepreneurs in the business will be actively courted by C&W to work on a range of joint media ventures alongside the development of a new range of wireless technologies. This latter facility will eventually enable Mercury to build up radio-based local telephone networks in the UK that will avoid interconnection payments to British Telecom.

Deregulation is the hoped-for key to the emancipation of all radio waves, fibreoptic cables and even old-fashioned telephone wires, wherever they exist or are planned to exist. But the pace of change is making it more and more difficult to define what it is that should be regulated. Should it be non-discriminatory access to the rush-hour on the electronic superhighway; should it be a regulation of ownership, using limitations such as nationality and residence; should we try to regulate content; should it be in limiting the number of hours that suppliers can broadcast; or a maximum percentage of revenue from, say, the total advertising income available? Even in America, home of the most dynamic changes in both distribution and content, major uncertainties still persist. The Clinton administration had seemed to make deregulation and the development of an electronic super-highway a serious part of its long-term policy, and the Vice President has taken a number of opportunities to state that the administration will not let the existing regulatory structures impede or distort the welcome evolution of the communications industry. Operators are, however, having difficulty imagining the final shape of the promised deregulated environment which, since the reregulatory effects of the 1992 Cable Act, looks in dire need of a 'quick fix' if it is to stimulate the required investment and return confidence to an increasingly confused marketplace.

Last but not least, Italy

Even a highly selective sample of media concentration would be incomplete without reference to the colourful history of media ownership and control in Italy. Long the home of manufacturers and industrialists who have felt that it was only natural to have a mix of newspaper and television vehicles in close support of their main business, the web of media manipulation in Italy almost defies categorization. Not so much international media moguls as domestic tycoons, the names of Benedetti, Berlusconi and Agnelli have dominated the business and media worlds of Italy since the Second World War. All of them share the secret of privileged relations with Italian finance and, at various times, even more privileged relations with political leaders. All see politics as a continuation of business by other means, and all have received the accolade of a public nickname: 'His Transmittance' (Berlusconi); 'The Lawyer' (Giovanni Agnelli); 'The Engineer' (Benedetti). Given the rise of the single European market and a growing aversion within Italy to the Americanization of so much television output, we can expect to see these domestic giants flexing their muscles in the wider media arenas. In key areas of the economy it is occasionally difficult to detect where industrial and media power in Italy ends and where government begins. Carlo de Benedetti is a giant in the economic history of postwar Italy. As well as owning Olivetti he is also the main shareholder in Editoriale L'Espresso, which publishes the left-wing daily newspaper *La Repubblica* and the weekly *Espresso*. *La Repubblica* in turn owns a stake in the Mirror Group-led consortium that now owns the UK's *The Independent* and *The Independent on Sunday* newspapers.

Returning to Italy from exile in Switzerland after the Second World War, Benedetti transformed Olivetti from a moribund office machinery company with 50 workers to a £1 billion telecommunications and computer giant. Typical of the self-made entrepreneurs who have risen to prominence and notoriety in the world of Italian business, he has been accused of many things, notably of bribing politicians to pass laws obliging shops to have cash registers which would itemize every purchase receipt (which Olivetti could of course supply). In October 1993 he was also accused of paying £5 million in bribes to the Post Office minister in return for contracts to computerize parts of the Italian postal service; he was also accused of charging more than the market price for the equipment. He was involved in the collapse of the Banco Ambrosiano, Italy's largest private bank, and he has been sought for questioning, along with Cesare Romiti, Fiat's chief executive, in connection with contracts given to Intermetro, the consortium charged with building Rome's new subway. By Italian standards these are typical, almost reasonable qualifications to run a newspaper. Indeed, Benedetti is regarded as a rather modest media tycoon with a reputation for a 'hands-off approach' to editorial matters, unlike his fellow media dabblers Gianni Agnelli and Silvio Berlusconi.

During April 1991, after a bitter legal battle, Benedetti and his arch rival Silvio Berlusconi presided over the division of Italy's then largest publishing group, Mondadori. Benedetti kept control of a publishing unit called L'Espresso, which embraced the best-selling liberal daily newspaper *La Repubblica*, Italy's second largest news magazine *Espresso* and a stable of 15 local papers. Berlusconi retained control of most of the old Mondadori empire, including the name, the political weekly *Panorama* and the weekly *Epoca*. As well as now controlling all the Mondadori publishing imprints and a chain of newspapers and magazines, Berlusconi also controls three of Italy's six nationwide TV channels, with access to over 40 per cent of all Italian viewers. He also owns the AC Milan football team, Standa, the largest supermarket chain in the country, Europe's biggest advertising agency Publitalia 80, and a vast feature film and local television empire. As a prologue to his wider ambitions he also owns a minority share in the French La Cinq television channel, as well as stakes in TeleFunf in Germany and TeleCinco in Spain.

During early 1994, despite some serious (£1.8 billion) debt problems within his main holding company Finivest, Berlusconi spotted a gap in the market for a political leader, particularly one who had the style and dynamism to banish the Left. In characteristic unabashed Italian fashion, he promptly enlisted all parts of his media empire to promote him as the political saviour of his country. His campaign war cry 'Forza Italia' (Come on, Italy) was one that all Italian soccer fans would recognize, and no space in his vast media machine was left untouched by it. More of an employees' club than a political party, Forza Italia candidates sought election by promoting family values, efficiency, anti-communism, a free market and, above all, an honest and corruption-free Italy. Although, unlike many other Italian tycoons, Berlusconi has never been officially named in any corruption case, his acquisition of a virtual monopoly of Italian commercial television, his highly secretive business dealings and his association with members of Italy's infamous and most secret Masonic Lodge, Propaganda 2, will always breed suspicion and doubts as to his political sincerity. Having achieved considerable success in the elections of March 1994, Forza Italia, and its allies the federalist Northern League and the neo-Fascist National Alliance, now have an outright majority in the lower Chamber of Deputies but only a relative majority in the upper Senate. As Prime Minister of the world's fifth largest industrial economy, Berlusconi now faces the major task of convincing the Italian public, not to mention the rest of the world, that he can deliver his political promises while standing at a distance from his own business interests. What is good for Italy might also be good for Finivest, but without a clear and believable separation of his business from his political interests Berlusconi risks having broken one political mould (Italy's old corrupt guard) only to replace it with another that is just as suspect:

> It is as though John Major owned all the ITV franchises and ITN, as well as the *Sunday Times*, a brace of important provincial daily newspapers, the Emap publishing house, Penguin Books, a mid-sized insurance group such as Royal Insurance, and Tesco, all wrapped up as the country's third largest private-sector concern with sales last year of 11.6 trillion lire, equivalent to £4.8 billion. And of course Manchester United as well. [12]

Early disagreements with his allies have dogged Europe's first media Prime Minister, but if he survives, observers will be particularly interested to see how he now relates to Benedetti and the 'royal family' of Italy, the Agnellis.

In 1994 the Agnelli family, the owners of the industrial giant Fiat, still own or control two of Italy's three most influential newspapers. de Benedetti's ownership of *La Repubblica* has denied them the third, although Gianni Agnelli's brother-in-law was once its managing director. The Agnellis have controlled the Milan-based *Corriere della Sera* since 1984 through their majority stake in Rizzoli-Corriere (RCS), now, with the breakup of Mondadori between Benedetti and Berlusconi, the biggest publishing group in the country and one that has proved hungry for acquisition. They have also owned the highly respected Turin daily paper *La Stampa* since 1920, and while they would not claim to be in the Berlusconi and Benedetti league when it comes to more widespread media holdings, they continue to use the power of print to support their interests whenever and wherever it is needed.

As the country's single biggest spender on advertising, through Fiat and their other industrial holdings, the Agnellis also have a major impact on the revenues of other media apparently outside their direct sphere of influence. It is an invisible power that they are known not to shirk from exerting, especially when offended by unsympathetic journalists or proprietors. The Agnellis have deliberately kept out of the television business: indeed, Gianni Agnelli is thought to have vetoed some proposed moves into TV during the late 1980s, preferring to let Berlusconi hold the field. It was noticeable during Fiat's controversial acquisition of Alfa Romeo from the government in 1986 (the government wanted to sell it to Ford), that the Berlusconi media said nothing. Friedman [13], after reflecting on how Italian newspaper proprietors love to fill the front pages of their own newspapers with material on themselves and their families, also notes the seriousness with which they ensure that the flavour of discourse that emerges from them is clearly their flavour:

By owning substantial portions of the media, Italian entrepreneurs are able subtly and indirectly to condition the coverage and help define the terms of debate. They exert vast amounts of time and energy cultivating 'friends' in the media, in a way which goes far beyond the wildest dreams of an American public relations man. Ownership, advertising and news-making: it is a powerful combination.

In Italy three or four men control the flow of most hard information without breaking any laws. They have cultivated an acceptable image of the industrialist as power-broker and legitimized the use of the press and television as a naked lever of that power. During the period after the dismantling of the state television monopoly, between 1976 and 1991, this select group ruthlessly exploited a regulationless home market presided over by toothless political coalitions. Clearly profiting from bureaucratic incompetence, political corruption and weak governments, they have in many ways operated nationally in a way their bigger brothers would like to operate globally. In more recent years, though, Italian governments have been growing less patient with the home-grown family dominance of their media. The Agnelli family have twice faced official criticism for their violation of newspaper circulation rules, the broadcasting law of 1990 for the first time set down understandable limits on who could own what, and since the beginning of 1993 clear limits have been placed on the timing and duration of television advertising. Whether a Berlusconi-led coalition will be as interested in pursuing excesses of media power will be a key test of his government's credibility.

This snapshot of media activity in the early 1990s suggests a business that is often moving so fast that even those deeply immersed in its workings are not always clear what is going on. While this book was being printed some major changes will have taken place in the partnerships and alliances noted above. While you have been reading this section, a chief executive somewhere will have been on the telephone clinching a new partnership, merger or buy-out, that will have changed the landscape again. Blink, and an independent media business disappears, blink again and a bigger media corporation is born.

What does it all mean?

Where I could, I have deliberately included the sums of money involved in the examples of media mergers and concentration given above. Although such figures may not mean much to most of us, the staggering size of the finance involved is always going to be an issue when considering the content of, and access to, information via these media. These billions lie at the root of what is offered and why. As well as funding the vital programming exclusivity that distinguishes one media combine from another, they also smooth the path through the laws and regulations that are the inevitable barrier to all moves into new markets. Billions are also required to keep up with the competitive possibilities offered by the new technology, to fund new acquisitions and possibly to buy the influence with politicians and political parties that can reduce the interference level with regard to monopolies commissions or anti-competitiveness committees. Many of the companies noted above are in direct competition and yet they often hold financial interests in each other. At times competitors, at times friends, at times seeming to be both, these relationships are not easily understood. That we are often only able to identify a small portion of their total business 'iceberg' is no doubt a great comfort to them. It is an interesting irony that we gain much of our information about media concentration and the workings of the corporations that fuel it, from commentators who are also employed by parts of it. As media mergers and acquisitions are now often significant news items in their own right, these great corporations increasingly mediate a lot of news about themselves.

To most people of course the business of media concentration is just high finance on a distant plane. Despite their patronage being what it is all about, they generally just get on with life, making daily choices from the media available. In reality this is often a mixture of one or two newspapers, a clutch of favourite television programmes, selected wavelengths on a radio, an occasional visit to the cinema or the theatre, books, magazines, films or other programmes on video, and recorded music. The use of these media is often determined by habit and routine. Changes in behaviour are often slow and there is still a considerable element of inertia in the way that we cling to particular forms of media.

This 'brand' loyalty poses both threats and opportunities to the media conglomerates. People may be reluctant to change but once they do they are likely to stick with the new offering long enough for it to grow on them. Change is usually brought about by one or a number of factors: variation in individual economic circumstances, new entrants to the market, a reduction in the time available to consume the media's offerings, increased variety, e.g. an increase in the number of television channels, and reductions in the cost of reception might all stimulate change, but despite its part in the rhetoric of free-market economics the exercize of raw consumer power is rare. When it is brought into play it is usually seen in the curtailing of an unpopular TV series, the decline in the sales of a particular artist, poor viewing figures for a one-off programme, the migration of audience share to a similar offering and, most dramatically, in the closure of a national newspaper. Consumers of information and entertainment are generally passive, and once 'plugged in' take quite a lot of unplugging. Advertisers, on the other hand, go where they believe the audience is: if they believe the audience is moving then they move. As they are increasingly targeting particular economic groups the suspected migration of quite small groups of consumers from one form of media to another can trigger serious losses in advertising revenue. The challenge thus facing all providers of information and entertainment is how to get people regularly plugged into their media conduit rather than that of a competitor. They are also keenly concerned to keep their costs low and their profits high, and to spread the risk, and hence the source, of their income across as broad a range of audience as possible. They want their media families to be at once independent and dependent. They want them to feed into and off each other when things are going well and they want them to be capable of independent survival should one or another experience a downturn in demand, hence the need to 'collect' as many varieties as possible beneath one corporate umbrella.

For those who think more deeply about the origin of the information and entertainment that most of us now consume, the issue of media concentration is one that still gives rise to serious concern. This is not shared by everyone and some commentators would question the need to worry at all. After all, big corporations are not new: why should the collection and integration of information into the ownership of fewer hands worry us any more than the corporate concentration that determines the cars we drive, the fridges we use and the clothes we wear? The worriers retort that media concentration is about the increasing centralization and control of a lot of the information that we process to construct meaning; that the modern media are the source of much of our understanding of both our local and global worlds, and that they increasingly create our reality for us. More and more it is they who define the issues that loom large on the agendas of public debate. As the construction of meaning influences all of our key behaviours, the issue of how we construct it is generally thought to be more important than cars and jumpers.

In one form or another the media, controlled by the kind of large combines noted above, have become the major source of our everyday information. We access some of it directly, but just as often indirectly through conversation. These media increasingly provide the ingredients from which we build up our picture of social reality, and, like the credibility that written information once gained over oral information, many people believe that information from these sources is impartial, authoritative, trustworthy and politically neutral. Is it our fault that we fall prey to such beliefs or is the raw power and the mix of new media now so strong that we need protection from it, as well as access to alternative constructions of the world? Higher levels of education all round might help to answer the first, and governments not afraid to take on the media conglomerates via creative and robustly monitored regulation, could help mitigate the worst excesses of the second. The ability to discriminate between that which is beneficial and that which is harmful is a skill that advanced societies have always celebrated. The new world of information concentration perhaps demands new and more sophisticated levels of preparation for which our current secondary school curriculum does not, as yet, cater.

The worriers also worry because they fear that, in the hands of fewer and fewer people, these powerful conduits will be manipulated by equally powerful interests, interests that may wish us to view the world from a particular perspective, to form or reform our opinions in a particular way, to encourage us to use our votes for a particular party, or to gain our support for the wars and military interventions that we are told are necessary to sustain world peace and world trade. The media owners would reply that it has all grown too big and too diverse for one person or small group of people to control and direct, that the media now does no more than reflect an already well established public opinion, and that they have little or no serious role in shaping it. They would point to the regular publication of material critical of governments and establishment figures as evidence of the diversity of ideas and opinions that they present to their audiences. At the same time they clearly believe in and promote a particular view of how society should be organized, and they are unlikely to let any media they own be used as a platform for opposing views, although Rupert Murdoch's future relationship with the Chinese government may well test this theory to breaking point.

The media may occasionally practice a little blast of moral indignation, as the British press did in early 1994, to remind the Major government of what 'back to basics' was supposed to mean, but normal service is always resumed as soon as possible. The media are also often critical of one-off isolated abuses that occur within the prevailing political and economic system. Some of these explorations have opened eyes, liberated new ideas and changed public perceptions about false leaders, false assumptions and antisocial conventions. The media also, at times, pose as the last repository and custodian of our moral and ethical values, but they are never critical of the nature of our economic organization or the basis of our political system. Any discussion of radical alternatives in these areas is always packaged within strictly limited boundaries. When 'big' alternatives, e.g. in areas like interpretations of democracy, transport policy, poverty, environmental economics or electoral reform do raise their heads above the parapet they are portrayed as unrealistic, extreme and unworkable. Dissent is always reported in the UK media as an unsavoury form of 'politics', never the healthy manifestation of democracy, and most of the time serious dissent from the dominant orthodoxy is just not covered. Such a narrow definition of the parameters of choice must, in the end, undermine any comprehensive attempt to approach political or economic literacy:

> Democracy, fundamentally, implies the right to choose between alterna- tive ideas, policies, people and even systems. Where the media present only a limited spectrum of ideas and foster uniformity of values and atti- tudes they severely constrain our ability to exercize genuinely free choice. Our 'pluralist' 'liberal' democracy is threatened by the tyranny of the mediocre, moderate majority which the great 19th century liberals feared above all. [14]

I suspect that many liberals in the 19th century would have been very happy with a good slice of the 'moderate majority', but this quote from Moyra Grant's *The British Media* is otherwise spot on. Although always the first to be called on to answer charges of manip- ulating public opinion, media proprietors are often guiltless of some of the misuse or misrepresentation of information that occurs in their various organs. Their employees are not always averse to using their positions to influence the style and content of feature or editorial material in return for a favour or a little consideration. Indeed, in some parts of the world journalism has long been regarded as little more than an extension of commerce. In Italy it is not unusual for Zanussi to offer journalists a free television set, for Benetton to fly a horde of feature writers to Havana for the opening of its new shop there (with a weekend in New York thrown in), for car companies to 'forget' to collect the vehicles that they left for testing, and for top designers to routinely cover the backs of fashion journalists with their latest gear. Writing positively about particular companies or products, because of the paid advertising that they have already taken, or in lieu of the advertising that they might yet be persuaded to buy, is almost universal in Italian news- papers and their even more popular magazines. For a journalist used to complying with the grander kinds of corporate partisanship, a little action on their own behalf would seem no more than a natural extension of the norm:

> When police arrested Carlo Sama, former chief executive of the Ferruzzi group, magistrates reportedly found a list of journalists' names among his papers. It emerged that the Ferruzzi family, anxious about their image, had earmarked a budget of more than a billion lire to bribe journalists 'able to influence the major papers'. Although Milan's attorney-general

later denied the existence of any such list, Sergio Cusani, one of Mr Sama's sidekicks, has insisted that the Ferruzzis not only made a practice of subverting the press, but that the press insisted on being subverted. [15]

The thin line between editorial and advertising is becoming a major challenge for newspaper readers in the 1990s. The crass signals put out by some sections of the Italian press is possibly less of an affront in a culture where the public is used to seeing 'thank you' written between so many lines. More problematical is the presentation of information which is packaged and presented in a way that could pass as neutral, where the sponsorship, while not hidden, is embedded in the proffered objectivity, and where the depth of the partnership between the sponsor and the media is at best opaque and at worst completely hidden. Late in 1993 the *Sunday Times* produced a supplement dedicated to 'Health care: a consumer guide to medical services' produced in association with Norwich Union Healthcare. Although offering around 13 pages of signed features on health care issues, it also carried two full-page advertisements for Norwich Union, an opportunity to win two weeks at a health hydro worth £2,000 sponsored by Norwich Union, and it carried the words 'Norwich Union' at the top of each page. One feature entitled 'More caring means a lot more sharing' drew particular attention to the way that the Norwich Union's own 'Trust Care' scheme fitted neatly in with the independent sector of the NHS in partnership with the new NHS trusts. There was no mention of any alternative schemes and none of the articles were headed with the words 'advertising feature', which is the conventional way of describing sponsored column inches in the UK. The feature material had a distinct flavour of 'the plain fact is that the traditional NHS has become too expensive for the country' about it, and the overall message was clearly intended to compare a vibrant and efficient private health sector with an inefficient, expensive and floundering public one.

Clearly the *Sunday Times* found that the 'special, sponsored supplement' approach worked, as it repeated the format, this time in association with IBM, in May 1994. Entitled 'Groupware, a guide to the next big step in information technology' this supplement also carried the name of the sponsor at the top of every page. Although the editorial content was not quite as blatantly one-sided as the Norwich Union piece, informed readers could be excused some surprise at the triumphant representation of IBM as a serious groupware player. Indeed, IBM, hardly noted for its dynamic role in networking or groupware at all, was portrayed as a key force in this domain, capable of sourcing all the networking needs of a modern business. While it was impossible to write 13 pages of editorial without including material on the main providers of groupware support, such as Lotus (Lotus Notes), Novell (Unix) and Microsoft (DOS and Windows), the IBM name was liberally sprinkled about the piece.

In future the potential moulders of opinion will concentrate a lot of time and effort on the 'received' component of 'received wisdom'. They will at all times be seeking to maximize audience figures and thus the value of the advertising or, increasingly, the subscription income, that they can attract. For television companies to do this cost-effectively their programming must have a global appeal, which is at odds with the current technological imperative of 'interactiveness', which theoretically allows for greater diversity and more choice. Although future providers may use 'increased choice' as the catch-phrase of the new 'interactive' information age, highly tailored options, apart from video on demand, will inevitably require a wide and diverse funding base that can operate on very many levels. The future economic basis for this is by no means clear. Catering for all the diverse choices that potential audiences might require is clearly not going to be economic: a limited choice within a clearly defined menu is the more likely outcome.

Many commentators believe that 'narrowband' opinion formation is already in full swing, and that it is destined to become even narrower in the future if the information journey from creation to presentation continues to be in the hands of a small number of big corporations. This view would generally equate diversity of output with diversity of input, with a concomitant access to a wider range of biases. Such a range of providers would require some form of subsidy to insulate them from the ravages of economic downturns and predatory pricing, and this is definitely not the flavour of the decade. We have seen how business and financial targets tend to be measured in telephone-like numbers; in the UK BT alone is forecasting an annual turnover of £2 billion a year by the end of the decade from its video-on-demand service, while SG Warburg the investment advisors have estimated the global media market to be worth US$3 trillion by the end of the decade, with roughly a third of this total ending up in Europe. During October 1993 the German film director Wim Wenders led a delegation of European film directors and producers to the EC Commission in Brussels, to demand a 'cultural exclusion' clause in the free trade rules of GATT to protect the European market from complete domination by Hollywood. He maintained that the situation with regard to European cultural production was now getting desperate:

> By the year 2000 the audiovisual sector would become the world's biggest industry . . . Europe will become a Third World continent because we will not have anything to say on the most important medium

... There is a war going on and the Americans have been planning for it for a long time. The most powerful tools are images and sound. [16]

Despite an existing EC Broadcast Directive that urges all member states to ensure that at least 50 per cent of programming is produced in Europe (France has its own requirement of at least 60 per cent), Wenders' vision of a future film and television industry swamped by American software played on Japanese hardware is not difficult to imagine. From a base of US$750 million in 1980, US film exports rose from US$3,750 million in 1990 (EC film exports to the US stood at just US$250 million in that year), to a total of US$5.5 billion in 1992. Of these sales no less than US$3.7 billion were made in Europe. With American films taking almost 80 per cent of EC box office receipts back home with them, the figures do look like a 'war' against indigenous film makers – if indeed there is any truly indigenous film making going on. Despite a market that is now equal in scale to that of the US, film and programme makers in Europe have a cultural strength, the richness of their many languages, which is unfortunately a big disadvantage in the film business. Although the 4441 cinema screens in France may still give over nearly 40 per cent of their time to European films, the 1787 screens in the UK spare only 15 per cent of their market to European output [17]. Subtitles rarely make for block-busters on the Hollywood scale:

> The European [Film] Academy thinks that, despite the continent's illus-trious history, it is going to be increasingly difficult to save the European cinema from permanent art-house status or even virtual extinction. And that, if an outstanding European film-maker comes along, he or she is more likely, in Bertolucci's immortal phrase to 'suck the tits of Hollywood' than try to fight a losing battle at home. [17]

As it turned out, the European fear of a post-GATT North American media tidal wave was considerably allayed by the continuing protection afforded to the European film and media business at the final GATT round held in Geneva during December 1993. Prior to this, the Spanish commentator Mario Vargas Llosa [18] highlighted the futility of any quota system, as well as noting some of the less attrac-tive, racist and vested privilege features of a closed media market:

> For there is nothing that corrupts, vitiates, mediocritizes creative work as much as state parasitism does. There is abundant proof of this in the audio-visual field. If not, then what about the staggering volumes of films pro-duced at immense cost by states bent on defending their 'national culture'? Not one in a thousand of such films is remembered today, or salvageable from the rubbish dump of oblivion on account of its artistic value.

The French would not agree. They take their indigenous cinema and television output seriously, as representing key ingredients of French cultural identity, the pastoral evocation of which was most recently brought out in the filming of Marcel Pagnol's 'Jean de Florette' and 'Manon des Sources'. Encapsulating a deep Frenchness in their traditions, behaviour, routine and language, the French film industry represents something very important to French morale and cultural identity. Vargas Llosa recites the protectionist dirge without sympathy:

> The central argument of these adversaries of the total opening of markets is that 'culture' is a matter apart, and that products of the artistic spirit and fantasy of a nation cannot be put in the same bag with washbasins, computers, automobiles and other manufactured products. Unlike these other wares, artistic and cultural creations must be protected, shielded against a competition in which they might disappear, thus depriving the nation that created them of its tradition, its idiosyncrasy, its spiritual identity. [18]

However, as we have seen, cultural and information products are increasingly being sucked into a global test of their attractiveness and value against which local protectionism can only be temporary. Indeed, the denationalization of European audiovisual media is already a reality: the search for a truly authentic English, German or French production is now rather like a search for unicorns, not many of them about. What now defines national authenticity? Is it the actors? Is it the writers? Is it the technicians? Is it the director? A random look at the rolling credits of any non-American production reads like a European Parliament, and why not? European and international cooperation has been one of the most important sources of funding for big media projects since the Second World War, often facilitating work that would never have seen the light of day via strictly nationalistic avenues of enthusiasm.

Europe may feel that it has its own problems of cultural 'swamping' by US programmes, but the rest of the world tends not to differentiate too much: they are still the receivers of a highly rationalized and edited view of the world which excludes or marginalizes their own cultural achievements which, they are told, do not have the same potential for commercial exploitation. Equipped with vast resources, the media moguls now stand ready to invade the recently liberated airwaves of eastern Europe. Together with the likes of Time Warner, TCI and Turner Broadcasting, News Corporation has the opportunity to explore all the possibilities of 'infotainment'. With vast stocks of information and entertainment stored in a variety of media, NC can convert any of it into a new form of electronic package for onward distribution to any viable market. Once a business like NC has the rights to a piece of information it can more or less sit back and wait for the technology to provide new ways of distributing it. The word 'library' has taken on a new meaning in the global media context. Stocks of books, maps, news headlines, sports information, magazine features, financial information, feature films and documentaries, all originally packaged in one format for one audience, can now be digitally compressed and repackaged for different audiences in a more convenient or more portable form.

It is getting increasingly difficult to know what comes first in the modern information world, the need or the technology. Does the perceived need for up-to-the-minute information accelerate the development of smaller and more sophisticated electronic devices, or does the existence of such devices generate a desire for more accessible and up-to-date information? Marketed in the first instance to techno-friendly youngsters, the more attractive and time-specific information of this kind will soon be available via portable handheld equipment that is capable of instant updating via cordless networks. As the amount of information that the silicon chip can store gets bigger, so the world gets smaller. Hard-headed businessmen shake with excitement when they see a chance to get in on the global media action, often cheerfully ignoring their once powerful corporate accountants. Time shareholders have yet to see anything like the US$200 per share that they would have got if they had joined with Paramount rather than Warner in 1989. Five years after their acquisition of Columbia and MCA, Sony and Matsushita still live with the negative equity of having bought expensive and temperamental assets at the top of the market and, given the Chinese government's recent clampdown on the erection of satellite dishes and their general nervousness at the boldness of his Asian pretensions, Rupert Murdoch may have to wait many years before his major investment in Star TV brings home the expected bacon.

The US$10 billion enthusiasm for Paramount Communications drummed up by two experienced media men, Barry Diller and Sumner Redstone, at a time when few others ever rated the company at more than US$8 billion, is probably the most recent example of the crazy–brave acquisition syndrome. The returns will come, but reflect on the corporate shareholders of BSkyB who had to wait four years before receiving their first dividend.

Currently none of the media conglomerates is yet so large as to be able to monopolize the great range and variety of services needed to meet worldwide demand, or to bar other potential players entering the business. However, some real barriers to entry could now be on the horizon. Suppose a newly established news provider seeks to compete with CNN in the US. As the guardian of 40 per cent of the cables going into American homes, and with a 23 per cent stake in CNN, TCI would have to be persuaded that, even though the newcomer could pay the necessary 'tolls' to use its wires, it should compromise its own investment in an existing news service. Once those that control the wires are also allowed to own and control the programming, new entrants to the market are going to find it hard to get in. This is not the stuff of unfettered competition or the much-heralded unlimited consumer choice!

If TCI's partnership with QVC to acquire Paramount had been successful, the urge to keep even more programming within this particular family would have been very strong, and a key gateway to Al Gore's 'superhighway' might suddenly have closed shut. As an aside, it is interesting to note how quickly some of these North American players are moving into the UK, both to lay cable and to provide programmes. The QVC 24-hour shopping channel is now available on BSkyB, and TCI is heavily involved in the construction of cable television and telephone networks throughout the UK.

Concentration: hospitality or restriction?

Small publishers, radio stations and television companies are finding it increasingly difficult to survive in modern market conditions. Their strengths – freshness, irreverence towards the received wisdom, independence, individual attention to their audience and their contributors – are highly valued but expensive to maintain. Without subsidy their unit costs will be very high and to cut labour costs they need access to the very best in state-of-the-art technology, which requires serious capital investment which in turn requires steady and secure income flows to service. Customers now generally demand greater sophistication in both content and presentation from their media. The big corporations have the financial muscle to deliver this: they can call on reporters and presenters from enterprises within the same group from all over the world, with a cost-effectiveness that a smaller, independent provider would find impossible to emulate. They are also less likely to be susceptible to the ebb and flow of market conditions, and hence more reliable in terms of promised delivery, but there will probably be some restrictions on choice arising out of the limited coverage of some programming: the supplying company may own the film stock of a specific studio or group of studios and may not wish to buy in material from elsewhere, and this principle might also operate with regard to other forms of information.

Viewers and listeners often assume that the media they are using offers them a thorough and comprehensive coverage of anything they might want to use. They are rarely aware of limiting factors such as restricted licences or a requirement to draw only on certain in-house stocks of film or other media. Their perception is that, through this one channel, the world is their information and entertainment oyster, and of course individual media combines do nothing to disabuse them of this. Customers now do get some prenotified niche delivery of services when they subscribe to film, sport or music TV channels, but they have no idea what might be included or excluded in the service of a general, commercial provider.

Other kinds of less welcome synergy might also come into play as a conglomerate makes use of its power to promote some parts of its empire at the expense of others. The censoring of information about potentially embarrassing issues arising in parts of their non-media business is an obvious concern: when media groups do censor they will endeavour to do so subtly so as not to draw attention to it. They will take the same care over the promotion of causes which they believe will benefit other parts of the corporation.

Within print publishing it is likely that some small book publishers will survive in highly specialized niche markets, but the appetite for integrating all but the very smallest of these into bigger concerns will continue unabated. Virago in the UK is an example of a small publisher that is still independent and, more to the point, still profitable 20 years after its formation in 1973. Virago began by reprinting the works of often long-forgotten women writers in distinctive green covers. The acquisition rights of these early works were, by modern standards, quite cheap, and it remains to be seen whether Virago can continue its success with living writers, who may require large cash advances prior to publication.

The acquisition of Hodder and Stoughton by the smaller, leaner and financially fitter Headline Publishing in the UK is an interesting example of higher percentage profits being more than a match for big turnover.

There does not seem to have been a major reduction in book publishing as a result of the trend towards concentration: British book publishing's 80 000 titles turned over £2.5 billion in 1992, with exports accounting for some £500 million of that figure.

With the entry of the media conglomerates into publishing came new laws of efficiency: titles that just made profits were no longer enough, each unit had to have a clear programme of minimum profit set by someone who knew about profits rather than publishing. Then came the market researchers, the elevation of 'formula' to new heights, the airport bestseller (5 per cent of all 'trade' books sold in Britain are sold at airports), the personality books, the TV tie-ins. In retrospect the roots of the commoditization of western book publishing will probably be traced back to the age of imprint concentration but, like all trends in mass communication, the seeds were probably sown well before, both in the more competitive world that small publishers were having to operate in and the smaller margins available to invest in new books.

There is no denying that the popularity of certain sorts of books in the 1990s does seem disproportionate when considered against their expected place in the scheme of things. Some particularly repetitive appetites have been created (slimming, cooking and lifestyle books) via the enthusiastic media tie-in synergy that sees healthy profits from mixing up the same content in as many different forms of media as possible. This concentration must obviously squeeze other, less starstruck, titles out, but there have always been fashions in publishing and it has always found space for a less than profound popular item at the expense of something more profound. For instance, if a publisher's revenues are regularly tied up in funding £100,000 advances to the authors of blockbuster novels expected to sell in millions, this cash is not going to be available to fund the specialist authors who, for one-hundredth of such sums, would toil away on one or more of 'the 15 ancient civilizations of Africa'. Many publishers are caught up in this trap: having paid out so much money it would be foolish not to follow it up with a sensible marketing budget, to make sure they achieve the sales necessary to refund the advance and possibly make a profit.

Within media groups with diverse commercial interests there will undoubtedly be pressure at times to carry out policies and actions which will not be in the public interest, and which in other industries would warrant the appointment of a formal regulator. Aware of this, many governments have enacted laws and regulations to help retain some vestige of diversity and competition within their various national media. Such controls usually fall into one of two main categories:

1. Laws governing the cross-ownership of different forms of media.
2. Laws restricting the percentage holdings that foreign nationals can take in different media businesses.

They vary considerably both in their detailed provisions and in the intensity of their enforcement. They also still tend to be based on national sovereignties, whereas the big media operations increasingly defy categorization in national terms. There is, as yet, no organization charged with the international policing of media expansion. In the UK the 1990 Broadcasting Act restricted newspaper proprietors to a max-imum 20 per cent holding in television stations, but these safeguards do not apply to satellite television, which it defined as a non-domestic service and hence exempt from any ownership restrictions. Thus despite Rupert Murdoch's lack of European citizenship, his 50 per cent interest in BSkyB continues to be legally compatible with his ownership of five UK national newspapers. A wide-ranging review of cross-media ownership is currently underway in the UK. A first for such a review is that it is planned to involve some unified thinking about relationships between all the elements involved within the three main media, i.e. broadcasting, the press and telecommunications. Bringing together officials from the National Heritage Department, the Department of Trade and the Downing Street Policy Unit, it is expected to recommend a major liberalization of UK cross-media ownership rules for enactment some time towards the end of 1994. The review should take the opportunity to establish some durable principles, firm enough to cope with the build-up of pressure to diversify from the current operators, and imaginative enough to allow true consumer access and choice. One principle that should not be compromised is the need to ensure that there will be room for several rival delivery systems, available to both suppliers and consumers of information. A second principle should ensure that there is competition within as well as between different systems of delivery. A third, and most important, principle should be that those in the delivery business should not be permitted to be service suppliers as well. At the moment BSkyB in the UK and Canal Plus in France both deliver programmes via their satellite services and own the programmes that they deliver. They also operate technologically advanced conditional-access systems, which allows them to ensure that their services are only seen by those who have paid for them. The big question, as we have seen, is how to insist that space be found for newcomers while the existing players grow bigger, stronger and ever more exclusive.

These issues, complicated in Europe by the need also to seek and find a consensus within the European Union, defy the simplistic analysis of free-marketeers and bureaucrats alike. Despite its low-key start – no formal issuing of consultation papers, no commission of enquiry and no Green Paper – it is clear that the outcome of the UK government's review will have a major impact on the range and quality of entertainment and information accessible to all UK citizens in the future. One widely expected outcome is that the government will allow a larger role for newspaper publishers in television ownership. Politicians everywhere are growing increasingly concerned at the threat to democratic debate by the growth of powerful multimedia empires. The big media entrepreneurs invest a great deal of time, effort and cash seeking to overcome cross-ownership and foreign status restrictions. They employ armies of lawyers skilled in seeking ways around national restrictions. They are particularly interested in scouring the legal definitions of 'control' to find ways in which seemingly separate but close business associates or family members might take on the mantle of proprietor or owner, while both control and profits remain within the main company. Opposition parties who threaten to enforce media regulation when they come to power undoubtedly incur the editorial wrath of media proprietors who have prospered under a more *laissez faire* approach. The UK Labour party's declared aim to force a showdown with News Corporation over its cross-ownership holdings, when next in government, will inevitably result in editorial hostility to their policies during the next general election campaign. NC in particular has benefitted from the current government's hands-off policy with regard to the breadth of its newspaper and satellite TV ownership, and it will be expected to return the favour via obvious media support for the Conservative party at election time. Receiving and returning favours is something which the modern media industry clearly understands and rewards.

In 1992, in association with the BBC, BSkyB entered the bidding to televise live football from the newly formed 'Premiership' in the UK. Alan Sugar, the Chairman and Managing Director of Amstrad, the consumer electronics company that supplied satellite dishes to BSkyB subscribers, also happened to be the Chairman of Tottenham Hotspur Football Club. Tottenham was to play in the Premiership and its Chairman would thus be a legitimate party to the negotiations determining who would get the television rights. Sugar had little or no prior history of enthusiasm for football, or for Tottenham Hotspur. During the crucial and confidential meeting of club chairmen to discuss the bids, Sugar left the negotiations and phoned BSkyB to urge them to increase their offer, as the terrestrial commercial stations had put in a higher bid. BSkyB simply had to win if it was to gain the kind of subscription income it needed to keep it viable. It was a battle it could not lose. This scene, of Alan Sugar making an urgent phone call to BSkyB from a public phone in the lobby of a London hotel, captured the imagination of the non-Murdoch press. It seemed to characterize an almost total loss of integrity among media operators in the UK; a new level of grubbiness had set in. The role of the once mighty BBC, now a junior partner, set only to get the crumbs of recorded highlights from the deal, reinforced the feeling that not just sport on TV, but that TV itself would never be the same again. Whatever bid the ITV companies made BSkyB would have to top it. As well as the cachet of being associated with the national television channel, BSkyB would also gain access to the extensive equipment and facilities that the BBC already had in place at all the locations where Premiership matches would be played.

In the face of such complex 'favour' networks, and pending the outcome of the major review noted above, the UK looks particularly vulnerable to mogul manipulation, but capturing exclusive sports coverage for satellite channels is not confined to the UK. During late 1993 Murdoch's Fox Broadcasting Company paid an astonishing US$1.5 billion for the television rights to cover the next four seasons of the National Football League Conference (NFL). CBS, who lost the NFL rights to Fox, is now without football coverage for the first time since it started broadcasting the games in 1956. Although to many outsiders this deal looked like another bout of mogulmania, Fox, like BSkyB, is gambling on the longer term. Seeking to challenge the big three networks, CBS, NBC and ABC, Fox needs to raise its credibility with viewers and sponsors alike. Commentators on Sunday afternoon football games in the US traditionally plug the evening schedule of the channel, and Fox needs greater viewer familiarization with its schedules. The NFL will also attract new advertisers who, although drawn initially by the football, are likely to stay on to reinforce their message in association with other Fox offerings. Up until now Fox's attraction to advertisers has been small, but agents will now be seeking to allocate a larger slice of their budget to Fox's improved inventory mix, including the all-important 18–45-year-old males who make up the majority of football-watching Americans. Murdoch knows that American football is big business – advertising revenue during the 1993 Superbowl ran at around US$1.7 million per minute. He also knows that come the new ubiquity of cable and satellite links, owning the programmes will mean holding the pass, while owning the archives means holding exclusive access to all those future compilations and montages that have become so much a part of our popular culture.

In most countries at least, the state-run broadcasting authorities bear the semblance of being independent. Theoretically they have no special interest group twisting their arm, no dependence on the whims and fancies of advertising agencies, no reason to be partisan in a particular way. They are often strong on reflecting the diversity of their indigenous cultures and they usually have clear mandates to educate and inform as well as to entertain. Their sponsor, however, being a government of whatever political hue, will, in certain circumstances, want to exercise some control. Some exercize total control, feeding their citizens propaganda and misinformation as if in a constant state of war. They have failed to grasp that this only bores people into seeking both solace and information elsewhere. But even the so-called democratic governments have secrets: they and their agencies make mistakes, they will often want to minimize bad publicity, they will want certain things to go in a certain way, they want to look good and they want media criticism kept to a minimum. Given their temporary nature and the constant glare of the spotlight on their doings, the behaviour of democratically elected governments is generally more circumspect; censorship of one kind or another is the usual charge that is levied against them and it is an instrument that they use in a variety of guises. One approach is to bring about pressure to prevent the making of a programme, or to ban it for a specified period so that it does not appear at a time that might embarrass them, or to prevent it being shown at all. In the UK the BBC is, at various times, accused by parties of both the left and the right of extreme bias, but this has so far not prevented the BBC, the ITV companies or Channel 4 from continuing to produce material that is uncomfortable for the government of the day. The BBC can still be punished by a government squeezing of the licence fee, via which it acquires its £1.5 billion of main income, while pressure can be brought to bear on the ITV companies through the government-nominated members of the Independent Television Commission.

However, it is not only governments that impose censorship: each of us carries out acts of conscious censorship every day when we suppress bits of information that we feel we would rather hold on to for the time being, and possibly forever. Human behaviour with regard to sharing information, even among those ostensibly committed to the freedom of artistic expression, can often seem contradictory. Gaps between rhetoric in support of unimpeded access to information, and the eventual test of this in practice, are commonplace. The fashionable opportunism of the Thatcher years – just 'being economical with the truth' in the UK – and the serious discrepancies found within the 'absolute' statements by Presidents on issues from Watergate to the Iran–Contra affair in the US, have left us less surprised than we might otherwise have been at the now almost daily revelations of information tampering and suppression.

Towards the end of 1993 Channel 4 felt the pinch of censorship when Time Warner secured a court injunction to stop it from showing extracts from the Stanley Kubrick film 'A Clockwork Orange'. The extracts were to appear in a programme aimed at reviewing the film's relationship with the country that inspired it (Britain), together with comment on its continued exclusion from British cinema screens. In the absence of any evidence or statements to the contrary it has always been assumed that Kubrick had the film withdrawn from the UK in 1972, after some highly speculative press reports linked it with certain incidents of perceived 'copycat' violence. The injunction against Channel 4 was eventually overturned by the Court of Appeal, using Section 30 of the UK's 1988 Copyright Act, which allows for the use of film and television material for the purpose of review and criticism. Without this right the critical review of any material would be limited to that which a publisher or a distributor chose to make available, or that which the television company could afford to buy. It is not really known whether Time Warner was acting in support of Kubrick's

20-year-old ban. If they were, they would have done well to note his impassioned attack on the 'irrational diktat' of the *Detroit Times* after it had decided in 1972 not to carry any advertising or reviews for 'X' rated films such as 'A Clockwork Orange'. At that time Kubrick wrote to them in the following vein:

> There is no power, legal or otherwise, which should be exercized against the rights of adults to select their own entertainment. [It is] an act inimical to the principles of freedom. . . . A film is made to be seen by the public. [19]

Kubrick was understandably upset that an important regional newspaper was going to ignore his film, which had been nominated for four Academy Awards, including Best Picture, and one which he believed had important things to say about life in Britain in the early 1970s. Above all, he felt that the paper was arrogantly interposing itself between its readers and their ability to make up their own minds. It is interesting how censorious even artists of liberation can become: Waldemar Januszczak, Channel 4's commissioning editor for arts and music, was not slow to note the irony:

> Thus Channel 4 found itself in the curious position of defending the right of 'A Clockwork Orange' to be seen as a work of art in the public domain and that therefore can be reviewed properly and seriously, while its distributors were insisting that the film was a sellable product whose value we were undermining by reviewing it. [19]

Behavioural ambiguities, such as those faced by Channel 4 during this incident, have always lent a sense of fragility to our 'Athenian' value system. Given that human approaches to information access and availability can be so volatile, it should not surprise us that we carry this trait over into the institutions we create. If there is no guaranteed probity in our day-to-day information exchanges, even at the most mundane conversational level, why should it be any different within the communication systems we build? The UK is very much what I would describe as 'a great sins of omission' culture, where there is almost a predilection to say less rather than more in our everyday exchanges, a climate where reticence is natural and where secrecy is clearly embedded in all levels of our organizational and institutional arrangements. By choosing to highlight some issues and exclude others all authors act as conscious censors. They have preferences and build up a case or a story around these preferences. They would claim that they have no brief to be – in fact could never be – complete. They would say that if their omissions are so serious, so crass and so obvious, that others are bound to want to respond to ensure the publication of an alternative view. Libraries regularly fall prey to economic censorship in their choice of materials, one version of a work being more affordable than another and some authors being excluded simply because there are not enough funds to represent all. The issue of access to the different kinds of media by aspiring artists can also seem censorious by exclusion. It is a huge question.

The big media conglomerates are unlikely to seek, or to provide a base for, the experimental and the innovative: the imperative of their mass income base steers them towards the tried and tested. It is some testimony to the success of market demands that they do eventually engage avant-garde material that has been 'tried out' elsewhere. This is all the more reason to ensure that there are always locations for these 'trials' and that they do not disappear completely. We always assume that artists want the largest possible audience for their work, both to share their ideas with as many people as possible and to produce as much income as possible. Surprisingly, this may not always be true, but if their work amuses, delights, thrills and informs a select few, it will not be long before someone will want to bring it to the many.

Truth, reliability, distortion

During 1993 the widely respected journalist Julian Pettifer revisited Vietnam, 25 years after going there to report on the war. In a television documentary ('Frontline', Channel 4, 27 June 1993) he accepted that he, along with many other journalists, despite being present on the ground – in his case for nine years between 1966 and 1975 – had got much of what they reported wrong. Rather than the simple anti-American, anti-communist, colonial conflict that much of his earlier reporting emphasized, he now accepted that the true picture was much more complex. Denied access to what was going on among the Viet Cong in the north, the 'pack' mentality that often grips war journalists fed on and reinforced the idea of an American rather than a Vietnamese war. Obsessed with the Americans and all their doings, they failed to recognize that they were really in the middle of a civil war between one people with two very different ideas on how they wanted their futures to look.

With the wisdom of hindsight, Pettifer was exploring one of the big questions of information probity. However willing he may have been to find and export the 'truth', just being a part of the media business had cut him off from the thing he most wanted: however inadvertently, the good reporter became part of a badly distorted message. This was highlighted for him when his boss, on receiving what he regarded as some good film footage back in London, got a fast message back to him along the lines of 'all that we need now is some material showing you in serious danger'. Pettifer was not an obsequious servant of an uncaring conglomerate: he was simply not able to get to the crux of what was really happening in Vietnam. Yet what he said was being taken seriously by millions of people. Their constructions on the progress of the war, on the rights and wrongs of it, and on the behaviour of the various participants, were largely formed by the authoritative way in which he presented his reports.

News via brief, two or three minute television slices always has a tendency to trivialize, simply because to go deeper would need much more time and a wider range of viewpoints. Pettifer was both the creator and the victim of the growing homogenization of news. Like so many others, he was packaging information in readiness for yet further repackaging, which would ensure that it fitted the rituals and conventions, the viewpoints and angles that have become the accepted 'craft' of news presentation. In his *Who Stole the News* (1994), a follow-up to his equally incisive *Coups and Earthquakes* (1979), Mort Rosenblum [20], himself an Associated Press reporter for over 25 years, offers a merciless critique of contemporary news construction. Compulsive reading for anyone who is interested in judging just how much of the truth gets through to viewers and readers, his story is a catalogue of black humour and shame in equal proportions. Getting deep into the nitty-gritty of the day-to-day life of a news reporter, he exposes the crass interventions often required to get the sound and pictures demanded by the executives back home, the sometimes hideous reconstructions created to fit in with key time slots and, most saddening of all, some appalling examples of the treatment handed out to the victims of famine, fire and sword in the name of reporting from the scene. Some of this crassness seems unbelievable. In his Chapter 2, where he deals with the reporting of the famine in Somalia, Rosenblum notes how the US Air Force, in carrying out its initial aid flights to that stricken country, still managed to ensure that they scheduled in one journalist for every ton of food, and of how burly US marines mindlessly trampled on the bare feet of the children in an orphanage as they doled out food to their more fortunate comrades before the cameras.

Pettifer and Rosenblum are not alone in wrestling with the dilemmas of being inside a circus that they know can do better. Decoding the language of the everyday media is not easy when we are all part of the code itself. John Pilger, another well respected television journalist in the UK, has also spoken out strongly about the limits of public scrutiny that he sees being imposed by a relentless sameness in the 'objective' reporting of news. As illuminating illustrations of this he tells two stories drawn from external observers. One story tells of Russians visiting the US in the years before *glasnost*, how they could not believe, after reading the newspapers and watching the news on a variety of television stations, that all the opinions on the key issues seemed to be the same:

'In our country' they said, 'to get that result, we have a dictatorship. We imprison people. We tear out their fingernails. Here, you have none of that. So what's the secret? How do you do it?' [21]

Filming secretly in Czechoslovakia in 1970, Pilger was working with members of the Charter 77 group who were concerned to ensure that, in gaining freedom of expression, they did not mimic 'the illusions of the west'. The banned Czech writer Zdener Urbanak noted that:

You in the west have a problem. You are not sure when you are being lied to, when you are being tricked. We do not suffer from this; and unlike you we have been forced to acquire the skill of reading between the lines. [21]

In examining the origins of the First World War, the great communicator A.J.P. Taylor was convinced that, as all the plans for the mobilization of great armies in 1914 depended on railways, and as railways have to run to fixed timetables, it was railway timetables that eventually determined the resolution of the disputing nations to wage war. Any modification affecting one direction would ruin the plans for those coming in the other direction. Thus it is with information packaged as news. All around the globe, lunchtime, early-evening, mid-evening and late-evening news broadcasts occur at fixed times over rigidly controlled durations. Nearly all western political behaviour is organized around news opportunities and many important political or economic statements are timed in order to catch the most favoured news transmissions. US marines never seem to land anywhere in the world, whatever the urgency of the mission, at any other than a Pentagon-timed photo-opportunity, orchestrated to gain prime-time transmission, usually on a beach where the lighting would do justice to a Spielberg blockbuster. Satellite and cable news channels have made some of this timetabling seem less important, but despite this the news output of the established terrestrial television and radio stations is still regarded as the most important source of hard information available from these media, not least because, for most people at least, their timing is right. Given these traditions, it will be interesting to see whether the 'news on demand' experiment announced in mid 1994 by IBM and ITN attracts many takers from the business and commercial sectors.

So much a part of national life is television news in the UK that when the 14 regional ITV companies sought to change the timing of the late night 'News At Ten' they suffered severe rebukes, not just from the ITC but from politicians of all parties, the Prime Minister and the Commons National Heritage Select Committee. Interestingly, all of these groups saw the continuation of a hard news slot at 10 o'clock in the evening as a serious test of the new ITV franchisees' continuing commitment to quality news and information. We can assume that 10 o'clock in the evening of itself possesses no mystical significance for the nation as a whole, and that had the tradition been to put out the late evening news at 9.30 p.m. or 10.30 p.m. these times would have exacted a similar reverence when threatened. The House of Commons National Heritage Select Committee attempted some clarification of why 10 o'clock was such a critical information moment. They were concerned that 'News At Ten' had featured as part of the 'core information' submitted by the franchisees in their bids for their licences, and that:

> . . . an earlier bulletin could not offer coverage of any news that developed beyond the afternoon, including political news, sports results, news from America and hard-hitting news that is normally withheld from younger audiences. [22]

In fact only eight of the ITV companies had made a specific commitment to broadcast 'News At Ten' in their franchise applications, but as all 14 companies were required to broadcast national news bulletins from ITN live and simultaneously, this effectively tied the other six to the same policy. Unfortunately, this sentiment has to live in tandem with the strong competitive ethos that has emerged from the government-inspired bidding process for the commercial franchises which emerged from the 1990 Broadcasting Act. After a much criticized auction, the successful ITV companies ended up paying a collective £300 million to the Treasury for their licences. As more than two-thirds of commercial television advertising revenue is earned between 6.30 p.m. and 10.30 p.m., it should not surprise the government that scheduling for these four hours will become more and more critical. The new franchisees now have to compete more aggressively with the BBC, BSkyB and Channel 4, and this led them to re-examine the cost of 'News At Ten', which clearly gets in the way of more revenue-rich options like film and drama. The 'News At Ten' saga turned out to be something of a test case for the ITC, who had previously watched helplessly as Yorkshire Television took over Tyne-Tees Television, and as critical management and programme changes took place at Granada, all within weeks of the ITC accepting their new licence pledges. The storm-in-a-teacup news scheduling crisis is just a foretaste of bigger controversies to come.

The future place of news, information and current affairs in an increasingly American type of scheduling environment will crop up again and again as the old values of public-service television slip away in the face of shareholder demands. For the UK commercial television stations the mix of programming, public interest, commercial and legal issues arising out of this particular controversy served as a useful lesson in public relations. They learnt that media issues can assume a high political and public interest profile. Bloodied but unbowed, they will no doubt return to this particular fray later, probably with a much softer sell. They would certainly not want it to jeopardize their long-term goal of securing greater commercial television concentration in the UK. They did not have to wait long. In November 1993 the British government announced a cautious easing of the moratorium, established in the 1990 Broadcasting Act, on mergers between the 14 ITV operators. This paved the way for takeovers between the larger franchise holders, with the proviso that no one will be allowed to hold more than two licences, that they can only hold 20 per cent of a third company and only up to 5 per cent in any others, and that the two London licence-holders, Carlton and London Weekend Television (LWT), are barred from taking each other over. Within days of this relaxation of the rules, and before Parliament had even had a chance to debate the proposed changes, the first shots were fired. Carlton Communications, which provides the weekday commercial television service to the London area, launched a friendly bid for Central Independent Television, who hold the franchise for the west and east Midlands of England. Shortly after this, Granada, who hold the franchise for the northwest of England, made a less than welcome bid for LWT. Early in 1994 MAI, a financial services and media group that already owns Meridian, the ITV franchise holder for the south of England, gained a speedy exemption from referral to the Monopolies and Mergers Commission with regard to its takeover of Anglia Television. Thus within four months 14 ITV channels had become 11. Apart from heralding the beginning of a sea change in regional television in the UK, the Carlton–Central merger also raises important questions of principle for the ITC. Central is a regional television station of the old school. As well as a broadcaster, it was also a distinguished and award-winning programme maker. Carlton, on the other hand, is more of a new-style publisher–contractor, commissioning the bulk of its programmes from independent producers and buying in ready-made sitcoms and costume dramas. One consequence of such a merger could be a decline in the general quality of programming across the new network and a reduction in the number of programmes made in the Midlands with a distinctly Midlands flavour.

The joint company, worth around £1.5 billion in annual sales and serving some 20 million viewers, is easily the biggest commercial television station in Britain, attracting 31 per cent of ITV net advertising revenue, or 22 per cent of total terrestrial revenue if advertising income for Channel 4 is also included. The way this percentage is calculated is important, as it would keep the combined group's advertising income within the maximum 25 per cent rule set by the ITC and regulated by the Office of Fair Trading. The future potential for a joint Carlton – Central advertising rate, which in pounds per thousand of viewers would be cheaper than anything its rivals could provide, might seriously destabilize the economic fabric of the other regional franchises. Channel 4, only recently responsible for its own advertising, would also be a loser in any battle for bargain-basement advertising.

The British government did not really have much choice but to relax the rules on ITV takeovers by British firms. Under existing UK legislation, any company operating within the European Union would have been able to bid for any ITV company from 1 January 1994, the date that the moratorium banning foreign takeovers of British ITV companies expired. All the smaller independent television companies will become potential takeover targets as the larger ones look for suitable partners. By international standards most of the current ITV companies are tiny. Even HTV, with a market value of only £58.5 million, is defined as a 'large' company under the 1990 Broadcasting Act. Compared with Bertelsmann in Germany or Time Warner in the US, these companies are media minnows, and it is easy to see why the larger ITV companies want the opportunity to achieve more economies of scale. They want more synergy and bigger profits and they want to be able to compete more effectively in world, rather than local, media markets. The 40-year-long regional identity of commercial television in the UK will now inevitably give way to supraregional conglomerates serving much bigger, more advertiser-friendly populations.

The writing was already on the screen: in 1993 Granada owned 17.5 per cent of BSkyB, 18 per cent of ITN and 17.5 per cent of London Weekend Television. LWT owned 14 per cent of Yorkshire Television, 20 per cent of GMTV and 18 per cent of ITN. Carlton already held a 20 per cent stake in Central Television, 20 per cent of GMTV, an indirect stake in the south-coast broadcaster Meridian and 18 per cent of ITN. Central owned 20 per cent of Meridian and 18 per cent of ITN.

The great seduction now is that the home market, wherever it is, is no longer big enough to sustain quantity and quality in programme delivery, and if it is to have a viable home-based media it has to be one that can also compete on the world stage. We should not uncritically accept the 'bigger is better' argument; after all, the 'media minnows' of the UK have always produced programming that has been envied and bought all over the world. Their programme-making and engineering standards have often been emulated and their shelves groan with national and international awards for drama, humour and documentary productions. Bigger profits may require bigger media enterprises, but talent rather than size has always been the critical success factor behind excellent programming, and talent has never been the exclusive preserve of big corporations. The whirlwind that began with the Broadcasting Act of 1990 will be reaped within the decade by a complete change in the landscape of commercial television in the UK.

Something like five or six ITV companies are likely to go through into the 21st century, leaving probably no more than two or three in place before 2010 is out. In this vastly different climate the ITC will have an even more pivotal role in safeguarding viewers' interests and in ensuring that licence promises, including news and current affairs, are properly fulfilled and that supposedly regional programming is not really 'made in London' with a bit of an accent!

However, there are unlikely to be marches and demonstrations in favour of truly local, regional television in the UK. As with the dangers to individual privacy of mass computerization noted earlier, the deregionalization of television will be condoned and then tolerated. Most people will feel impotent to do anything about it, other than to switch off. The arguments against it can also seem too subtle, too precious or too marginal to inspire mass opposition. The 1950s regional split of ITV stations in the UK was as much about preserving cultural and regional identities as it was about making profits. Such quaint ideas cannot survive: the regional is quickly giving way to the national and the national to the global. Whether making bigger profits and servicing bigger debts proves to be incompatible with making distinguished programmes remains to be seen. There has always been a 'lowest common denominator' component in every form of popular news and entertainment; likewise, there have always been many producers, directors and artists who aspire to the highest levels of attainment in their work, who want to make programmes that they feel proud of and which also appeal to a wide audience. It is often said that aspiring to the highest is as much a driving force in the mobilization of human ingenuity as churning out the lowest. At this time in the development of UK television we can enlist a no more substantial ally than hope in foretelling the future quality of the output from the new regional combines.

The newly liberated media in eastern Europe and the former republics of the USSR face challenges not dissimilar to western concerns over concentration and cultural dilution. On the one hand released from the central diktats of old and censorious regimes, they have their first opportunity for many years to truly reflect the diversity of their various languages and culture. On the other hand, they are being wooed into joint ventures and partnerships by cash-rich western corporations who, armed with the 'bigger is better' ideology, seek the largest possible market for their products. As we have seen, local or regional flavours rarely figure in this scenario. Faced with these pressures the new media of eastern Europe will no doubt experiment at both ends of the spectrum. They have seen enough of western media behaviour to know how difficult it is to strike the right balance between solvency and probity. After being forced to adopt both Russian and German languages for 123 years during the state of partition between 1795 and 1918, the Polish government now see their language as a key symbol of national identity, and are urging their newly liberated media to avoid the worst excesses of western decadence in the language of advertisements. In order to uphold the dignity of the mother tongue the government is offering the television stations the 'support' of two language police. These arbiters have been given the job of monitoring the language of television advertisements to ensure that they do not drift into sloppy grammar and syntax or, worse, American Polish. It is important to note that it is the *use* of language they hope to regulate, not the idea of advertisements themselves. Such concerns have no place in the world of Vladimir Zelenzy, managing director of Nova, the new commercial television station in the Czech Republic and the first commercial television station to open in eastern Europe:

> We may soon realize that our illusion about the high standards of Czech culture and the intelligent taste of the people are just a long-perpetuated fallacy. [23]

This chapter is entitled 'Information concentration: more or less?' There is no doubt that the citizens of most developed economies would now regard themselves as having 'more' choice in the range of entertainment and information conduits available to them than at any other time in their history. This includes access to more radio frequencies, more television channels and more books and magazines, although they would probably perceive that their access to discrete newspaper titles had declined. Being better educated than their forebears, they would also claim that they were now better able to take advantage of all this information and better able to discriminate between forms of information. Most would guess that the organs of the media were owned by fewer corporations than they were ten years ago, and they would also guess that this trend was likely to continue. The concept of 'less' with regard to the range of opinion, ideas, theories and viewpoints available to them would be harder for most people to grasp. They would generally believe that they had the opportunity, should they wish, to access as wide a range of ideas and opinions as they would want or could cope with. In addition, most of them would display a healthy cynicism with regard to official sources of news and information, both as part of the age-old tradition of scepticism with regard to anything 'official' and as a part of a growing self-confidence in their own sifting and filtering capacities. In becoming accustomed to the way information is packaged and presented we become a part of the custom, a part of the narrowing that this inevitably brings. Custom, by its very nature, is slow to respond to innovation. It is lazy, and initially offers little hospitality to alternative constructions of the world. Media conglomerates gain their power and influence from this lethargy. They grew up and expanded within economic and political systems that allowed or even encouraged them to concentrate, and, currently enmeshed in a risky investment and acquisition cycle, they are not going to rock too many established boats.

To the issues already noted above, I would add the following. The 'information moment' is now likely to occur in the home, mediated by information which is increasingly owned by the owner of the distribution system. Providers will increasingly confuse our shortage of disposable time with poor attention span. Armed with this mistake, and seeking faster returns for every unit of information time, the media conglomerates will squeeze more and more into smaller and more digestible packages, arresting our attention with short, sharp information moments supported by sensational sounds and pictures. One outcome of this brevity is that our concept of 'serious' is nearly always being reviewed downwards. Issues such as war and invasion are either ignored or sanitized into drama by presentations that only have space for headlines. The entertainment value of the 'clean' and 'clinical' technology that is supposed to have won the 1990 Gulf War for the allies is probably the most notorious example of hard news packaged as excitement. Media treatment of this conflict seems to have been almost entirely choreographed by the allied authorities, avoiding any discussion of the underlying issues. Instead, their coverage was often indistinguishable from the kind of entertainment we would get from a war film like 'The Dirty Dozen'. The invasion of East Timor by the Indonesians in 1975, however, went largely unreported, due initially to the murder or banishment of all journalists. The estimated 200 000 Timorese dead (nearly a third of the population), have thus remained largely unnoticed and unmourned. John Pilger's 1994 exposure of the catalogue of US arms that continue to be sold to the Indonesians and the brutality with which they have been deployed against the Timorese, awakened, for the first time and nearly 20 years after the invasion, some real sense of horror and complicity among many British people [24].

Media concentration has clearly become a potent instrument in the process of the 'narrowing to fit' mentioned earlier. Then it was in the context of how societies increasingly celebrate specialism and focus, rather than richness and breadth in valuing the contributions individuals might make. Media corporations use the language of diversity because they know that it is what we want to hear, but behind their public statements they just get on with the economic reality of their business – making profits. The narrowing of expression they believe this requires, the normalizing of the unthinkable, the raising of brutality and cruelty to the status of the commonplace, and the trivializing of alternative constructions of reality, all stem from the imperatives of the market. This has never been a natural place for the highest ideals and is inevitably a place where the variety you get today is the variety that sold well yesterday and the day before. We should not forget, however, that the media owners did not invent the use of economic, military or political power. Alone or in tandem, governments and powerful industrial interests have always determined what information will be made available and how it will be conveyed. The media becomes both a victim and a collaborator of official information manipulation of this kind, and when it is run by a handful of players it is so much easier to control it. It was not the newspapers that suppressed the evidence that eventually took away 14 years from the lives of the Guildford Four: it was the UK Attorney General, the nation's chief law officer, not a conforming media, who urged six ministers of the Crown to sign public-interest immunity certificates which could have sent three innocent men to jail, rather than expose their own duplicity in the Matrix Churchill 'arms to Iraq' affair. The same law officer urged two more ministers to sign up in 1990–92, to prevent the release of information about links between overseas aid and a £1.3 million arms deal with Malaysia.

The people rarely have access to the tools and instruments necessary to secure the alternative story, and if there were more newspapers, more radio and television stations, would the range, quality and probity of information that we could access be so much better? The answer has to be an ambiguous 'yes, but . . .'. A wide range of small, independent carriers of news and information would be just as vulnerable to political and economic pressure as the large conglomerates are, but those applying the pressure would have to work a bit harder to achieve it. A smaller, more diverse range of information providers would also have to commit acts of selection and omission: the window of time available for most people's consumption of information would insist that they did. But there are alternatives. Back in the 1950s the Scott family set up a trust in the UK to protect the future of the *Manchester Guardian*. This is a unique form of newspaper ownership in the UK, one where five of the nine owner–trustees are professional journalists. It is an approach which, if it is not too late, could form a template for the newly freed and evolving media operations in the former USSR and the countries of eastern Europe. From the relatively straightforward management of two newspapers, the *Manchester Evening News* and *The Guardian*, the Scott trust has grown into a large commercial business. Now embracing three dozen local newspapers, trade magazines, radio interests and television production, its annual turnover of £200 million makes it a sizeable and influential domestic player which, although still a minnow in global terms, retains respect and strength from its unique place within a hands-off trusteeship. Recently renamed the Guardian Media Group plc, and divided up into a national newspaper division (the trust acquired *The Observer* in 1989) and a publications and communications division, the trust continues to insulate its newspapers from the cruder pressures of short-term commercialism and makes no intervention whatsoever in editorial matters. One result of the Scott trust's mandate to support *The Guardian* is that it is able, as long as its other enterprises prosper, to retire from the cyclical winds of the marketplace. It can withstand serious drops in circulation or cuts in advertising income without being at risk from takeovers or having to consider cutting its daily cover price.

A configuration more typical of a modern media conglomerate, but one that seems to walk the tightrope between managing a business and a hands-off style of proprietorship, is the German-based Bertelsmann group. Bertelsmann, a family-owned company founded in 1835, is now one of the world's largest media combines, with interests in commercial television, book and record clubs, film companies, a string of book publishers and, through the publisher Gruner und Jahr, the owner of the biggest collection of general and special-interest magazines in Europe. It also owns at least six companies involved in digital information development and delivery, some minor shares in local radio and a growing interest in cable operations throughout Europe. Via its ownership of RCA Music it also exerts considerable influence in the world of music and musical copyright. Bertelsmann is owned by one family, the Mohns, who seem happy to adopt a low-profile hands-off approach to the business, which they see as being a place for making profits for both owners and employees. Publishing vehicles that support the left, the right and the centre within German politics, the Mohn family have gained a reputation for political openness which they have turned to their advantage while pursuing steady business growth. Stability and continuity are provided for by arrangements that prevent the Mohns being removed by any other shareholders, and by a policy of decentralization which allows many of the individual units to operate independently, i.e. a large company that celebrates the ability of its parts to behave like small companies. Whether this non-politicized independent family approach can continue into the future remains to be seen. The past record of Bertelsmann suggests that it gains strength, even competitive advantage, from a known stance of business growth allied with proprietorial non-intervention. Smaller examples, e.g. Katherine Graham's ownership of the *Washington Post* in the US and the old Fairfax family approach to its newspaper holdings in Australia, have worked well in the past, although transferring such values or principles into the mega league seems a disproportionately difficult challenge. The bigger the media business, the bigger the temptation to interfere and the bigger the effort to blame other influences for such behaviour. Blaming the technology helps to draw critical fire away from the human origin of the intervention, but it is not very convincing. The satellite may beam the signals but we all know who fires the rockets!

The impact of media concentration on the poorer economies of the world cannot really be seen as anything but a continuation of western colonialism by other means. The rise of the US to superpower status is almost entirely coincident with the rise of media like radio, film and television, and, more recently, the introduction of satellites and fibre-optics. The US has also contributed most to the development and future structure of these media, e.g. by developing a near monopoly in film making and distribution. The most powerful nation of our times has thus been able to project its views, its beliefs, its economic ideas and its political obsessions way beyond its national borders via the most potent communication technologies that have ever existed. As with other kinds of manufactured goods, poorer countries have had to import both the hardware and the software of the media technologies they wish to use. They seem cast forever in the role of recipients, with little chance of ever becoming creators and distributors. This distinction is doubly important because those who develop, produce and sell such technologies also hold deep information and knowledge about the social and economic changes they are likely to bring about. Transferring them to another, poorer, spot on the globe may be a good 'sell' but does nothing to integrate the technological potential with the potential of a particular culture or the needs of a particular geography or educational mix. I emphasize the role of the US here because, although a nation like Japan may now be well established as an economic superpower, manufacturing much of the media hardware that poorer countries might seek to acquire, not many of their peoples want to think Japanese. By the same token the many languages of Europe will clearly prevent its hard information, films and music from dominating programme provision far outside the European Union. Some Eurocentric spheres of influence, e.g. French-influenced north Africa and Spanish-influenced South America, may resist for a time, as may those Arab and non-Arab countries with strong links to Islam, but the footprint of the media conglomerates will eventually embrace them all. By being closer than its North American counterparts, both physically and culturally, to the opening up of the media in eastern Europe, a European group like Bertelsmann may be able to use both its financial muscle and its reputation for political independence to upstage North American media interests in that area, but it will not be easy.

For better or worse the urban populations of the poorer countries of the world have come to desire the American dream, in English, as it has been presented to them. The disappointments have been great as many of the expectations created have rarely been fulfilled, except for a very elite few. Frustration, fuelled by prosperous images that seduce without satisfying, is the inevitable consequence of the media 'bombing' of poor countries. The continuing concentration of media technology and programming in the west offers little in the way of change or respite from this one-way traffic. The conglomerates will continue to deliver whatever can be paid for now, and to hover around in space to see how things might pick up in the future, but they do not see themselves as having a role in helping to pump-prime infant media enterprises and they have no intention of transferring any significant technology to these countries in a way that makes local sense. Although some of the technical developments look as if they will be quite exciting, it is difficult to be optimistic about the long-term impact that continued concentration of the media will have on both the rich, comfortable economies or the yearning, developing ones. The issues that make up the bulk of this chapter continue to generate some of the most robust debates of our time, even within organs that are clearly a part of the subject under discussion. Reporters and commentators like John Pilger, Julian Pettifer, Mort Rosenblum and Michael Buerk continue to bring honour to their profession while also disseminating a wider understanding of its power to omit, distort and oversimplify. Any public exposure of the worst aspects of media concentration will have to be done by that small band of vigilant and independent journalists who manage to earn a living outside the mainstream networks, or that even smaller band who work within the limited protection of state broadcasting systems. Of course there will also be those who, though working within one of the big commercial corporations, will break cover now and then in the face of what they perceive as unacceptable behaviour. Although these groups may be small, and are probably getting smaller, I believe that they will always exist. Their members are – and will become more so – the new tribunes of the people with regard to the moral incontinence of the big operators. It is the bounden duty of all those who treasure the freedom and values of a truly pluralist information culture to help ensure that they survive.

References

1. Reed and Elsevier: bigger, better? *The Economist*, 19 September 1992
2. Buckingham, L. (1993) Reed Elsevier success shines through ERM fog. *The Guardian*, 6 August

3. Longman aims to extend influence in Far East. *The Bookseller*, 7 May 1993

4. Longman's profits surge. *The Bookseller*, 14 May 1993

5. Buckingham, L. (1988) Maxwell nears US victory. *The Guardian*, 3 November

6. BBC 2, 'Inside Story: Tiny Rowland, the Rebel Tycoon', 26 May 1993

7. Simon, B. and Gibbins, R. (1993) Power Corporation lets its money do the talking. *Financial Times*, 4 June

8. Murdoch in Asia: third time unlucky? *The Economist*, 26 March 1994

9. Nisse, J. and Poole, T. (1993) When the stardust finally settled. *The Independent on Sunday*, 1 August

10. Snoddy, R. (1993) Paramount Pays $553 for US publisher Macmillan. *Financial Times*, 11 November

11. Glover, J. (1994) The Forza's man who has too much. *The Guardian*, 16 April

12. Friedman, A. (1989) *Agnelli and the Network of Italian Power*. London: Mandarin

13. Grant, M. (1984) *The British Media*. London: Comedia Publishing Group

14. Glover, J. (1993) Pens dipped in dirty ink. *The Guardian*, 4 October

15. Wim Wenders, quoted in *The Guardian*, 14 October 1993

16. Malcolm, D. (1993) Europe's lost picture show. *The Guardian*, 1 December

17. Vargas Llosa, M. (1993) Fields of dreams. *The Sunday Times*, 31 October

18. Januszczak, W. (1993) Defending a critical freedom. *The Sunday Times*, 31 October

19. Rosenblum, M. (1994) *Who Stole the News?* Chichester: John Wiley

20. Pilger, J. (1993) The brave new media world. *New Statesman and Society*, 11 June, 14–15

21. Quoted by Anthony Bevins, *The Independent*, 3 June 1993

22. In 'Kiosk', *The Guardian*, 31 January 1994

23. Pilger, J. (1994) *The Guardian*, 12 February and 'Death of a Nation: The Timor Conspiracy' made for Central Television and shown on the ITV Network on 22nd February 1994

Chapter 6

Epilogue: some final thoughts

Disentangling information from being is not easy. We are born with genes whose information content was established hundreds of thousands of years ago. For a million years or more, while the anatomy and brain size of our ancestors continued to develop the stone-based technology that they used hardly changed at all. Then, around 40 000 years ago, humans began living closer together, seeking more comfort, convenience and kinship from the larger social group. In these 'societies' they needed new ways to exchange information, to share experiences, give out warnings and indulge in communal rituals. They began exploring ways to externalize what they felt and thought through new uses of old materials, and information technology was born. These ancient triggers now coexist with electronic multimedia, as they once did with the stone and wooden artefacts used for so long by early man. Today things are dramatically reversed: the technology changes rapidly whereas the capacity of humans has remained more or less as it was 40 000 years ago. The new information available to us is changing all the time; our senses access and process it and our experience is determined by our use of it. We grow up, move around, absorb more and become different: living is a constant process of information processing and acquisition. Despite the proliferation of all kinds of devices to store what we know, our deaths, after even a moderately eventful life, still represent the loss of a small mobile library.

There are still many links in the information-knowledge chain that we are not quite sure about. Whether, like all physical adaptations, the form and very existence of knowledge is explicable because it reflects an aspect of the world outside is still a big question. Issues such as the origin of instinct, the relationship between knowledge and natural selection, the prerequisites for successful learning and the origins of the widely different cultures that evolve from the combination of all these are still wide open for debate. Given the vast quantities of information that we gather about the world we live in, it is chastening to consider how little we still know about the information build-up that makes us who we are. The debate between sociobiologists, who believe human traits derive from information that is inherited, and cultural anthropologists who insist that all information is culturally fashioned, has become particularly acrimonious in recent years without doing much to illuminate the middle-ground that is the natural territory of the inquisitive lay person. The latter might be forgiven for giving credence to a dual or multi-inheritance theory, that is an alliance between gene codes that carry both specific (fixed) information and those carrying looser information supporting a number of potential characteristics and information which is learned and then deeply assimilated within a culture, i.e. the 'meme', which together source the messy complex which we call human behaviour.

Similarly, although Chomsky's theory of 'innateness' has become part of the conventional wisdom of modern psychology, there are still major differences of opinion as to the precise nature of the embedded information that translates thoughts into language and babies into speakers and readers. Biotechnologists and computer scientists still stand humbly before the 10 billion nerve cells and the 6 trillion connecting synapses that link them to fuel the magical link between the brain, the mind and human consciousness. We have learnt also that language can imprison as well as liberate information. As Harry Lutz, the brother of the hero Oscar in William Gaddis's 1994 novel *A frolic of his own* explains, language can still be hijacked by one group in order to confuse and impoverish another:

> Every profession is a conspiracy against the public, every profession protects itself with a language of its own . . . till it all evaporates into language confronted by language turning language itself into theory till it's not what it's about it's only about itself. [1]

Humans as information processors have come a long way in a short time, and although our ability to process and transfer information between domains has developed quite recently, it has developed fast, as has our ingenuity in storing and processing it. Nonetheless we are still often surprised by important information moments which we experience in all kinds of situations and on many different intellectual levels. Although sometimes not even aware of it, we also instigate important information moments for others. 'The unlocking of dilemmas through insights gained in unlikely places' [2], though one of the most powerful realities of our lives, continues to be seriously underestimated as a source of information gathering. Because we are not yet sure how to nurture the tacit knowledge that forms the link between established wisdoms and innovation, we have branded this particular component of the information-knowledge chain a mystery that is best left outside our formal educational processes. Hence our obsession with the 'technology' side of 'information technology' at the expense of the optimum conditions that humans need for processing information. The cult of so-called incontrovertible, hard information (facts, statistics and declarations), however brittle, however much it has been found wanting, still dominates, it still retains a limpet-like grip on our lives. Such information may help us to carry out inspired ideas but it rarely instigates them: it is difficult to observe an apple falling from a branch on the Internet! As an information system the world remains a capricious place, with all of us experiencing as many information 'misses' and 'near misses' as direct hits. The old adage that 'you never know what you don't know' is a conundrum which remains at the centre of the debate about how much information we really need to operate as complete citizens. It is possible that much contemporary information access and exchange has as much to do with habit, ritual and oneupmanship as it does with real needs. Whether social or anti-social, the transaction, be it watching television, chatting with colleagues or silently logging on to the Internet, has become as important as the outcome. In a world where the message is now often stored invisibly in a computer, it is not surprising that we have become over-fascinated with the devices that access it. As books became objects to stroke, to hold and to personalize, so now the plastic case of the lap-top computer carries the scribble of our most used instructions. We have become addicted to the sensing sensation: logging on, watching, reading, listening, scanning; we need to be doing it to confirm our status as engaged citizens. In 1984, Richard Schickel in his *Common fame*, a study of the invention and uses of celebrity, opined that almost nothing happens outside our own lives that requires our immediate attention. His book offered an antidote to the uncritical acceptance of the information osmosis that feeds our claims to understand more because it makes us feel better informed. He raises the question of whether our level and depth of understanding have really improved simply because we know more about the wider world. It is a question that, ten years later we still cannot answer satisfactorily. Knowing and understanding are not the same thing, but without knowledge and the information that guides it, the reflection that feeds understanding may itself remain underfed. Optimizing the information needed is one, much sought-for, solution; learning how to select from even that is another.

Despite the growing sophistication of all the technologies involved and the speed with which information can now be transmitted, what we might call 'normal' channels of communication often disappoint us. They rarely give us advance warning of major economic or political upheavals. Neither the structure of the modern media nor the boundaries of the thinking that informs it generally offer much opportunity to explore anything significant that has not already been opened up somewhere else. The deeper causes of events tend to be traded for simple analyses built on surface information, or information only one or two stages below the surface.

One consequence of expecting every action and every outcome to be 'informed' is that we have great difficulty in dealing with randomness. Our Newtonian-based education, which urges us to seek equilibrium and balance in all things, allied to the continuous stream of information provided by a prolific but conservative media, implies that we inhabit a world where old and new packets of information always merge comfortably into rational outcomes. The strength of these expectations can dull our senses to the often irrational connectedness of events, as when apparently trivial causes produce startling or discontinuous change. Of course, events that we currently perceive as random may actually be deterministic. After all, we now understand the causes of many of the natural phenomena which the ancients regarded as acts of playfulness by the gods. As computing power expands, the number of dimensions within which calculations can be made will grow to further diminish the catalogue of phenomena that are currently perceived as purely random.

As they develop over time all cultures exhibit contradictions in the way that they encourage, tolerate or restrict information access and exchange. Many commentators assume that these contradictions will dissolve in the face of unprecedented technological forces, and that the instruments once used to inhibit access to information will wither. Although true in parts, this assumption underestimates the tenacity with which the powerful have always clung on to the instruments of power and profit. Once it is perceived as a threat to either, the delightful anarchy of the Internet will eventually be threatened by encryption, encoding, prevention and restriction, in order to control information flows or claim intellectual ownership. Such a resource, operated without marginal costs is a nightmare to those who seek to commoditize information. Already a sophisticated lobbying organization, the Electronic Frontier Foundation (EFF) is active in the US. The EFF 'open platform' mission faces the dilemma of seeking social policy goals e.g. a wide diversity of information services, universal service, free speech and common carriage to support political, cultural and personal communications, within an environment where such goals can only be achieved in collusion with market forces. So far its main campaign effort has been centred around extending civil liberties in cyberspace, by lobbying to protect the constitutional rights of individuals using private networks from possible eavesdropping and intervention by the US security services [3]. The security services maintain that they are only interested in reading material which they suspect of disseminating criminal information such as might be used to facilitate illicit arms and drug deals. So sensitive an issue is this that the US government has banned the export of encryption programmes under regulations governing the export of arms, and is actively seeking the acceptance of its right to intervene in networks where it 'suspects' that laws may be being broken. Frustrated in its desire to impose a hard-wired 'Clipper' chip encryption device, that only officials from law enforcement and intelligence agencies would have been able to access, the US administration now seems likely to embrace a less technical 'knock and announce' formula for security service interventions on the Internet. Given that there are now more than 260 foreign encryption products available worldwide, more than 80 of which offer encryption which is stronger than that which US companies are currently allowed to export, it seems that the international market will continue to meet its network security needs without help from US manufacturers [4]. In an interesting testament to the effectiveness of eyeball-to-eyeball contact over electronic-only lobbying the EFF moved its base to Washington to be closer to the seat of government. Although encryption programmes will figure large in the future openness or otherwise of ongoing electronic superhighways, probably the biggest risk to the free status of the Internet will be the attitude of the telephone companies that own most of the networks. It is now possible to have a conversation over the Internet with anyone in the world in almost real-time. Such a feature could see an explosion in free international communication that the phone companies will undoubtedly want to stop. The phone companies will also be watching the growth of commercial users on the Internet. Tempted by the enormous quantities of cheap information available, millions of business users are now joining up in search of such information for repackaging and onward sale, or just to become better informed. Rupert Murdoch entering the fray in the UK with his Delphi Internet, offering the opportunity to read and comment on headlines in *The Times* as well as access to other parts of his media empire, suggests that a wave of populist exploitations of the network is just around the corner. Notwithstanding the concern among academics and other serious users that this commercialization may generate, it is important to remember that, despite predictions of 200 million users by 1995, the majority of citizens in developed countries cannot gain access to the Internet, and outside these countries it could be the name of a horse! Although replete with 'highway' metaphors the future 'superhighway' is rarely referred to as the information 'freeway'.

Whatever networking technology is in place British governments will continue to be 'economical' with information and US governments will continue to be 'open' after they have destroyed the embarrassing information. The Chinese will continue to violently suppress alternative sources of information for as long as they can and Silvio Berlusconi, the Prime Minister of Italy, with a monopoly of private television and effective control of the three state TV stations, will continue to both create and manage the consent of his countrymen. Cultures are definitely moulded by technology, but during the moulding men and women always emerge who are determined that it should serve them more effectively than the rest of us.

Although tempting fate, it is probably appropriate within any chapter entitled 'Epilogue: some final thoughts' to roam over a few predictions about the nature of the world in which future information access and exchange will take place.

Where we are now was once the future for past prophets many of whose predictions, particularly with regard to the distributed benefits of information technology, did not come true. Where we are now will also become the past for future historians who will seek to explain our contribution to their present. My guess is that western historians will see the 1990s as a decade when the old boundaries between work and non-work time really started to break up, bringing an enforced 'leisure' to many who did not want it, and a relentless impregnation of work into the lives of those high-level information and knowledge workers whose domains lay, as yet, outside the competence of intelligent machines.

One trend that now seems well established is that more and more peoples around the world will seek to take charge of their own destiny and their own resources. The Soviet Union, Czechoslovakia and Yugoslavia formerly represented three nation states; since their dissolution they now number more than 20. Whether in Quebec or Abkhazian, the idea of a global, free-market economy that all small states can operate in, because information and knowledge-based enterprise need not be related to size or the ownership of natural resources, is being encouraged. These small states seek the well-voiced desires of all nationalists: to empower themselves politically and to conserve important elements of their own culture, but most of all they have been seduced by a new idea; that access to economic wealth, such as that achieved by Singapore, Hong Kong, Bermuda and Taiwan, is no longer dependent on geographic size.

Interestingly, given the imperative of cultural conservation noted above, as the world of nations becomes more fragmented the media that influences and informs them is becoming more concentrated. Bigger, and highly centralized, media corporations will come to talk to smaller and smaller national groups. The turnover of a Microsoft, a Sony or a News Corporation will dwarf the GDP of some of the new central

European nations. Little and poor nations will face these global media networks much as the Lilliputians struggled to tie down Gulliver. Many of them will sell their moiety cheaply, granting licences for short-term gain and to satisfy populist demands for more consumer-led information. Other countries will resist for longer, seeking to protect their own political, spiritual or cultural ideals.

Future cultural filtering of this kind will be both difficult and expensive. Hughes Electronic's US$400 million deal with Malaysia to launch that country's first independent satellite 36km above Kuala Lumpur is a testament to the lengths that some nations will go to to ensure ownership of their own filtering technology. Nowhere are the contradictions between a conservative government and a satellite-hungry populace more marked than in the religiously conservative Iran. While more than 400 hundred satellite dishes a day, mostly imported from Turkey and Dubai, are being installed all over the country, the governing mullahs, some of whose rooftops display the biggest dishes, seem to be in total disarray as to whether or not this is something that they can, or want to, stamp out by legislation and religious policing. These tensions are set to multiply as people all over the world seek to escape into the seductive sounds and images delivered by western media. Sometimes the recipients themselves will rebel against inappropriate media exports. Television viewers in both Estonia and Lithuania, many of whom cannot afford meat for themselves let alone for their pets, have successfully protested against the screening of western made advertisements for pet-food on television. The sight of well-fed dogs and cats munching through tasty chunks of tinned meat has particularly offended scores of hungry Lithuanian pensioners.

More usually it is the official attempts at restriction that we hear about. In 1994, Malaysia banned screenings of Steven Spielberg's Oscar-winning film 'Schindler's List' on the grounds that it was propaganda in support of one race against another, and many Middle East countries exercize strict controls over the audiovisual images that they allow to be shown legally within their borders, the Cadbury's 'chocolate flake' advertisement being a celebrated Saudi Arabian exclusion. Although linguistic and cultural distinctions are resilient, they do not collapse before the cocktail of old movies and 'soaps', but they can be chipped away. We stand at a critical watershed where the culturally distinct is often being forced to compete with bland global-speak for status and attention. One problem with this kind of competition is that the language used to sell the values of distinctiveness e.g. 'classic', 'refined' and 'canonical' often labels it as elitist and inaccessible. We need a new vocabulary to market cultural distinctiveness, one which lays more stress on its accessibility, its warmth, its natural rhythm and its humanity. Social and educational awareness will help redress some of the balances that the new and largely unprotected mercantilism would tip over into the purely commercial chasm. That it will require energy, vigilance and vision just to keep some of the current balances in tact, however cannot now be in any doubt.

Alliances between individual media combines that we currently regard as big will continue. Entrepreneurs like QVC's Barry Diller, TCI's John Malone, Viacom's Sumner Redstone and Bell Atlantic's Ray Smith will roam the world restlessly seeking out deals. QVC may have failed to acquire Home Shopping Channel, Paramount or CBS, but a Comcast will get QVC and Canada's Maclean Hunter. British Telecom may fall out with Rupert Murdoch but it will get on nicely with the programming and marketing clout of an MCI; Bell Atlantic and TCI may have failed to tie the knot, but TCI will work together with Bill Gates, Rupert Murdoch and Viacom on projects whose eventual impact could dwarf that expected from the lost Bell Atlantic deal.

Although perhaps now at its zenith in the older developed economies, information about consumption will still dominate all forms of media. The newly industrialized economies of Asia, particularly those where the less religiously inclined Chinese and Japanese influence is strongest, will embrace this mantle with enthusiasm. Other cultures, drawing their moral strength, or deep prejudices, from alternative spiritual and religious sources, will continue to limit access to information which they feel reinforces decadent lifestyles. Some of this resistance will take the shape of violence against the journalists and commentators whom they see as being at the forefront of the process. The opening up of China, largely homogeneous and outside any other nation's sphere of influence, looks set to be the big economic event of the next decade. With greater affluence will come a greater desire for new sources of information, knowledge and entertainment. After the death of Deng Xiaoping another chapter will have closed on the Chinese revolutionary past, and the new Chinese entrepreneurs will want a greater say in opening up the way in which consumption and the information that fuels it is organized. In a demographic league of its own (its population is predicted to grow to between 1.62 billion and 1.86 billion by 2050), China's ability to support and feed its population is something of an alarming challenge. Over the next 25 years China's ratio of working to non-working population is expected to drop to fewer than four productive people supporting over six dependent people. It is unlikely that the tensions arising from these factors will be resolved without external effects of one sort or another.

With the worldwide decline in the value of mass production, Japan's economic strength, nurtured almost entirely on its genius in this area, will suffer some serious setbacks, as will those who have attempted to emulate it. High-quality information and intelligence embedded in sophisticated tailor-made smart devices, will be where the highground of future engineering and manufacturing lies. Mass production will migrate to where the labour is cheapest, until there is nowhere else to go. As western countries have had to respond to Japan, so Japan will have to learn to trade up, think quicker, be lighter on its feet and cherish the creativity of individuals. More ballet than sumo!

All societies reproduce themselves through education. In order to begin exploring ways to prize individuality, the Japanese have begun to look seriously at their rigid educational system. They have also begun investing in opportunities to conduct more pure research and, using the cash surpluses from their manufacturing successes, to stake a claim in global finance: already the top six of the world's 15 biggest banks are Japanese [5].

The faster-developing countries of the world will couple their growing economic independence with less tolerance towards the hypocrisies of the old colonial powers, particularly with regard to the latter's newly acquired conscience on environmental issues such as deforestation. Asian resistance to western concepts of human rights, civil liberties and social welfare will continue to give them major advantages in global trade. In seeking to emulate these looser and less well-protected work practices, European politicians and businessmen will face hostility from political and cultural systems that are unprepared for such radical change. This will result in the migration of more capital to countries where business governments are in power. In a lecture during 1994 Sir Ian Vallance [6], the Chairman of British Telecom, noted that all businesses were operating in a context of a 'new world disorder', with many new 'players' challenging the old hands, a context where certainties were few and far between and where complacency would lead to extinction.

> These changes present a huge challenge to the traditional powerful economies of North America, Europe and Japan. The era of exclusive control over the means of wealth production in the hands of privileged and established western countries and companies has come to an end. The competition is better capitalized, better educated, better equipped, better informed and more numerous than ever before. [6]

The cost-cutting, labour-reducing dynamic of post-Fordist, lean manufacturing has now become a supra national drive which threatens us with the lean state, lean education, lean health and lean welfare. If 'lean' is to become the *leitmotif* of a world whose population is still growing and whose workers seek economic activity to sustain themselves, radical ways of defining an individual's economic contribution to society, and society's obligations to them, will have to move off the drawing board and into acceptance. Although really no different from the old challenge of redistributing wealth, the numbers involved, the depth of restructuring needed and the levels of tolerance required to effect such a massive redistribution have never been faced before.

Without underestimating the influence that changes in economic balance can have, we should not forget that most of the big changes that occur in the world are still the result of violence.

The miniaturization of the tools of violence will continue a trend which has seen the cost of violence fall while the cost of resisting it is increasing. Portable rocket launchers, mini bombs and pocketable bio-weapons will give small groups the power of big groups. Future terrorists will have access to cheap and lethal sources of violence that will give them easy ascendancy over whole slices of territory.

> The democratization of the means of destruction dramatically raised the costs of keeping unofficial violence under control. The British government faced with actual combatant forces among the Catholic and Protestant paramilitaries of Northern Ireland of no more than a few hundred, needed something like 20 000 troops, 8000 armed police and an expenditure of £3 billion a year in the province. [7]

Global trafficking in the kind of high grade plutonium that is capable of supporting the proliferation of 'home-made' nuclear weapons must be the single most disturbing threat to what has passed for peace in the world since 1945. Information concerning the whereabouts and availability of these materials will be sold at a premium. In June 1994 five agents of North Korea were expelled from Russia for trying to obtain components for nuclear weapons. Four discoveries of weapons-grade nuclear materials being smuggled or offered for sale were made by the German authorities between May and August 1994, all reportedly originating from inside Russia. With modern compression techniques it is possible to squeeze the equivalent of the 21 000 tonnes of TNT that destroyed Nagasaki in August 1945 from just over 2kg of plutonium, with 1kg you could get a blast equivalant to 2100 tonnes. It has been estimated that there were some 35 000 nuclear weapons scattered around the territories of the former Soviet Union before it split apart, many of them still unaccounted for [8]. The breakdown of large power structures into smaller groups has left some considerable firepower in the hands of countries not much larger than Wales, and the accidental discovery in July 1994 that a used-car salesman in Idaho was openly hawking parts of a nuclear reprocessing plant which could produce weapons grade uranium ('original instructions thrown in'), while embarrassing for the US Defense Department and somewhat uncomfortable for the rest of us, probably succeeded in cheering up a hi-tech terrorist or two [9].

In August 1994 the UK Policy Studies Institute noted that expenditure on private security was one of the fastest growing sectors of the UK economy. With expenditure already running at over £2 billion a year, it employed more people (176 000) in 1994 than the publicly funded police forces, who employed 143 000 [10]. The UK's 20 per cent of telephone users who currently choose to stay ex-directory, one of the highest such populations in Europe, already suggests a degree of insecurity that is well on the way to US levels. The use of comparatively cheap technology to commit violence and the investment in expensive technology to protect ourselves from it looks like being one of the most common features of the next two decades.

There can be no doubt that the widening gap between the incomes of the richest and the poorest citizens in many developed countries will help feed dissatisfactions that seek outlets in violence. In Chapter 3 we noted that the high-abstraction workers in the top quartile of earners might not want to redistribute some of their growing wealth among those whose access to the information moments of education and training had been more frugal than their own. Given the issues touched on above, some form of wealth sharing between workers and non-workers might be a better option than living restricted, if select, lives just a high fence away from danger. A report by the Institute of Fiscal Studies in June 1994 [11] identified that hourly wages for those in the poorest-paid jobs in the UK had seen no real increase since 1975. This study revealed that the unprecedented restructuring of wage differentials over the last 15 years had engineered the biggest difference between the highest and the lowest paid workers in the UK since the first comparative statistics on wages had been gathered in 1886:

> There is much evidence that not only are UK workers less skilled on average than those in the rest of Europe but also that they lack the general skills obtained from basic education that are necessary for further training. . . . The collapse in the labour market opportunities at the lower end of the skill distribution has been so drastic that some men can no longer provide for themselves through employment. [11]

Any pretence that the deprivation stemming from such a reality is unrelated to increasing violence, rising crime and the creation of inner-city 'no-go' areas is now beyond belief. The spellchecker in my wordprocessing software has no reference to 'Internet' or 'cyberspace' but it clearly lights up if I spell 'underclass' incorrectly.

The near future will see a tremendous rise in every kind of computer crime. Hacking into other people's files, distributing viruses for fun or for advantage, and the theft and copying of every kind of software will become commonplace. All applications – music, images, indeed anything that can be digitized – will be stolen, re-packaged and redistributed for gain or for wider public access.

A large amount of human time and effort has always been spent laying claim to original, unique or exceptional information and then setting up systems to ensure that it is properly rewarded and protected from predators. Yet information ownership has always been a fragile affair and copying the information that someone else holds, in order to replicate its benefits is one of the oldest professions. Establishing the originality and ownership of intellectual property in the future could be extremely difficult. For instance, tracking down the precise owner- ship of intellectual property in a case where a software engineer creates a program that is able to design other programs, one of which eventu- ally writes something that we would recognize as a document, looks like a nightmare in cyberspace. If bits of this computer- generated document then appear incorporated in other computer- generated material on the Internet, or embedded within other pieces of software, the precise identity of the author or the exact components of the original 'edition' will pose something of a Gordian puzzle for those charged with compiling the bibliographies of the future.

Other computer-based activities will continue to create new ethical, legal and institutional dilemmas as the technological possibilities run way ahead of legal and regulatory frameworks. Invasions of computer privacy will continue with impunity as the actions against such viola- tions remain isolated and sporadic, while the peddlers of pornography will become skilled in manipulating the intricacies of worldwide net- works. Children at one in ten secondary schools in the UK are already reputed to have easy access to computer-generated pornography, and the growth of fast global networks of computer sleaze are likely to become highly profitable, and legally elusive, features of future elec- tronic networks.

The computerization of the workplace will continue and, although there will be some incremental growth in the number of telecom- muters, most people with jobs will continue to 'go to' work for a few decades yet. Harnessing intelligent knowledge-based systems to exe- cute some higher orders of processing and analysis will transfer many more basic tasks from humans to machines leaving many thousands of people currently operating at the lower end of the information handling spectrum without work. The differences in energy and raw materials needed for certain kinds of work will be quite marked.

A systems analyst or computer programmer, whose energy source might be two meals a day, is not tied to time or place; he or she can work where they please and they can offer their skills to a variety of clients in a variety of contractual arrangements. Transfers of higher levels of intel- ligence to both manufactured and bioengineered products will continue to reduce the need for the physical exertions traditionally associated with maintenance, e.g. intelligent glass that can count raindrops and sense when to let in or cut out sunlight; genetically engineered grass seed that grows to an optimum height and then stops; a tyre that notifies the driver of its air pressure; engines that retune themselves; and the automation of just about every kind of fault-finding process.

Biotechnology will continue to shift the settled parameters of those social relations which derive their bonding from biological realities. The scientific possibilities of DNA manipulation will pose ethical and moral questions about the construction of human identity and talent that, although often discussed in abstract terms, have only recently had to be put to the test in practice. The potential to create super-humans, constructed according to a preferred menu of qualities and physical attributes will, like the harnessing of atomic energy, test the depths of both the dark and light sides of human desires:

> Early stages of genetic engineering will make possible the elimination of many of the approximately thirty-five hundred genetic-based diseases that now plague humanity. As the specific genes that control human development are identified, it will be possible for parents to determine at conception the race, sex, height, hair colour, eye colour, complexion, intelligence and athletic abilities of their offspring. Designer children will be a reality after the millennium. [12]

As with the evolution of all human endeavours the world of information access and exchange will be characterized by a plurality which while disseminating great benefits to many will also aggregate great power to a few. Bill Gates with his 90 per cent global monopoly of MS-DOS and Windows, and his intended launch of 840 low-orbit satellites to deliver every form of communication anywhere on earth, Rupert Murdoch with his encryption technology, and Intel with their aggressive world dominance of semi-conductor production, together with a few other individuals or corporations, will own, or seek to own, most of the information worth having. National regulatory bodies will become increasingly impotent as powerful corporations infiltrate and manipulate government policy. International regulatory bodies will fail to construct effective controls in the face of national jealousies and desperate concerns to protect local employment. As all developed economies emphasize investment in information and knowledge infrastructures, invariably via private rather than more benign public agencies, less developed countries will be locked out of regional networks and global systems. They will be hindered by a quartet of factors: debt, poor access to rapidly changing technologies, inadequate infrastructures and, paradoxically, a lack of information about information. As soon as they begin to crack the combination someone else changes it.

The 'information revolution' is clearly confined to certain very well defined sectors, both locally and globally. Mexico City's towering glass stock market, packed with the latest in electronic information technology, saw its trading grow by 48 per cent in 1993. Its members were also host to most of the US$7 billion in new money that flowed into Mexico in the first three months following the US Congress's approval of the NAFTA agreement. However as in many other developing nations this urban ostentation is accompanied by a much larger slice of rural squalor. Ironically, the gap between rich and poor in developing countries often seems to widen as the per capita GDP increases. In Mexico this latter has grown from US$2525 in 1989, to US$4324 in 1993, while the poorest Mexicans' share of the national income declined in real terms from 5 per cent in 1984 to 4.3 per cent in 1992. Many new communication technologies will reinforce the already deep differences in regional, economic and social benefits. Making it easier for the already information-rich to communicate and transact with other information-rich operators is not always commercially compatible with extending the family.

In the UK the evolution of a broadband, fibreoptic superhighway capable of carrying all kinds of visual and data services is largely in the hands of a few US-owned companies such as TeleWest (owned by US West and TCI), Nynex (a regional phone operator in the US) and Bell Cablemedia. They are intending to invest around £6 billion between now and the turn of the century in the hope of generating around the same figure in income every year thereafter. It will be a gradual, patchwork process and the information, as opposed to the entertainment, services that will eventually flow over it are still largely undefined. British Telecom's promise to invest £15 billion to provide a cohesive and unified, fibre optic infrastructure, in return for an earlier review of its restrictions on broadcasting, has so far gone unanswered, and it looks as if the patchwork mentality will prevail. Whether this will be in the wider public interest or an efficiency enough motor to spark off productive innovations in information-based commerce is difficult to predict. The role of regulation will probably be crucial in ensuring that the eventual network reaches all parts of the country and does not end up simply redefining existing regional inequalities.

The digitization of information promises to bring tremendous resources to all those who can obtain access to it. Chadwyck Healey's *English Poetry Full-Text Database*, compressing roughly 4500 volumes of verse on four compact discs for £25 000, is just one example of a major commercial publishing project that is destined to become an indispensable research tool for scholars. The great libraries of the world will thus travel to researchers on compact discs and down telephone lines rather than the other way round. But most of us are not scholars, our information needs are less well defined and we may not be able to afford computers, software, modems and subscriptions to on-line hosts. To access these, we will need a new definition of the public library. Given that it has always been a place where we spend our time rather than our money, it needs a major rethink about the way it offers access to electronic information. In 1989 I suggested that librarians:

1. Watch over the pacing of the transition from hard-copy to digitization, so that users of (up until now) cheap forms and packages of information are not disenfranchised by the sudden disappearance of material which they can then access only electronically.

2. Form consortia among themselves to improve their own purchasing power and influence in the face of the growing centralization of information production and distribution, among both hard-copy and electronic providers. [13]

Six years on, these ideas, particularly the second, seem just as valid. Libraries will need to cooperate on a much greater scale to bring the resources of electronic publishing to their economically highly differentiated public. Those who can afford it will pay for their own discs or for online connectivity; for those who cannot the motivation to make the journey to a publicly funded information node should guarantee them the same kind of access. Although this seems an obvious need, and a reasonable definition of public information provision, there are few signs that any philosophy other than that of free market competition will prevail. Despite all the good that it has done and continues to do, the future funding of public information services, in the UK at least, continues to lack anything that might pass for a passionate and coordinated advocacy. The showering of information moments among non-profit purposeful populations via public investment is definitely in decline with a clear move to an information of the private, by the private, for the private steadily replacing it.

For all the current excitement that it has generated in the world of multimedia, Compact Disc publishing is very much an intermediate technology. Although CD publishing is here to stay, alongside hard-copy books and journals, the real information breakthrough will come when publishers and communication companies have the bandwidth and critical mass available on cable networks to put all of their materials up online to offices and homes. Charging a small amount for each one of millions of transactions, a few cents or pence every time someone consults a database, downloads a movie, checks their bank balance or joins in a video conference, all of which will be repeated *ad infinitum*, is where the real money lies. Microsoft, as well as launching its own online data service (Marvel) has been buying up the digital rights to the world's most famous paintings in readiness for just such a time. Bill Gates knows that those who capture a slice of these billions of transactions will enjoy revenues that the providers of one-off pieces of software and traditional wired services could only dream of.

The deep penetration of telecommunications infrastructures in the developed countries of the world has made it easier to transact on an almost infinite range of issues over vast distances. In the past, if we wanted to be at the nerve centre of these transactions we made our way to a city, as from the Middle Ages on this is where the action has been. Cities are still the great information nodes of nations: London, Frankfurt, New York, Tokyo and Hong Kong all gain their prestige and high property prices from this reality. As an example of the scale of economic activity that cities are still capable of, some recent research suggested that London, with a GDP bigger than that of Turkey, transferred about £7 billion to the rest of the UK in 1993 [14]. Although place now seems largely redundant as far as many transactions are concerned, living in the information 'mud' of a city gateway is still something that is valued by those standing at similar gateways in other places. Financial market-makers orbiting the earth in bubbles that had no geographic contact with the markets that they make would soon become out of touch, unreliable and broke. Despite the continuing ghettoization of many cities and the increasing versatility of telecommunications, I suspect that the future of cities as concentrations of education, business and commerce, and as the premiere centres of the information that flows from them, is assured for many more decades yet.

The growing intolerance of many followers of Islam towards what they perceive as the corrupt and materialistic foundation of many Western or Christian sources of information and entertainment poses one of the most serious threats to future international relations. Interestingly, in the context of information access and exchange, the future of Islam is not so much about the future of countries or nationalism, as the relevance and popularity of an idea:

> The idea, Islam, ignores the frontier that most people draw between religion and politics. It may be the last such idea the world will see. Or it may, on the contrary, prove to be the force that persuades other people to rediscover a connection between day-to-day life and a moral order. Either way, it denies turn of the century western conventional wisdom. [15]

Many countries, such as Algeria and Egypt, where Islam is an active or dominant creed, are already experiencing varying degrees of political and social disturbance as extremists vie with liberals to posit new criteria for salvation, fuelled by poverty and stagnating economic conditions. Whatever the *via media* may be between the austere world of communism and the sometimes value-free images portrayed by western capitalism, the *Via Dolorosa* of a new crusade, to bring the severest interpretations of the Koran to populations that for 80 or 90 years have subsisted on a mixture of western pragmatism and soft Islam, is unlikely to be it.

However we envisage our future, confidence, or lack of it, will continue to be the most visible manifestation of access to an information rich or an information poor environment. Those without access to information will remain hesitant, backward, reticent, disorientated and unable to achieve their full potential. We have all seen how lack of confidence has fuelled the myths and illusions that a culture can build up around the routes to self-actualization and achievement. How many people, for want of quite simple information, have gone on believing the construction of their own inadequacy? Equally how many, often to their own astonishment and surprise, have travelled through one or a series of information moments to discover the rich range of endeavours that they can succeed at?

Amongst the media geared up to exploit the lowest common denominator we should remember that much of the information and entertainment that sells well and returns big profits will also enrich and inform, and that in the future enriching and informing could turn out to be as profitable as light entertainment and trivial diversion. Big audiences for home-based education and for information that enriches the soul and illuminates previously dark corners will develop, as traditionally organized job opportunities are reduced and new definitions of productive time become accepted. Also, if past examples in history are anything to go by, the digital superhighways of the future stand a good chance of being pressed into a multiplicity of unexpected modes of community service, just as the building of railways in the nineteenth century, carried out primarily to exercize political control and to generate profit from the carriage of goods and passengers, often had popular political and 'hidden property' consequences for the public good which were not predicted at the time. The Tsar of Russia began building the 5800 mile long Trans-Siberian Railway in 1891 because he wanted better control of eastern Russia and Siberia. With these new lines of communication came a new industrial working class where there had previously been isolated peasants. The railway became a conduit for disaffection and revolution, joining the once remote city-based revolutionaries with new and distant bands of workers. Similarly, the British Raj built the railways in India to reinforce and distribute the power of empire, enabling some 60 000 soldiers and bureaucrats to control 600 million subjects. Built to help troops and administrators move faster around a sub-continent that was twenty times the size of England, these railways were also used by Mahatma Gandhi to travel around India preaching his messages of civil disobedience and independence. Like these old railway lines, future information conduits will carry information and ideas which their creators never imagined. Messages that will enrich and ennoble, messages about decency, justice, selflessness, the right to freedom of speech and assembly, and the rights of all peoples to dignity in life and death, just as fast as they will carry the trivial and the manipulative.

We know that, when linked with existing community concerns, radio and television, as well as feeding some sympathetic voyeurism, can also catalyse political action. In 1966 Ken Loach's TV film 'Cathy Come Home' sent out a cry that nine years later resulted in the UK Housing Act of 1977 which for the first time gave homeless people access to permanent housing. In 1989 the speedy distribution of television pictures of Thai troops violently suppressing a lawful demonstration in Bangkok undoubtedly lead the Thai government to restrain the brutal enthusiasm of its security forces. Most Americans are convinced that the nightly television pictures depicting the horror and lunacy of the war in Vietnam between 1963 and 1974 made a major contribution to mobilizing public opinion against an infinite continuation of the war.

The greatest challenge for all of us is to prove that we, not the owners of the technology, are in control; that important as information is to each of us as individuals, it is the communities we belong to and the bonding they provide that make it worth something. The new monasticism that encourages us to see ourselves as totally independent actors who need no more from life than singular access to the communications port on a computer or an interactive TV, is the enemy of collective reason and debate and we must not fall for it. Testing and reviewing information within lively and articulate communities is still the most important safeguard of our democratic freedoms. Most community-based activities that involve meeting in real space e.g., attending specialist clubs, voting, attendance at political, trade union or voluntary group meetings have already become a minority interest. Accomplishing things jointly looks like becoming a forgotten art, associations of humans striving to achieve common goals look like becoming extinct. The vital connectness between hearts and minds that once so animated social and informational exchange in the US and Europe is in danger of losing the important sparkle that it always gained from humans engaging with each other in small spaces. Zinberg has noted some of the, often underestimated, benefits that accrue to societies from being socially connected, including it being 'good for your health':

Areas with high social connectedness produce better government services – less corruption and more efficiency. The drop in membership in voluntary associations is marked by a concomitant rise in cynicism and alienation.The convergence of these two growing trends – dropping out and logging on – exacerbates the serious consequences of a drop in political involvement and a rise in social isolation. [16]

Whether tapping on a keyboard or turning over the pages we must remember that it is us, churning it over inside our heads, discussing it with colleagues and sharing it with neighbours, that for better or for worse, makes things happen. In 1987, a May Day editorial in *The Guardian*, concerned with the 'there is no such thing as society' attitude then being sponsored by Mrs Thatcher, and within which it was becoming easy to trivialize or deny any form of community investment, noted:

Without a communality of effort, however there will be no true progress. Without widespread anger and alarm, we shall sit back and watch swathes of industrial Britain and the rotten cores of our inner cities become the hopeless homes of a fifth of our citizens, an underclass without prospects or decent education or any sense of belonging to a society that they will one day in pockets of fury, turn against. It is the greatest challenge to our political system. Some day the system will react. Some day the voters will care. But as the nation folds its arms and turns on the snooker, not quite yet. [17]

Unimpeded access to information alone will not change this grim scenario, but it can be one of the great liberating keys. Those who work within the day-to-day bustle of information access and exchange in the public domain have been 'unfolding their arms' for a long time. They change people's lives every day simply by revealing and sharing what they know; by exploring sources of information that illuminate hitherto unknown choices; or just as importantly, by directing people to where more powerful information might be found. When the sharing of information is regarded as a self-evident truth, when economic and censorious obstacles are removed, and when all governments play their part in ensuring access to it, then it can deliver hope and opportunity. Confidence and high self-esteem are fuelled by many motors, and easy access to information is undoubtedly one of the most important. It can take individuals and peoples to new heights and it can remove many inequalities. Given that we can be sure that someone, somewhere, will always be busy leaving someone else info-poor, all of us need to ask ourselves on a daily basis what we are doing to make someone else info-rich? If we are unhappy with the answer, perhaps we should try harder.

References

1. Gaddis, W. (1994) *A frolic of his own*. Viking

2. Peters, T. (1994) Nuggets in the network. *Independent on Sunday*, 24 July

3. Bowcott, O. (1994) The fight for civil rights marches on. *Guardian, 'OnLine'*, 11 August

4. Berman testifies on computer security (1994) *EFF Networks and Policy.* **II** (1), 2 and 9–10.

5. Financial Indicators (1994)*The Economist*, 23 July

6. Vallance, I. (1994) Lecture at University of Central England, Birmingham, 6 July

7. Hobsbawm, E. (1994) Towards the new millennium. *The Sunday Times*, 16 October

8. *The Economist*, 12 February 1994

9. *The Guardian*, 4 August 1994

10. Lynn, M. (1994) Crime pays for security industry. The Sunday Times, 28 August

11. Institute of Fiscal Studies, June 1994

12. Dale, D. J. and Rees-Mogg, W. (1994) *The great reckoning: How the world will change before the year 2000*, 2nd edn. London: Pan Books

13. Haywood, T. (1989) *The withering of public access*. London: Library Association

14. London: yet it moves (1994) *The Economist*, 20 August

15. Survey of Islam (1994) *The Economist*, 6 August

16. Zinberg, D.S. (1994) Drop out and log on. *The Times Higher Educational Supplement*, 7 October

17. Editorial (1987) *The Guardian*, 4 May

Index

ADS 6812